MW00861806

Historic Sites in Virginia's Northern Neck and Essex County

A Guide

Edited by Thomas A. Wolf
Preservation Northern Neck and Middle Peninsula, Inc.
Warsaw, Virginia

Distributed by the University of Virginia Press

The Northern Neck Region

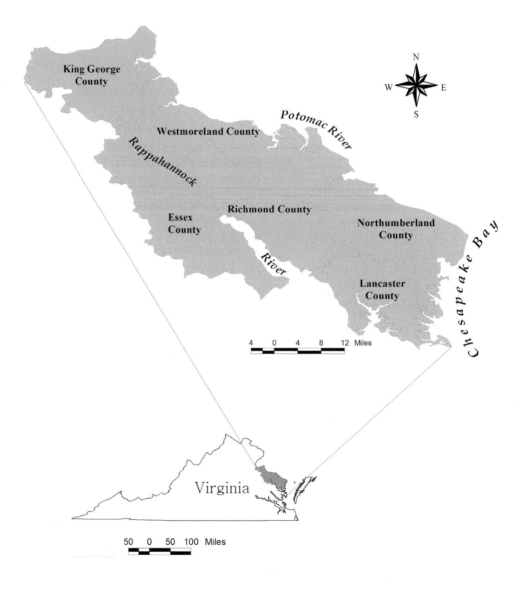

Project Volunteers

Steering Committee

Gerald Abbott (Lancaster)
John F. Bott (Northumberland)
Jean M. Graham (King George)
Anita Harrower (Essex)
Gordon Harrower (Essex)
Elizabeth N. Lee (King George)
Rebecca W. Marks (Richmond)
Robert N. McKenney (Lancaster, Northumberland)
Priscilla M. Wellford (Richmond)
Edward J. White (Westmoreland)
Thomas A. Wolf (Chair, Northumberland)

Other Contributors

Phyllis Ashton (King George)
Francene Barber (Richmond)
John Barber (Richmond)
Brenda Boidock (Richmond)
Virginia Felts Brown
  (Westmoreland)
David Deputy (King George)
Beatrice England (Westmoreland)
Alma Gaddis (King George)
Jean Hudson (King George)
Carolyn H. Jett (Northumberland)
David I. Jett
  (Northumberland, Richmond)
Meade N. Kilduff
  (Northumberland)

Bobbe King (King George)
Kathryn Murray (Richmond)
Lynn Norris (Westmoreland)
Walter B. Norris, Jr.
  (Westmoreland)
Sabrina Prescott (Richmond)
Marvin LeRoy Ransone
  (Lancaster)
Delores Shea (King George)
Ruth Taliaferro (King George)
Darlene Tallent (Westmoreland)
Eloise Toulson (Northumberland)
Sue Williams (King George)
Barbara Yancey (King George)

A Special Recognition

This book could not have been written and published without the tireless efforts of Thomas A. Wolf, who served as Chair of the Steering Committee. He was also the editor and compiler of the book and author of several chapters. We believe that his countless hours of work, leadership and miles of travel will be an inspiration to all who appreciate our heritage and desire to preserve it.

Rebecca W. Marks
Robert N. McKenney
Elizabeth N. Lee
Jean M. Graham

Edward J. White
John F. Bott
Anita Harrower

Gerald Abbott
Priscilla M. Wellford
Gordon Harrower

—Steering Committee members

First Edition

Third Printing

Published in the United States by Preservation Northern Neck and Middle Peninsula, Inc., P.O. Box 691, Warsaw, Virginia 22572

Library of Congress Control Number: 2010938880

ISBN 978-0-692-01167-6

Printed in the United States of America

Distributed by the University of Virginia Press
www.upress.virginia.edu

Historic Sites in Virginia's Northern Neck and Essex County

A Guide

Acknowledgements

The idea for this *Guide* began to take hold in 2006 and early 2007, as momentum was building for the celebrations surrounding the 400th anniversary of the founding of Jamestown. At that time, the Reverend Michael Malone, then director of the Board of Trustees of the Northern Neck Branch (NNB) of Preservation Virginia (PV)—still known at that time as the APVA, or the Association for the Preservation of Virginia Antiquities—suggested that an "inventory" might be taken of historic sites in the Northern Neck of Virginia. Over time, the notion of compiling an unpublished inventory—copies of which, it was realized, might simply languish, unread, on office shelves—evolved into the idea of publishing *Historic Sites in Virginia's Northern Neck and Essex County: A Guide*. Early enthusiasm for this project was also influenced by discussions with staff of the Virginia Department of Historic Resources (DHR) in Richmond in the late spring of 2007, and an initial perusal of relevant DHR archival holdings.

In early 2008, the NNB board formally decided to proceed with the *Guide*. A Steering Committee for this project, made up of representatives of the six counties to be covered, was established, and thereafter reported periodically to the NNB board. The project was enthusiastically embraced by Jerry W. Davis, Executive Director of the Northern Neck Planning District Commission (NNPDC), on which are represented the boards of supervisors of Lancaster, Northumberland, Richmond and Westmoreland counties. The Steering Committee also received important encouragement from Susan Smead, the then Manager of the DHR's Survey and Cost Share Program. In the course of 2008, the DHR, the NNPDC (representing the above four counties), and the boards of supervisors of Essex and King George counties, together committed the critical financial resources which, in addition to the efforts of many volunteers, have made this project possible.

By the end of 2008, committees had been formed in each of the six counties, and their chairpersons (or in some cases, co-chairs) were represented on the Steering Committee. In the meantime, the DHR had given the Steering Committee extensive access to its archives, including the files and quad maps that helped provide a systematic basis for inventorying the historic sites in each county.

Drawing on these archives, and the archival resources of the local organizations listed below, the county committees during 2009 carefully researched and selected those sites that they wished to propose for inclusion in the *Guide*, and these sites were presented to the Steering Committee for its approval. Once the sites had been selected, the county chairs prepared succinct descriptions of all their sites, which were then edited for general consistency. In the early months of 2010, the other chapters of the *Guide* were written and edited, the selected sites were photographed, and the various maps appearing in this book were prepared.

Thanks are due to all the volunteers, in all six counties, who have contributed countless hours to researching, helping select, describing and photographing the historic sites to be included in this book, and for their writing and editing of its various chapters.

We would also like to express our deep gratitude to Jerry W. Davis of the NNPDC; Susan Smead, Robert Carter, and E. Randolph Turner of the DHR for their support throughout this entire process; Quatro Hubbard and his very helpful colleagues for their invaluable continuing assistance at the DHR archives; Camille Bowman of the Tidewater Office of the DHR for her early comments on the scope and approach of the project; and Pamela Schenian of that Office for her very helpful review of the entire manuscript. Finally, but not least, thanks are due to Stuart McKenzie and Grant Turner of the NNPDC for lending their mapping expertise to the project, and to Kathryn Murray for her many helpful suggestions and for undertaking the design and production of the *Guide*.

We are also very grateful to the following local organizations for lending their support to this project, whether in the form of archival material, publications, photographs, physical facilities or the many hours put in by their staff or members: the Essex County Museum and Historical Society, King George County Historical Society, Kinsale Museum, Mary Ball Washington Library and Museum, Northern Neck of Virginia Historical Society, Northumberland County Historical Society, Preservation Virginia-Northern Neck Branch, Reedville Fishermen's Museum, Richmond County Museum, and the Steamboat Era Museum of Irvington (Terri Thaxton, Executive Director).

While a number of published sources were also drawn on for this book (see the selected bibliographies at the end of Chapters 2-8), it should be mentioned that the descriptions of most sites in Westmoreland County have drawn heavily on Walter Biscoe Norris, Jr., *Westmoreland County Virginia, 1653-1983* (Montross, Va.: Westmoreland Board of Supervisors, 1983, Fourth Edition, 2008). Likewise, the descriptions of most home sites in Essex County have relied heavily on Robert LaFollette, Anita Harrower and Gordon Harrower, *Essex County, Virginia: Historic Homes* (Lancaster, Va.: Anchor Communications for Essex County Museum, 2002).

List of Maps

Table of Contents

The Northern Neck Region

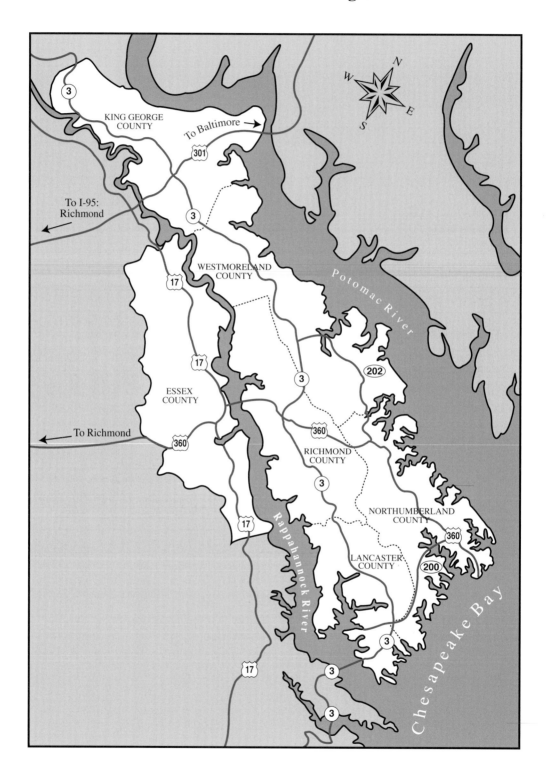

Chapter 1
Introduction

This *Guide* to historic sites in the Northern Neck of Virginia (and including the important "gateway" of Essex County), is meant for all those who want to know more about the history of this region and about the physical structures that survive to help us interpret this history. Interested readers will include natives and other long-time residents of the Northern Neck; those so-called "come heres" who have discovered the charms of this region and moved here either permanently or as weekenders; and travelers to this part of the world who seek a well-researched, conveniently organized, highly readable and portable "guide" to historic sites in this unique area of Virginia's Tidewater Region. Those with a particular interest in colonial and antebellum architecture, and its preservation, should also find this to be a handy guide to architectural trends and the state of historic preservation in this region.

It is sometimes forgotten that some of America's greatest early leaders — including George Washington, James Madison and James Monroe — were born in the Northern Neck. It was also the birthplace of the most revered leader of the Confederate forces during the Civil War, Robert E. Lee. But it was likewise the birthplace of a number of local leaders, and of countless more or less ordinary men and women, whose descendants today — some 375 years after the first English settlement in the Northern Neck — number in the hundreds of thousands or possibly millions, and live throughout the United States and to some extent abroad.

This is the first book in more than 75 years to provide a systematic guide to historic sites in this region as a whole. The earlier volume, H. Ragland Eubank's *Touring Historyland: An Authentic Guide Book of the Historic Northern Neck of Virginia*, was published in 1934. Although a highly readable and intriguing guide to this region, Eubank's book was heavily focused on the genealogical connections among those families who, by the 18th century, had come to dominate the economic, political and social life of the Northern Neck. The reader was introduced to their homes, but in most cases more was said about the family connections of their occupants than the houses they inhabited or the historic events in which many of their owners had participated. Generally ignored, as well, was the history of the Native Americans who had once dominated the Northern Neck region, and that of the African Americans living here and descended from either blacks who were already free prior to the Civil War, or the slaves who became free as a consequence of that conflict.

This *Guide* provides a kind of inventory of historic sites from the period of initial European settlement in the Northern Neck region — in the 1640s — through the turmoil of the Civil War, more than 200 years later. But it also includes a few of the known, but now lost, sites inhabited by Native Americans when Capt. John Smith undertook his voyages of exploration up the Potomac and Rappahannock rivers in 1608. And it also contains descriptions of a number of historic sites that date from after the Civil War, including many of the churches and schools established by emancipated slaves, and sites integral to the economy of the region in the late 19th century, including menhaden fishing and the steamboats that connected this region to the larger world of Chesapeake commerce.

Unfortunately, many of the sites still standing when Eubank published his book, in 1934, are now no longer to be seen. Indeed, the research for this *Guide* has brought home only too clearly how much of the tangible human-built environment has been lost, and continues to fade away. Several historic structures even disappeared during the preparation of the *Guide*, either due to neglect and ultimately abandonment and collapse, or to the encroachments of commercial or housing developments. Many of those sites that appear to be in a serious state of neglect at the time of writing are marked "endangered" at the end of their site descriptions.

Another threat to our better understanding and appreciation of the past is the loss of open land, whether to commercial or residential development, or to more "natural" phenomena such as shoreline erosion. This *Guide* has focused on the historic structures—homes, churches, schools, public buildings—of this region, and in most cases there has been little scope for also describing the natural environment in which these sites were initially constructed. Yet it must be recognized that while preserving, say, an 18th-century house in and of itself is an immensely worthwhile endeavor, much may also be lost if its agrarian or rural village context is not also preserved. Thus historic preservation and land conservation must go hand in hand if the unique character of this still essentially rural region is to be preserved for this and future generations.

Criteria for Selection of Historic Sites, and the Organization of the *Guide*

It is certainly true that not all "old" sites are necessarily "historic," and by the same token not all "historic" sites need be necessarily "old." It is also the case that a site deemed historic by one person or group may hold little if any historic interest for others. And while some sites have a clear national or regional significance, other places may only be considered "historic" by the most local of constituencies.

In selecting 460 sites for stand-alone description as historic sites in the six counties covered by this *Guide*, several criteria have been followed. First, it was recognized that a general cutoff line would have to be drawn, for despite the continuing deterioration of old homes and other buildings in the area, not all could possibly be included in one easily portable book. The dividing line chosen roughly coincides with the Civil War.

Second, it was observed that certain exceptions to this general rule would need to be made, reflecting important historical developments in the various communities making up the Northern Neck region after the Civil War. For example, the end of that conflict and emancipation meant that black churches and schools now came into being, although unfortunately most of the earliest of such structures could not be built in a way to survive the ravages of time.

Third, it was noted that many of the really significant historic sites had long since disappeared as structures, or had been replaced by newer ones, and yet the historical significance of such sites demanded that they be included, even though they are, strictly speaking, visually "lost." A number of these "lost" sites are included in this *Guide*, and in some cases old photographs or drawings of them are shown, sometimes as "cautionary tales" about what can happen to tangible markers of our heritage.

Fourth, it was also recognized that a number of sites from the post-Civil War era, whether still standing or "lost," could be usefully portrayed as "representative" examples of those important social and economic trends that emerged in the Northern Neck during the century following the Civil War. Many of these places, while not included among the 460 "stand-alone" sites, are still noted—and some are portrayed by photographs, old and new—in the latter part of Chapter 2, which presents a compact narrative history of the region.

Finally, although the dating of old structures often involves conjecture, even by professional architectural historians, it is believed that very few, if any, errors of commission have been made in the selection of sites for this *Guide*. In other words, virtually all of these sites are thought to be as old as is stated, and where some doubt prevails, only very rough estimates of the time of construction are presented. On the other hand, it is quite probable that there have been errors of omission, in that some very old extant structures have been left out. This is because in some cases essentially no professional attention has yet been given to these buildings, local "traditions" concerning their age could not be readily found, or a possibly very old structure was essentially inaccessible due to being remote and overgrown with vegetation, or to the reluctance of its owners to permit some on-site examination.

Following the brief narrative history presented in Chapter 2, the 460 historic sites are presented county-by-county, in separate chapters. As indicated on the frontispiece map to this chapter, today there are four main "gateways" to the Northern Neck: (1) south on U.S. 301 from southern Maryland, crossing over the Nice Bridge into King George County; (2) east on State Highway 3 from Fredericksburg, also into King George County; (3) southeast on U.S. 17 from Fredericksburg into Essex County, connecting with U.S. 360 coming to the northeast from the state capital of Richmond, and then traversing the Downing Bridge into Richmond County; and (4) north and west on State Highway 3 from Middlesex County over the Norris Bridge into Lancaster County.

The individual county chapters have been arranged in a way that takes the traveler through the Northern Neck region on essentially a clockwise tour, although as noted there are of course alternative gateways that may be used, and within the region many different routes that may be taken. In particular, the county chapters begin with the historical sites to be found in King George County (Chapter 3), and this is then followed by Chapters 4 through 8 on Westmoreland, Northumberland, Lancaster, Richmond and Essex counties respectively.

Chapter 9, the concluding chapter, presents some general observations that have come out of the research for this *Guide*. In particular, it calls for renewed attention to the preservation of those sites described in the book, as well as of other old structures that are worthy of preservation for future generations.

The Northern Neck region has a number of historical societies, history museums and preservation societies, and these are listed, by county and with contact information, in the Appendix. The *Guide* contains two indexes. The first is an alphabetical listing of the 460 historical sites with their page numbers. The second index is both a subject and proper name index. Also included is a brief Glossary of architectural and construction terms frequently used in this book.

How to Use this *Guide*

Each of the 460 historic sites has been assigned an identifying number specific to the county in which it is located. On the second page of each county chapter, the reader will find a countywide map showing the order (A, B, C etc.) of the "local" maps for that county on which the different sites may be located, by their site numbers. In a few cases, a site will appear on more than one local map. At the very end of each site description, the reader will find noted the local map(s) on which that site appears. For example, at the end of the description for Stratford Hall (site number 26 in Westmoreland County — see pages 83-84), the reader will see "(*Map B*)." This local map for Westmoreland appears on page 82 (see the List of Maps on page ix), and the location of Stratford Hall is easily found on Map B by looking for site number 26.

At the end of each site description, there is further information provided in italics. This includes whether that site has been placed on the Virginia Landmarks Register (*VLR*) by the Virginia Department of Historic Resources (DHR), and on the National Register of Historic Places (*NRHP*) by the U.S. Department of the Interior through its National Park Service. It is also indicated whether an historic easement on the property has been granted to the Virginia Board of Historic Resources (*BHR*). Also noted is whether there is a corresponding roadside *Historical Marker*.

This is followed by italicized information about whether the site is *visible* from the public road, and whether it is *privately owned*. Readers are reminded that they should not venture onto private property without the owner's permission, and that so doing in the presence of posted *No Trespassing* signs is punishable under the law. Sites deemed to be *endangered* are so labeled.

The Northern Neck region includes several state- and federally-designated Historic Districts: Kinsale, Heathsville, Reedville, Irvington, Lancaster, Morattico and Tappahannock. Each of these are ideal venues for walking tours, and the *Guide* includes detailed maps for several of these towns.

Enjoy your travels in and around the Northern Neck!

Chapter 2
The Northern Neck Region: Historical Overview

Introduction

The Virginia Tidewater region has three peninsulas (lower, middle and upper) separating its four great rivers (the James, York, Rappahannock, and Potomac). The Northern Neck is the northernmost of these peninsulas, and lies between the lower reaches of the Potomac and Rappahannock rivers as they make their way southeast into the Chesapeake Bay.

The six counties of the Northern Neck region (King George, Westmoreland, Northumberland, Lancaster, Richmond and Essex) considered here together comprise 1,184 square miles of land, making this region a bit larger than the land area of the state of Rhode Island. Moreover, the boundaries of the six counties also encompass another 276 square miles of water. Each of the counties has an extensive tidewater shoreline, which in turn is punctuated by a host of tidal estuaries, locally called rivers, creeks and coves.

With such extensive tidewater frontage, this region was an important area for early Indian settlements relying heavily on fishing, and also proved to be highly accessible — at least along the shoreline — to the early English settlers of Virginia. Once English settlement had been made, travel by water, whether within the region or south to the colonial capital at Jamestown, was the easiest way to move about, particularly while most of the land was covered with trees, and paths and roads were few and far between.

It is well known that Jamestown began as essentially a commercial venture, financed by shareholders of the London Company of Virginia (in modern times commonly referred to as the Virginia Company of London). It is equally well known that Jamestown came close to complete failure within a couple of years of its founding in 1607, due to a host of factors. Nevertheless the settlement survived, at least for almost a century. Not only was it the earliest permanent English settlement in the Americas, but also in 1619 it was the site of the first elected legislative assembly in this part of the world.

Despite the growing economic success of the young colony with the export of tobacco, hostilities between the early European settlers and the Native Americans continued. Following the Indian massacre of 1622, the British Crown revoked in 1624 the charter of the Company, and Virginia now came under the direct rule of King James I. European settlement gradually expanded outward from the James River valley. This was facilitated in large part by the headright system, originated in 1618, by which a person could claim and receive a patent for 50 acres of unsettled land for each person (including himself) for whose passage to Virginia he had directly or indirectly paid.

European settlement in the Northern Neck region began by the 1640s, and by the time of the first U.S. federal census in 1790, the region had a population of about 46,000, or almost 1.2 percent of the population of the infant United States. By 1860, however, on the eve of the Civil War, its population had dwindled to about 45,000, while the population of the original thirteen states had risen more than $3^{1}/_{2}$ times from its 1790 level. By 1940, the region's population stood at close to 48,000, having grown by only four percent in the intervening 150 years, while the population of the original thirteen states had grown during that entire period by almost 14 times.

In 1790, the free population of the region accounted for about 20,000, or less than 45 percent of the total. At that time, the average white household in this area consisted of about six to seven free persons, which meant that on average (including villages) there were only about $2^{1}/_{2}$ white households per square mile of land. Of the 3,000-odd dwellings then lived in by the white population, research conducted for this book suggests that no more than about four to five percent appear to have survived—either in their original form or, as is much more frequently the case, through incorporation into larger dwellings. Until the end of the Civil War brought emancipation, more than half of the population of this region remained enslaved, and largely lived in relatively cramped and poorly constructed dwellings, very few built to survive a long time.

Along with the industrial revolution, much of even rural America became crisscrossed by railroads. Although there were some plans to that effect in this region, no railroad was ever built. This not only severely restrained the degree of industrialization, but until the age of the automobile, it meant that links between the region and the outside world remained almost exclusively through steamboats.

In effect, right up to the mid-20th century, the Northern Neck and Essex County remained relatively sparsely populated, and also isolated, with the economy largely dependent on agriculture, fishing and timber. Even by the year 2000, the population had not yet doubled from its 1790 level, having grown to 76,000,

or only a two-thirds increase over 210 years. But within the region, there have been some important differences in recent population growth. For example, Essex County's population in 2000 was only ten percent higher than in 1790, whereas in King George County, largely due to the expansion of the Dahlgren Naval Proving Ground, the population more than tripled between 1940 and the end of the century.

Native Settlement and English Exploration

Archaeological evidence suggests that Native Americans may have inhabited parts of Virginia as early as 15,000 B.C. It is unclear, however, when they first might have appeared in the Northern Neck region. Greater evidence of Indian culture in Virginia, including stone spearheads, mortars and pestles and chipped stone axes, appears from the so-called Middle Archaic period (6,000 to 2,500 B.C.). By the Late Archaic period (2,500 to 1,200 B.C.), there were possibly tens of thousands of Native Americans living in what is now Virginia. It is thought that by this time the Indians were beginning to settle in hamlets and to focus more on the cultivation of the land. In the Tidewater region, oysters were an important seasonal source of food.

The evolution towards a more sedentary existence continued during the Early Woodland period (1,200 to 500 B.C.), for which archaeological findings have included fired clay cooling and storage vessels, and post holes suggestive of round or oval houses with thatch and bark coverings. During the Middle Woodland period (500 B.C. to 900 A.D.), woodworking techniques continued to improve, bows and arrows began to replace spears for hunting, and trade among regions was increasing. Through expanded trade, Indians in the Tidewater region were able to obtain the stones needed for projectile tips. During the Late Woodland period (900 A.D. to 1,600 A.D.), the Native Americans in Virginia began growing tobacco, which had originated in what is now Mexico. They developed fairly complex economic, social and political structures, and many of the thousands of Indians in Virginia now lived in large towns.

At the time of their initial contact with the Europeans, the native people of the Northern Neck spoke languages that belonged to the Eastern Algonquian language family, although the farther individual groups lived from one another, the more their Algonquian dialects were likely to differ. These Algonquian speakers are believed to have migrated into the Middle Atlantic from the Great Lakes region in several waves between about 100 and 900 A.D., during the latter half of the Middle Woodland period.

Those Indian groups living in this region always established their towns along the waterways, where canoeing back and forth was easy and fish relatively plentiful, and in places where there was food to be gathered and also reeds that could be used for mats. Given that the soil would tend to be worked out over just a few years, these Indian settlements usually were rather fluid in their boundaries, as the residents would shift their crops of corn, beans, squash and tobacco from one set of fields to another.

Even when full of people, these towns usually had populations of fewer than 100, and the largest usually had no more than a couple of hundred residents. Compared to the early settlements of the Europeans in Virginia, however, some of these towns were actually quite populous. The houses were typically bent-wood frameworks that were lashed together with twine made from Indian hemp, with mat or bark coverings. In the late spring and again in the fall, the Indians would tend to leave their towns for a while in order to take advantage of wild foods growing in the broader vicinity. Thus there were times when their villages may have seemed totally abandoned, but were only temporarily empty.

Most of the native people in the Northern Neck region lived within the territory of the Powhatans, who were ruled over by a "king," or paramount chief, of that name. Each district within the Powhatan Confederacy had its own werowance, or chief. These chiefs had a governing role locally in religious matters, in diplomatic relations with other chiefdoms and the paramount chief, and in military operations. The latter were important long before the arrival of the English, for the Powhatans were engaged in a military competition with tribes from outside the region, particularly the Massawomecks who lived in northwest Appalachia. Some of the Indian settlements were therefore actually fortified towns that were surrounded by pole-and-bark palisades.

Under instructions from the London Company, Capt. John Smith and some of his men made two extensive exploratory voyages around the Chesapeake Bay and up some of its tributaries in 1608. The first voyage, carried out over a seven-week period in June and July, included travelling up the Potomac River as far as the fall line (near present-day Washington, D.C.). It was on this trip that he encountered, or at least was made aware of, among others, the *Sekakawons* (later anglicized to Chicacoan) Indians living near what is today called the Coan River in Northumberland County.

Only several days after their return to Jamestown, Smith and his compatriots left on their second voyage, which included a two-week expedition in the second half of August 1608 up the Rappahannock River. Here they encountered, among others, the *Cuttatawomens* (or Corrotomans) in what is present-day Lancaster County; the *Moraughtacunds* (or Moratticos) in present-day Lancaster and Richmond counties; the *Topahanocks* in present-day Essex County; the Pissasecks in present-day Westmoreland County; and the *Nandtaughtacunds* (or Nanzaticos), in present-day King George County.

English Settlement to the American Revolution

It is not known exactly when the first English settlement was made in the Northern Neck region. Col. William Claiborne's attempt to settle and claim Kent Island in the upper Chesapeake Bay for Virginia had been forcibly thwarted by agents of the Maryland Proprietary by 1636, and a second feebler attempt to retake the island fizzled in 1646/47. The names of many of those living on Kent Island in the 1630s and early 1640s are mentioned as neighbors or patentees in the land patents on the Potomac side of the Northern Neck of the late 1640s and early 1650s. They also appear in the court records of York County (the then frontier county facing, to the northeast, the Middle Peninsula and the Northern Neck) in the mid-1640s, and of Northumberland County by the late 1640s.

Col. John Mottrom, frequently mentioned as the first English settler in this area—on the Coan River, a tributary of the Potomac in what is today upper Northumberland County—was almost certainly not the first resident, but he appears to have been the first recognized leader. He was seated in the House of Burgesses as the representative of Northumberland in 1645, even though a county had not yet been established for this region. Representation in the assembly was then denied "Chicawane *alias* Northumberland" in 1646, because the district had not contributed to the costs of the defense against the Indians. William Presley represented Northumberland in the House of Burgesses the next year, but it was not until 1648 that the General Assembly actually called for the formal establishment of a county on the "Neck of land between Rappahanock River and Potomack River," to be called Northumberland.

Although Kent Island was an important source of early migrants to the Northern Neck, settlers such as Mottrom and Presley, and many others, including John Carter, Epaphroditus Lawson and others who had settled along the north shore of the Rappahannock in the 1640s, had actually come up from the lower or middle peninsulas of Virginia. Other early settlers, including probably the majority of the indentured servants, had come more or less directly from Britain, typically as headrights (see above).

Relations with the Native Americans in this region remained tenuous, although outright warfare was avoided. Following the second major conflict with the Powhatan Indian alliance, in 1644, Sir William Berkeley, the royal governor, negotiated a pact with the Indians whereby in return for giving up most of their Tidewater homelands to the colonists, they received a reservation north of the York River. This area, though, came under continual settlement pressures from the colonists, and periodically the General Assembly acted to try to rein in what were perceived as some of the more egregious exploitative practices.

One target of the General Assembly's rather loose monitoring of dealings with the Indians was Col. Moore Fauntleroy, immigrant and progenitor of the Fauntleroy family of the Northern Neck region. At first settling on the south side of the James River, by 1650 Fauntleroy had received land patents for more than 8,000 acres in what today is Richmond County, and appears to have been one of the first European settlers in that area. Indeed, Farnham is named after the town in County Hampshire, England near his birthplace. (This practice of naming new settlements in the New World after former British places of residence was, of course, quite common.) Between 1660 and 1662, the General Assembly, meeting in Jamestown, admonished Fauntleroy—who had long been a Burgess—for possibly unfair dealings with the Rappahannock Indians as well with the governor, and he was ultimately dismissed from sitting in that august body. (The Rappahannocks and several other Indian tribes have recently received official recognition by the Commonwealth. The Rappahannock Tribal Center is located in King and Queen County, and the Rappahannocks still look upon Essex and Richmond counties, as well, as part of their aboriginal territory.)

In any event, by the late 1640s and early 1650s, Englishmen in some cases had bought land from the Indians, or had otherwise claimed land and received land patents from the colonial government. Individuals had settled all along the south shore of the Potomac, the tip of the Northern Neck along the Bay, and up and down both sides of the Rappahannock River. Frequently, land patents were only issued a number of years after settlement, so the date of earliest settlement—especially before the formation of counties—is often impossible to determine with any precision. But certainly by 1650—a year after the beheading of King Charles I and the establishment of the Commonwealth in England under Cromwell—settlement along the shorelines was quite widespread.

The formation of the six counties covered by this *Guide* was not at all straightforward. In essence, as in the rest of Virginia and most of the nation at large, counties in this region were initially established to cover very large, but only sparsely populated territories. As European settlement moved inland, and to the west, residents living increasingly far from the old county seats petitioned the legislature for their sections to be broken off and established as new counties. These new counties, in turn, were usually partially broken up as the internal migration continued apace. In addition, there were a number of minor adjustments of county boundary lines in later years.

The Table indicates when, and from what already established jurisdiction, the six counties in this *Guide* were established, but does not mention later, minor boundary adjustments. Whether technically justified

---

Formation of Northern Neck Region Counties

Northumberland: formed in 1648 from the Chickakoan Indian District.

Lancaster: formed in 1651 from Northumberland and York counties.

Westmoreland: formed in 1653 from Northumberland.

Rappahannock (Old): formed in 1656 from upper Lancaster (lower Lancaster, on the south side of Rappahannock River, became Middlesex Co. in 1669).

Essex: formed in 1692 from (Old) Rappahannock Co. south of the Rappahannock River.

Richmond: formed in 1692 from (Old) Rappahannock Co., north of the Rappahannock River.

King George: formed in 1721 from Richmond County.

or not, Northumberland has come to be called the "mother county" of this region. The county courts, made up of a dozen or so justices, effectively combined some local legislative, as well as executive and judicial functions. Particularly given the distance from the capital at Jamestown (and, from 1699, at Williamsburg), these county courts oversaw local affairs with a high degree of latitude.

As in the rest of early Tidewater Virginia, the main crop was tobacco, but its cultivation rapidly wore out the soil. This meant that those who, through some combination of ingenuity, industry, inherited wealth and political connections, were able to keep acquiring new land for cultivation, were going to do relatively well, while the others lagged behind. Over time, the planter class split into a small "gentry" group, which sought to mimic the ways of the landed class in England, and a class of so-called middling planters, perhaps doing well but not well enough to win increased economic or political influence. A third group was composed of tradesmen and craftsmen of various kinds, and those who had become tenant farmers or overseers for the wealthier planters. Increasingly, those who had achieved gentry status tended to preside over the county court, and it was these same planters who tended to compose the vestries of the local Anglican parishes, the Church of England being the established religion. In this way, both the secular and religious seats of power became in many cases virtually hereditary in nature.

In the earliest years, the plantations of the large and middling planters were worked mainly by white indentured servants. While in some cases these servants were men of some education who could serve in clerical capacities or as needed coopers, shoemakers, tailors and the like, the vast majority became field hands. If they survived the terms of their indenture—typically seven years—these men at least had the potential to become planters or paid craftsmen themselves, and many did. (The same may be said, as well, for many of the slaves who during their bondage had become skilled craftsmen, and who later proved that they could support themselves once emancipated.)

By the late 17th century, planters—especially the larger ones who could afford the initial outlay for their purchase—were turning increasingly to slave labor from Africa. By 1705, various laws had been passed by the General Assembly which basically codified the separate and enslaved role of blacks in Virginia. As noted in the introduction to this chapter, by the time of the American Revolution, slaves made up more than half of the population of the Northern Neck region.

Tobacco, the universal crop, was painstakingly grown, then harvested and dried, and put into hogsheads to be rolled to a nearby river landing where it would be inspected and shipped, almost always to England but, by the early to mid-18th century, increasingly to Scotland for re-export to continental markets. Tobacco also became the basic unit of account in an agrarian society starved for sterling, literally the coin of the realm. Most planters plowed their earnings from tobacco back into their farms, both to improve and, if they had the means, to expand them.

The pioneering generations struggled hard just to survive. Families subsisted on home-grown vegetables, cattle, hogs, and game. Small cotton and flax patches would have provided the material, along with wool, for weaving garments and bed linens. Most families lived in shacks, lean-tos, pole huts and other primitive structures, although some were able to erect simple frame houses with wood chimneys daubed with clay or plaster, known as "Virginia houses." All of these were of earthfast construction, and did not last long in the humid and termite-inviting climate of the Tidewater.

As living standards improved for many, they borrowed from their Anglo-Saxon heritage and built more durable homes, whether one-over-one room houses or, if more affluent, a hall and parlor type dwelling which had two rooms downstairs, a sleeping loft above, and frequently a root cellar or perhaps even a high English basement below. These houses typically had gable roofs, often with dormer windows, and one or possibly two end-chimneys that often served large fireplaces for heating and sometimes cooking, to the extent meals were not prepared in separate kitchen buildings.

Court records from the 17th and 18th centuries are replete with references to ferries used to cross major creeks and even rivers. Among the earliest of these ferries, which were usually run by one individual or his family, was the *Chowning* ferry, which operated from the 1670s to around 1800, and connected upper Lancaster County with the port town of Urbanna, in Middlesex County across the Rappahannock River. Another early ferry, a semi-private operation known as *Whiting's*, connected *Woodlawn* in King George County with *Camden*, a plantation on the south side of the Rappahannock just below the town of Port Royal in Caroline County, and ran from about 1690 to the 1740s. Of the major ferries that have operated here over the past 3¹/₂ centuries, almost 50 have been identified by name. And there were undoubtedly numerous other, smaller and less permanent ferry operations that permitted the easy crossing of the tributaries of the smaller rivers. Two ferries remain in operation today in this region: *Sunnybank Ferry* over the Little Wicomico River in Northumberland County, and *Merry Point Ferry* over the western branch of the Corrotoman River in Lancaster County.

Periodically, from the mid-1600s until the early 1700s, the General Assembly, under pressure from the Crown or Commonwealth, enacted legislation designed to encourage the establishment of towns in what remained an overwhelmingly rural and agricultural society, dominated by the growing of tobacco. The larger planters tended to be against the establishment of towns, since they typically had their own wharves and sought to monopolize the local trade in tobacco and to escape paying tobacco duties by shipping their product directly to England and to ports elsewhere. The Crown wanted just a few port towns, thinking in terms of economies of scale as well as minimizing the avoidance of custom duties, and typically pushed for just one port town on each of the four great Virginia rivers as well as one on the Eastern Shore. But this ignored the important role played by the "county" and county leaders in early Virginia, and when the burgesses representing the different counties finally did endorse the idea of establishing towns, they tended to propose one town for each county.

The General Assembly passed acts for port towns four times between 1662 and 1705. The act of 1680, for example, specifically identified the sites where the new ports were to be established. In Northumberland, there was to be a town on the Coan River. In Lancaster County, the town was to be on the Corrotoman River at a creek site near the then county courthouse. In Westmoreland County, the port was to be "on the mouth of the Nominy." Finally, the port town for (Old) Rappahannock County (then still encompassing what would become Essex and Richmond counties in 1692—see the Table) was to be established at a place named "Hobses" Hole, and this is the only one of these towns that actually took hold, later to be known as Tappahannock. Today's port town of Kinsale, in Westmoreland County, dates from a similar act passed in 1705.

Sessions of the very early county courts were typically held in the residences of the justices, but over time, as the population grew and land transportation improved, courthouses were constructed in what were deemed fairly central locations. But as the center of population tended in some instances to shift, some counties likewise relocated their courthouses. For example, in Lancaster County, the court originally met near today's White House Creek, off the west bank of the Corrotoman River, then later at Queenstown, which had been legislated into existence in 1705, but finally, from 1743, in the present village now known simply as Lancaster.

There were typically two or three Anglican parishes per county. In Essex, St. Anne's (formerly Sittingbourne) Parish was the "up-county" parish, having two parish churches, *Vauter's* and *Sale's*. In lower Essex, down-river, the early parish was known as South Farnham, and it was served by *Upper* and *Lower Piscataway* churches. Across the Rappahannock, Richmond County had Lunenburg parishes for its northern section and North Farnham Parish for the southern part. While the parish church wardens attempted to ensure church attendance, and many an errant soul was "presented" by them to the county court for non-attendance (or Sabbath drunkenness) and a consequent fine, attending church also provided an important social occasion for otherwise isolated families living in relatively remote locations.

Another opportunity to get together, at least for men, was the local militia muster. The General Assembly decreed that all able-bodied men between 16 and 60 had to be available for military service. Companies numbering between 30 and 70 men each, led by their elected officers, were required to train once a month. Early on a Saturday morning they would assemble at some central location, and following roll call, prayers, and inspection, undergo daylong exercises in the manual of arms and close order drill. At sundown, the exhausted troops were usually rewarded by their officers with beer, whiskey and victuals.

The selling of liquor to militiamen, however, was sometimes the subject of a court action. In 1763, William Trussell, who was licensed to keep an ordinary at his house in the Cherry Point area of upper Northumberland County (and, incidentally, was regularly hauled into court for non-attendance at church), was sued by a Scottish firm, with which he presumably had some sort of agreement, for allowing his assistant to sell liquor to the militia company drilling across the road!

With the restoration of the British monarchy in 1660, in the person of Charles II, Sir William Berkeley was renamed the royal governor of Virginia. In his second term, Berkeley remained quite popular among the colony's emerging elite, but as settlement expanded westward, many believed that he was not doing enough to protect them against the Indians whose habitats to the west had become increasingly threatened. Sparked by an incident at the Stafford County plantation of Thomas Mathew, whose primary residence was actually on Cherry Point in Northumberland, and led by an upstart young immigrant from an influential English family—Nathaniel Bacon—many of the small planters and those recently settled to the west rose up in 1676 in what is called Bacon's Rebellion.

The issue began as how best to defend the frontier settlements against Indian incursions (defensive forts, as Berkeley proposed, or through offensive operations), but it also developed class overtones, as Bacon and his confederates challenged the authority of Berkeley and many of the new landed gentry, and seized control of the General Assembly at Jamestown in June 1676 (but then ultimately burned down the capital). The June session of the Assembly called for each county to send a militia contingent to engage in direct battle with the Indians (and, in many instances with the supporters of Berkeley).

Northumberland County, for example, was ordered to send 49 soldiers. At some point, however, these and many other troops probably sided with the supporters of Berkeley, as the tide turned following Bacon's death in late 1676. Berkeley returned from exile on the Eastern Shore to take deadly revenge against many of those who had opposed him, but was soon recalled to London to answer for the disturbing rebellion.

While this conflict evidently did not directly intrude on the Northern Neck region, Berkeley's successor called for a revival of his plans, which were to erect forts at the "heads" (or fall lines) of Virginia's "Fower greate rivers," and during the next several years men were sent from the Northern Neck region to the heads of the Rappahannock and Potomac rivers to man those fortifications against the Indians.

The Northern Neck peninsula *per se* should not be confused with the Northern Neck Proprietary, although it did come to be included in the Proprietary. While in exile at the outset of the English Commonwealth, Charles II granted all the land between the Potomac and Rappahannock rivers to a group of loyalists. By the time their representatives visited Virginia to stake their claim, however, considerable settlement of this area in the Tidewater area had already occurred, secured by land patents from the colonial government. Moreover, the former government in Virginia had likewise been effectively deposed by the Commonwealth. Following the Restoration, however, negotiations between the two parties finally yielded an agreement in 1669 which in effect gave the proprietors a claim to unsettled territory in this region as of 1690.

One of the heirs of the loyalist proprietors was Thomas, Lord Culpeper, who briefly served as Virginia's royal governor in the early 1680s. Sensing a large opportunity, Culpeper managed after his return to England to receive a new proprietary charter, approved by King James II in 1688, in which he had written that the Proprietary would include all that land "bounded by and within the first heads or Springs" of the two rivers. In effect, the Proprietary would, beginning in 1690, have the right to claim rents on new settlements in an area amounting to more than five million acres, reaching all the way to the foot of the Alleghenies.

A principal beneficiary of this brilliant legal move by Culpeper (whose title to this land ultimately passed to the Fairfax family through marriage) was the already wealthy and influential Robert "King" Carter of Lancaster County, who managed to have himself appointed agent for the Fairfax family from 1703 to 1712, and again from 1722 to 1732. Indeed, Robert Carter is thought to have been the wealthiest man of his generation in the colonies. Having reputedly amassed something of the order of 200,000 acres of land in fourteen Virginia counties, and some 700 slaves, and with the building of his home, *Corotoman*, Carter in effect epitomized the degree to which the planter society in the Northern Neck region was now being divided between the very wealthy and the merely well-to-do.

Indeed, the half-century or so before the Revolution saw the construction of a number of mansions for the very affluent, men who not only had accumulated vast wealth, but many of whom also served on the Governor's Council, an elite group who effectively operated as both councillors to the governor and the upper house of the now bicameral legislature.

Among these grand homes were Robert "King" Carter's *Corotoman* in Lancaster County (built in the 1720s); Thomas Lee's *Stratford Hall* (1730s) and *Nomini Hall* (ca. 1730) built by "King" Carter for his son Robert, both in Westmoreland County; Charles Carter's *Cleve* (1740s) in King George County; Landon Carter's *Sabine Hall* (1738) and John Tayloe II's

Mount Airy (1750s) in Richmond County; Robert Beverley's *Blandfield* (1774), Muscoe Garnett's *Elmwood* (1774) and Sarah Taliaferro Brooke's house *Brooke's Bank* (ca. 1751) in Essex County; and Kendall Lee's *Ditchley* (ca. 1762) and Thomas Gaskins' *Gascony* (pre-1776) in Northumberland, and a number of smaller, but still quite opulent houses. Of these large original residences, all but Corotoman, Nomini Hall, Cleve and Gascony still stand today.

Meanwhile, the merely well-to-do were now improving their old homes, or building new ones, effectively raising the roof to two full stories, adding a flanking wing or so to the sides of an existing structure, or even relegating the old house to tenant farmers or servants and building for themselves much more commodious and pretentious houses. In Essex County, the second and third quarters of the 18th century witnessed a very interesting architectural development. Particularly in the Millers Tavern and Dunbrooke areas, gambrel-roofed three-bay homes, sitting atop a high English basement, now became quite popular among the middling planter class. Other homes of like size but with traditional hip or gable roofs were also built during this period throughout the Northern Neck region.

During these middle decades of the 18th century, several men who were to have an enormous impact in national affairs were born in the Northern Neck region. Most notably, George Washington, Commanding General of the Continental Army during the Revolutionary War and the first president of the United States, was born in Westmoreland County in 1732. That same year, Richard Henry Lee—author of the Leedstown Resolves (see below), and of the resolution, offered before the Continental Congress on June 7, 1776, that the colonies "are, and of right ought to be, free and independent States"—was born at *Stratford Hall*, also in Westmoreland County.

Although of a Piedmont family, James Madison, often called the Father of the Constitution and the fourth president of the United States, was born at the home of his maternal grandmother, near Port Conway in King George County, in 1751. James Monroe, the fifth president, was born in Westmoreland in 1758.

Relations between the colonies and Britain became more and more strained following the successful conclusion to the French and Indian War (1754-1761). Those colonists and colonial governments seeking new lands to the west were outraged by the King's Proclamation of 1763 which prohibited westward expansion, and yet the colonists at the same time fought any and all attempts by the Crown to tax them in order to help pay for their own defense.

This rising tension was brought home most directly to the Northern Neck in 1765-66, after the British parliament had levied the Stamp Act, intended to tax virtually any piece of paper that contained writing or print, including newspapers, pamphlets, and legal and shipping documents. In early 1766, Richard Henry Lee, then of *Chantilly* in Westmoreland County, penned the Leedstown Resolves, and these helped inspire many of the local Sons of Liberty to demand that the Scottish merchants Archibald Ritchie and Archibald McCall of Tappahannock do an about-face and oppose the Stamp Act. Ritchie complied, but McCall did not and was forced into exile in Scotland, from which he did not return until well after the Revolutionary War had ended in 1781. These forceful protests, and others called earlier in the northern colonies, helped lend weight to the repeal of this hated Act, but more importantly seemed to crystallize a growing sentiment towards independence from Britain.

Although many from the Northern Neck served either in local militia groups, the Continental Line or in the Virginia or Continental navies, this region saw little military activity during the Revolution. Some of the more conspicuous plantations near the shoreline of the Potomac River or the Bay, however, were the targets of raids by British privateers who stole their slaves. In at least one instance, late in the War when it had shifted to the south, British privateers shelled and destroyed *Gascony*, in Northumberland County, the bay side home of Col. Thomas Gaskins.

From the Formation of
A Nation to the Civil War

One consequence of the winning of independence was the disestablishment of church and state. Thomas Jefferson's Statute for Religious Freedom, first introduced in the General Assembly in 1779, was finally enacted into law by Virginia in 1786, and its message was later enshrined in the first amendment to the Constitution of the United States.

Although a successor denomination to the Anglican Church had been formed in 1784, this Protestant Episcopal Church met with hostility from the vast majority of citizens, who in the meantime had opted for a more evangelistic approach to religion and in any event believed that the taxes they had paid to maintain the old state-established church during the colonial era entitled them to ownership of its properties—not only its buildings, but the glebes or farms that had supported its ministers.

The glebe lands were sold off in the early 1800s by the overseers of the poor appointed by the county courts. The churches and glebe houses mostly fell into ruin or were vandalized to provide building material for other uses. The best way to do this was often to set fire to the interiors, which loosened the mortar so that bricks might be pried loose, and nails made more accessible.

The Episcopal Bishop William Meade reported in 1838 that *Wicomico Parish Church*, in Northumberland County, was at that point in a worrying state of disrepair, and that what remained of the enormous church was now the storage-place for "the carriage, the wagon, the plow, the fishing-seine, barrels of tar and lime, lumber, and various implements of husbandry. The cattle have free admission to it…and the old bell which once summoned the neighbours to the house of God is lying in one of the pews near the falling pulpit." Its last bricks were sold for a relatively nominal sum to a wealthy farmer who was building a new house, *Ingleside*, across the road.

It was the rare old church or glebe house that escaped this fate. The very few survivors in this region are *St. Paul's Episcopal Church* in King George County; *The Glebe* and *Yeocomico Church* in Westmoreland County; *Christ Church* and *St. Mary's White Chapel Church* in Lancaster County; a much-restored *Farnham Church* in Richmond County; and *Vauter's Church* and *St. Anne's Glebe* in upper Essex County.

In the meantime, the bulk of the population had responded to the Great Awakening of the mid-18th century, which emphasized an experiential, or more personal religious experience than was encouraged under prevailing church doctrine. But even before mid-century, and preceding the more revivalist movements, the Presbyterians, no doubt due in part to the rising importance of Scottish merchants in the economy of the Northern Neck region, had been able to make headway against the Anglican monopoly in some areas, particularly in Richmond, Northumberland and Lancaster counties.

By the time of the Revolution, the Baptists had also become a force to be reckoned with, and itinerant preachers led by the Rev. Lewis Lunsford were already active in several Northern Neck counties. The *Morattico* congregation, the "mother church" of the Baptist denomination in the lower Northern Neck, was organized in Richmond County in 1778, but its present church was built later in Lancaster County close to the boundary with Northumberland. It was followed soon thereafter by *Nomini Baptist Church* in Westmoreland County, whose congregation was formed in 1786.

In 1778, Lunsford baptized, in the waters of Totuskey Creek, Robert ("Councillor") Carter III of *Nomini Hall* in Westmoreland County, a grandson of "King" Carter and one of the wealthiest men in Virginia. But Carter, who had been bucking tradition and conformist opinions all along, also proceeded to leave the Baptist church within about a decade. Before ultimately moving to Baltimore, where he had joined the Swedenborgian church, Robert Carter arranged in 1791 for the controversial gradual emancipation of his more than 450 slaves, located on a number of plantations in Westmoreland County and beyond.

The Methodists arrived on the Northern Neck soon after the Baptists. Bishop Francis Asbury first visited the region in 1785, and in 1787 he preached in a barn that the Fairfields Methodist congregation was using for its meetings in Northumberland County. In 1789-90 that congregation erected its first meeting house or church, and this was followed in 1792 by the deed for the site of the *White Marsh Methodist Church* in Lancaster County.

On June 25, 1788, the Virginia convention narrowly ratified the Constitution of the United States. All the delegates from the Northern Neck region, except those from Essex County, voted for ratification. Indeed, Essex delegates James Upshaw and Meriwether Smith of *Bathurst* outspokenly opposed ratification, although Smith's opposition did not prevent him from later running, unsuccessfully, for the first U.S. Congress.

The early years of the new republic were generally not prosperous ones in the Northern Neck region. As the cultivation of tobacco, with its exhaustion of the soil, became less and less profitable, and with only limited amounts of virgin land locally, most planters still appeared to be slow to diversify adequately and to adopt some of the new farming techniques developed in the North. The lack of opportunity awaiting the younger generations led to continued and indeed accelerated migration westward and, increasingly, beyond the borders of Virginia.

Some of the wealthier planters, however, realized that diversification, into other crops, ironworks and some other manufacturing activities, held out the promise of maintaining their wealth. The Tayloe family, of *Mount Airy* in Richmond County, was particularly successful in this regard. Overall, however, the profitability of slavery was falling in the Northern Neck region, and many planters began to consider whether simply freeing their slaves, or at least some of them, would not make sense. In order to help keep the relative value of slaves from dropping further, the General Assembly in 1785 banned the further importation of slaves, either directly from Africa or from the West Indies.

The value of existing holdings of slaves also was then greatly enhanced by the invention of the cotton gin by Eli Whitney in 1793, and the enormous impact that had on the profitability of growing cotton in the Deep South. Now the selling of slaves southward became a potentially important source of income for Northern Neck planters. It is probably no coincidence that about this same time the General Assembly amended the above 1785 legislation with the provision that all free blacks had to register with their local county clerk, so as to discourage the hiring of blacks "who pretend to be free, but are in fact slaves."

In 1806, further legislation was passed requiring that any slave henceforth emancipated in Virginia would have to leave the state within one year. If the freed slave did not adhere to this law, he or she would be sold at auction to be sent out of the state, while the proceeds from the sale would be turned over to the county's overseers of the poor. This law, although not strictly enforced, aimed at restricting the growth of the free black population in the Commonwealth (and other states), and it was complemented by the creation of the American Colonization Society in 1816, which promoted the voluntary return of blacks to Africa by means of the colonization of what later became known as Liberia.

These trends and laws appear to have resulted in a modest decline in the enslaved population in the Northern Neck region more generally, but the population of free blacks increased. By 1860, on the eve of the Civil War, the enslaved population had fallen to about 23,000, compared to almost 26,000 in 1790, although it still made up about 51 percent of the region's total population (versus about 56 percent in 1790). Over the same period, the number of free blacks increased by more than 2,500, to about 3,400, or about 7 $1/2$ percent of the total population. (In Essex County, however, the proportion of the population enslaved actually increased over this period, from 60 percent in 1790 to 64 percent in 1860. On the eve of the Civil War, Richard Baylor Sr. of upper Essex is thought to have been the largest owner of those slaves who were then living in Virginia.)

The War of 1812 is generally viewed as one of the less necessary wars fought by the United States. Although at war's end, many touted it as a great American victory over the British, the U.S. had been fortunate to emerge from that conflict with barely a draw. As it turned out, the Northern Neck region was much affected by British naval raids. In 1814, after the British had ransacked Washington, D.C., including the White House, and having

unsuccessfully attempted to take Baltimore, their ships proceeded to sail up both the Potomac and Rappahannock rivers looking for targets to pillage.

On the Potomac, a number of residences and other buildings along the river were shelled and in some cases totally destroyed. These included, in Westmoreland County, virtually everything in the lively port town of Kinsale, Justice Bushrod Washington's *Bushfield*, and *Nomini Church*. Northumberland County also suffered badly, with the British landing at Mundy Point in the upper part of the county and burning all but the chimneys of the Davis house, now called *Burnt Chimneys*; burning to the ground *Cypress Farm* on Cherry Point; and raiding the Coan River where they captured or sank a number of local boats and then pillaged the county seat of Heathsville.

The destruction was no less awesome along the Rappahannock River valley. In Lancaster County the British are thought to have bombarded the residence known as *Pop Castle*, perhaps accounting for its unusual name. Essex County, and particularly its county seat of Tappahannock, was also the subject of British retribution. The British troops, arriving in eight armed schooners, sacked the town for three days, not only stealing and vandalizing as they went, but also taking away slaves.

With the war over, life returned basically to normal, but generally the economic situation did not improve. Several planters in the region took the lead in promoting increased diversification of crops and the use of improved agricultural techniques, among them James M. Garnett of *Elmwood* in upper Essex County (one of the founders of the Virginia Agricultural Society), and several members of the Baylor and later, the Taliaferro families of that county. In Westmoreland, Willoughby Newton Jr. of *Linden* served as a U.S. congressman and was president of the Virginia Agricultural Society in 1852.

Despite the general lack of economic prosperity, the construction of large plantation homes continued into the early decades of the 19th century, although none—with the clear exception of Richard Baylor's magnificent *Kinloch* (1840s) in upper Essex County; and possibly also Robert Payne Waring Jr.'s, *Edenetta* (ca. 1828) also in upper Essex, as well as James M. Smith's enlarged *Mantua* (1820s) and William Harding's *Springfield* (1828) in Northumberland—could quite compare with those earlier mentioned mansions of the mid-18th century. These and other large plantation homes frequently blended both Federal and Classical Revival architectural influences. By mid-century, a number of new church buildings in the area, as well as some residences such as *Wirtland* (1850) and *Roxbury* (1861) in Westmoreland County, were drawing on the Gothic Revival style and early Victorian influences.

At the same time, well-to-do but not fabulously wealthy farmers and merchants were building two-story five-bay houses that were both architecturally attractive and commodious. Families of more modest means, referred to at an earlier time as yeoman farmers, might have had 100 or 200 acres and several slaves, and raised and sold enough wheat and corn to pay for their families' wants that exceeded what could be provided by their ample gardens and a few head of cattle.

For generations, some of the wealthiest planters in the region, such as the Lees and the Carters, had sent their sons to England for their education. Many more, however, had educated their sons, and to some extent their daughters, through the use of tutors (Philip Fithian at *Nomini Hall* in 1773-74 being the best known of these, through his famous diary). They often held their classes in a separate brick or frame schoolhouse right on the plantation.

Although various private schools for a larger collection of pupils had also been established, these really only came into their own in the early- to mid-nineteenth century.

Indeed, various private academies that generally provided a classical education were begun and financed by the wealthier families throughout the region. They were numerous, and included the *Northumberland Academy* (1818-1864) in that county (although it was also evidently, and somewhat controversially, supported during its first three decades partly by public funds); the *Tappahannock Female Seminary* (1818-ca. 1860) in Essex County; the *Washington Academy* (1834-44) in Westmoreland; and the *Farnham Academy* (established in 1850) in Richmond County. Other, much simpler schools, were also commonplace in the region, and were often called "field schools" because they were usually small wooden structures built in worked-out fields by neighborhood groups of concerned parents, who would then hire a teacher.

Although public education was promoted in the earliest days of the Commonwealth by Thomas Jefferson, it was very slow to gain support in Virginia. In 1810, the General Assembly enacted a law calling for the establishment of a Literary Fund, to be supported by the proceeds from the sale of former glebe lands, fines, escheats and various confiscations by the state. Through later legislation, this Fund was empowered to help support, among other things, the establishment of local schools for the children of indigent parents. Such school systems—with a county school superintendent and a court-appointed school commissioner for each school district—were founded in subsequent years in several of the Northern Neck counties, and some of these schools survived even through the Civil War.

Very soon, however, there emerged a lively debate over whether public education ought to be extended to all free white children, whether indigent or not. After legislation enacted in 1829 failed to stimulate the voluntary establishment of such schools in more than a few counties, debate continued over whether and how to establish a more universal public school system. New legislation was enacted beginning in 1846, which more concretely spelled out the way in which a county—with the approval of at least two-thirds of its white male adults—could establish a so-called free-school system for all white children, presumably whether indigent or not. Funding would come from both the county and the Literary Fund.

Although a number of counties in the Commonwealth at one time or another tried this new free-school system, it fell far short of becoming a universal system of education for even the white school-age population. Local opposition to such schools frequently came from both the more well-to-do, who were opposed to being taxed for such a purpose, and from many indigent parents, who were loathe to send their children to school and thereby lose their help on the farm. Nevertheless, in King George County, ten so-called free-schools had been opened by 1850, but lack of local financial support led to their demise by the outbreak of the Civil War. Closures of these free schools in King George and most long–established schools for the indigent in other Northern Neck counties were accelerated not only by hard times locally, but by the diversion of Literary Fund resources to the defense effort.

An important antebellum civil reform, which had significant local implications, was the judicial reform incorporated in the Virginia Constitution of 1851 which mandated the popular election of county justices. In addition, many of the other local officials, who had previously been appointed by the still somewhat "hereditary" county courts, were now also to be popularly elected.

The Civil War and Reconstruction

The Northern Neck region can claim no well-known Civil War battleground, but large numbers of its male residents went off to fight in that conflict, many never returning. And while not the site of major conflicts, the location of this region, just south of the Potomac, meant that it was the scene of numerous Union gunboat attacks, foraging, smuggling and to some extent espionage. Moreover, the relative calm in this region did not mean that its residents did not feel strongly about the main issues that brought on the war—slavery and its extension into the western territories, and states' rights.

Significantly, following the secession of the seven states of the Lower South, and prior to the convening of the Virginia convention to consider secession from the Union, delegates from Essex and neighboring King and Queen counties met at *Millers Tavern* in Essex in early February 1861 and adopted the so-called "Millers Resolutions." These contained three important points: (1) the right of states to withdraw from the Union; (2) Virginia was committed to the defense of the South; and (3) a call for Virginia to leave the Union.

After several votes not to secede, the statewide convention finally did vote to secede on April 17, 1861, just days after hostilities began at Fort Sumter in South Carolina. Many young men in the region already belonged to a county militia company, such as the 37th Virginia militia in Northumberland, and the Essex Sharpshooters and other similar companies. But these were soon incorporated into the regular Virginia regiments, mainly the 40th Infantry, the 55th Infantry and the 9th Cavalry. Each of these regiments had distinguished records during the four long years of the bloodiest war in American history.

One of the first tasks of the 55th Infantry was the construction and manning of *Fort Lowry*, in the Dunnsville area south of Tappahannock on the Essex side of the Rappahannock River. Its purpose was to help defend Fredericksburg from Federal naval forces. It included an eight-gun battery, powder and shot magazines, and barracks to hold several thousand troops. Already in March 1862, however, orders came to abandon the fort, and the 55th was assigned to General A. P. Hill's division of the Army of Northern Virginia.

Essex County also was the home of several leaders of the Confederate army and government. Robert Mercer Taliaferro Hunter Sr. (1809-1887) of *Fonthill* was Speaker of the U.S. House of Representatives and a U.S. Senator prior to the Civil War, but with the outbreak of this conflict he became the Secretary of State of the Confederacy. Robert Garnett of *Champlain* and his cousin Richard Brooke Garnett, born at *Rose Hill (Rouzie)*, were both graduates of West Point. Donning the Confederate gray with the onset of the Civil War, they both became brigadier generals. Robert Garnett was the first Confederate general to be killed in the war, and Richard Garnett, who succeeded Thomas "Stonewall" Jackson as commander of the famous Stonewall Brigade, was later killed at Gettysburg.

Of lesser rank but probably better known today was Capt. William Latané of the Essex Light Dragoons of the 9th Virginia Cavalry. Raised at *The Meadow* in central Essex County, Latané achieved figurative immortality locally due to the poem, painting and lithograph "The Burial of Latané" inspired by his death during J. E. B. Stuart's daring cavalry ride around McClellan's Union forces in October 1862.

Virtually no part of the Northern Neck region was immune from minor raids from Union forces. Notable sites of Yankee intrusions or places of destruction include *Woodstock* on the Potomac River in King George County; *Buena Vista* in Westmoreland County, where Union troops captured a blockade runner in the attic; *Rock Hall* in Northumberland, which was raided by Union troops at one point and was located close to where the home guard burned the *Knickerbocker,* a Union steamer, in February 1865; *Pop Castle* in Lancaster County, this time the object of shelling from a Federal gunboat, and also *Greenfield*, which was shelled by Union gunboats after Confederate troops had stolen and sunk the Union ship the *Harriet De Ford* just days before the end of the War; and Tappahannock, which was the site of four incursions of Union forces between April 1862 and March 1865. Tradition has it that the residence known as *Claymont* in Westmoreland County was used as a clandestine headquarters by sympathetic southern Marylanders who ran the Federal blockade to bring supplies to the Confederacy.

King George County was also the route, for several days, of John Wilkes Booth during his escape from Washington, D.C. after his assassination of President Abraham Lincoln. During April 23-24, 1865, Booth and one of his accomplices paused briefly at the *Quesenberry* house and *Cleydael* in King George, before crossing the Rappahannock River from Port Conway to Port Royal in Caroline County. On April 26, Booth was shot and killed in a burning barn surrounded by Federal detectives, at the Garrett farm not far from Port Royal.

Each of the six counties erected monuments in the decades after the Civil War to honor those who had served the Confederate cause. King George County claims to have the oldest such monument in Virginia, dedicated already in 1869, and standing today outside the *King George County Courthouse*. Some, like this, are rather simple obelisks. The monument in Tappahannock, in Essex County, erected in

1909, is crowned by the statue of a Confederate soldier facing north. The monument outside the Northumberland courthouse in Heathsville was dedicated in 1873 and is topped by a classically-robed young woman with one arm reaching upward and another resting gently on top of a ship's anchor.

While heroes to their local populations, and despite the relative lack of military destruction in the region, the returning Confederate soldiers found an economy in shambles and their world for the most part turned upside down. Dandridge Cox, a wealthy planter on Cherry Point in upper Northumberland County, reported that half of his 34 slaves had escaped to behind the Union lines already in 1862, and one of his sons, having fought long and hard as a member of Longstreet's Corps of the Army of Northern Virginia and suffered a lifelong physical wound, noted upon returning home at the end of the War that he "found everything gone and everybody ruined."

Slavery was abolished by the Thirteenth Amendment to the Constitution, ratified in December 1865. Having not yet ratified the Fourteenth Amendment to the U. S. Constitution—which ensured citizenship for all African Americans and due process for all citizens—Virginia was designated the First Military District by the First Reconstruction Act passed by the Congress in March 1867. At the local level, this frequently meant that the U.S. Army interfered in the appointment of local justices and clerks of court. In some cases, this involved seating "carpetbaggers" from the North, or simply others sincerely wishing to carry out the more idealistic goals of Reconstruction.

A new state constitution was passed by referendum in 1869 (often called the Underwood Constitution, after the former New Yorker with radical reconstructionist views who had been named president of the convention), but without the strict loyalty oath and disenfranchisement clauses that had earlier been insisted upon by the radicals. Only then could a new government be established in Virginia that was acceptable to the U.S. Government. After its new legislature ratified the Fifteenth Amendment, which guaranteed the right to vote to all adult male citizens, Virginia was readmitted to congressional representation in January 1870. The military occupation ended and the traditional local interests were now in the position to oust the interlopers.

While radical reconstruction would effectively be sidelined in Virginia, changes were nevertheless in the making. The "plural" county court, which each county in the Northern Neck region had known since their beginnings in the mid-17th century, was now replaced by a single judge, who was to be elected by the General Assembly. At the same time, the county court was relieved of its remaining executive or local legislative duties, and these would be granted to a Board of Supervisors. Except for the fact that in the context of the Constitution of 1902 the county courts would be abolished forever, to be replaced by circuit courts at the county level (also with a single presiding judge), the local governmental and judicial system established in 1870 basically exists to this day.

The Underwood Constitution also provided for the first state-wide system of public education at the elementary level, although as noted earlier public education programs had already been initiated, before the Civil War, in some counties. Efforts to expand public education were seriously affected by the financial problems associated with servicing the state's public debt in the late 1870s, but by 1885 each of the counties in the Northern Neck was reporting growing local support for universal—if segregated—education, and a large growth in the number of schools and of pupils attending them.

The new elementary schools, usually

simply built frame buildings erected on brick piers rather than foundations, tended not to last for a very long time, and every few decades or so needed to be replaced. Examples of early public school houses that have survived in Northumberland County include the *Tellis Run School* on Cherry Point (built in 1873; now used as a dwelling), *Shiloh School* (1906) on Ball's Neck, and *Bluff Point Graded School* (1913).

While these constitutionally mandated changes in local governmental, judicial and educational institutions were still being debated and enacted, the various black communities in the Northern Neck region were establishing their own institutions. These initiatives took place in two principal areas—education and religion.

For the first time, schools were being established for African American children. The effort received strong early support from northern abolitionists who had come to the area and viewed education as an essential factor in helping newly-emancipated blacks become self-sufficient. In Northumberland County, for example, several schools for "the benefit and education of persons irrespective of sex, race, color, or previous condition of servitude" were begun with the financial backing and moral and educational support of white abolitionist schoolmistresses from upstate New York or New England. Within about a four-mile radius of the county seat of Heathsville, at least three such schools were established within just a few years following the end of the War and emancipation—the *Howland School* just south of Heathsville (1867), the *Holley School* to the northwest in Lottsburg (1869), and the *Stebbins School* (1870) just to the east of Heathsville.

After the end of the War, black members of established Baptist and Methodist congregations began requesting, and receiving, letters of dismissal allowing them to form their own congregations. Given the very limited financial resources

available to the black community, their earliest churches were built very simply from wood and have not survived. But many of the early congregations, and their early descendants, continue to this day. These include, among many others, *Good Hope Baptist Church* in King George County; *Zion Baptist Church* in Westmoreland County; *First Baptist Church* and *Galilee Methodist Church* in Northumberland County; *Mount Zion Baptist Church* in Richmond County; and in Essex County, *Antioch Baptist Church*.

1870 to 1940

In the wake of the Civil War and the uncertainties of the Reconstruction period that followed, the economy of the Northern Neck tended to languish. Agriculture was no more productive than it had been before the War, and indeed for awhile it suffered greatly simply due to the basic reorganization of production, with the system of slave labor being replaced by sharecropping and tenant farming. Over time, the new system proved itself, but in the meantime land values had plummeted and many once prosperous farmers or larger planters had become relatively impoverished. Recognizing this situation, the General Assembly enacted in 1870 a Homestead Exemption under which property owners could apply to the county court to protect them from the claims of creditors.

Within several decades, however, the economy of the region began to revive. This was due to two main factors. One was the growing influence of ever-improved steamboats in the Chesapeake region. Although steamboats had been plying the waters of the Rappahannock and the Potomac since the 1820s, technological improvements (including going from the paddle-wheel to propeller-driven steamboats, and larger boats), and growing post-war demand for agricultural products in the rapidly growing areas just to the north, led to stronger economic ties between the Northern Neck region and these former "Yankee" markets. Economically, the fast-moving steamboats were a boon to the region, as the Northern Neck region became an important source of fresh tomatoes, cucumbers and other vegetables, as well as of oysters, crabs and fish of various kinds, for the Annapolis, Baltimore and Washington markets. On their return voyages the vessels brought back traveling salesmen or "drummers," various types of farm equipment, and much of the merchandise that went to make up the inventories of the ubiquitous country stores in the region.

Aside from being commercial links, the steamboats provided connections to Baltimore and other urban centers for hospital access and various educational and social opportunities, and the possibility of attending the "floating theaters" that visited the region. At the same time, they provided a way for city residents to attend church camps and take part in recreational activities on the Northern Neck.

At each of the steamboat landings, which numbered in the dozens, wharves were built to accommodate deep draft vessels, and small villages tended to grow up around many of these wharves. Notable wharves included those at Boyd's Hole in King George County; Kinsale in Westmoreland; Lodge Landing, Cowart's and Coan Wharf in Northumberland; Irvington in Lancaster County; Sharps in Richmond County; and Bowler's Wharf and Tappahannock Wharf in Essex. Of the dozens of landings, only Saunders' Wharf in upper Essex still stands today, looking much like it did in the 1930s.

The steamboat wharves became the commercial centers of the region. Dunnsville, near Ware's Wharf in Essex County, was an example of a small but important local commercial center. In the late 19th century, Dunnsville boasted four stores (three of whose buildings have survived:

The Lancaster, *ca. 1930 (Courtesy of the Steamboat Era Museum, Irvington, Va.)*

Kinsale Wharf, 1904 (Courtesy of the Mariners' Museum, Newport News, Va.)

Lodge Landing, 1920s/1930s (Courtesy of the Mariners' Museum, Newport News, Va.)

Bowler's Wharf, ca. 1930 (Courtesy of the Mariners' Museum, Newport News, Va.)

Tappahannock Wharf, ca. 1930 (Courtesy of the Mariners' Museum, Newport News, Va.)

Ware General Store in Dunnsville (2010 photo)

Ware's Store, established in 1849; Atkins/ Dunn Store, dating from 1868; and Hoskins Store, another post-Civil War establishment), a hotel, and a blacksmith operation.

The region became linked to the northern Chesapeake and the upper Potomac as it never had been before. In fact, it was not uncommon to travel to Richmond (the state capital, after all) by first travelling northwards. Recalling her attendance at a private school southwest of Petersburg, just prior to World War I, a former resident of upper Northumberland County described many years later how she actually got there. It involved an overnight steamboat ride to Washington, D.C., a train ride the next morning to Richmond, a change of stations there, and two more train rides to her school. It was a trip of some 30 to 36 hours, which today could be made in less than three hours by car.

The booming market for vegetables also led to the widespread development of the canning industry in the region. Canneries, which became an important market for farmers and a major source of local employment, were numerous, and included in Richmond County the *Hammack Bros.* tomato cannery in Emmerton, and the *J. W. Welch Company*, which began its cannery operations near Downings, but also later had canneries in Lancaster and Northumberland counties. Other important regional canneries included the *King George Cannery* at Greenlaw's Wharf in that county, on the banks of the Rappahannock River, although the oldest cannery in King George was the *Mount Rose Cannery and Pickle Factory.* William Taliaferro Jr. of upper Essex County was a pioneer in various farming and pickling operations, and founded the *Rappahannock Valley Pickle Company.*

This great Steamboat Era lasted from the 1870s to the mid-1930s (the last run of the *Anne Arundel* between the Northern Neck and Baltimore took place in 1937). Its end was brought on by many factors, including (1) the building of bridges to the Northern Neck and of modern roads more generally, which made long-distance auto

Parks' Cannery, Westmoreland Co., 1930s/1940s (Courtesy of the Kinsale Museum, Kinsale, Va.)

Gillions and Coates Cannery, Westmoreland Co., 1960s (See Photography Credits.)

travel possible and long-distance trucking (including by ferry over the Potomac in the 1930s) economically feasible; (2) the Great Depression and the drastic fall-off of commerce; and (3) a spate of hurricanes that wiped out many of the important remaining steamboat wharves.

The other major economic factor of the time mainly affected just Northumberland and Lancaster counties in the lower Northern Neck. Northern fishing boat captains and entrepreneurs discovered the vast schools of menhaden in the lower Chesapeake Bay. These fish were prized not for eating but for the oil that could be extracted from them, and for the fertilizer and other products that could be made from the fried fish scrap remaining after the oil had been extracted. The first investments made to catch and process these fish in Lancaster and Northumberland counties took place just a few years following the Civil War.

Reedville, named for Elijah Reed of Maine who in 1874 had established a viable menhaden processing plant, became the main center of the region's menhaden industry. Other menhaden industrialists to make fortunes there were Albert Morris and his brother-in-law James C. Fisher, who had come down to the Chesapeake from New Jersey. Around the turn of the 20th century, Reedville, with its "Millionaires Row" of opulent Victorian and Queen Anne style houses, was reputed to be the wealthiest town per capita on the East Coast of the United States.

The menhaden industry also became very important in Lancaster County, with large processing plants erected on Dymer's Creek off of the Bay, and near Irvington and Weems on Carter's Creek off of the lower Rappahannock River. The largest such operations belonged to the

Bellows and Squires Menhaden Factory and the *Taft Fishing Company*. Both in Lancaster and Northumberland counties, the industrial orientation of the menhaden factories and the enormous wealth they created presented a distinct counterpoint to the agrarian hinterlands and the mainly smaller-scale seafood operations in these counties.

What we would consider "bank buildings" first started to spread in this region around the turn of the twentieth century. Examples of early bank buildings that are still standing, although now used for other purposes, include the *Bank of Kinsale* (1910) in Westmoreland County; *Peoples Bank* (1910) of Reedville and *Citizens Bank of Callao* (1919), both in Northumberland; and the *Bank of King George* (1919) in that county seat.

Even up to World War II and beyond, there were really very few "towns" or even villages in the Northern Neck region. Most of these had developed around the county

Bank of Kinsale (2010 photo)

courthouses, but exceptions included Callao and Reedville, both in Northumberland County; and Kilmarnock and Irvington in Lancaster County. Most of the other places with a very small post office and a store or two were very small villages or simply hamlets at crossroads. Examples were Hyacinth in Northumberland County and Farnham in Richmond County.

Among the earliest post offices in this region, dating from the early 1790s or in some cases even earlier, were those at Tappahannock in Essex County; Lancaster Court House (now Lancaster); Northumberland Court House (now Heathsville); Richmond Court House (now Warsaw); and Leedstown, Templeman's Crossroads and Kinsale in Westmoreland County. Most of the post offices in the "hamlets" have been closed over the past several decades.

To this day, one can see fine examples of farmhouses or village homes that reflect the architectural styles that became popular in the last decades of the 19th century and the first decades of the 20th century. In addition to numerous Queen Anne or other Victorian-era style houses (usually found in towns such as Colonial Beach, or Reedville), there are the many large vernacular "I" or "T" farmhouses dotting the landscape, the many examples of the American Four-Square style, as well as the ubiquitous rural

Farnham Store & Post Office (2010 photo)

Old Filling Station in Hyacinth (2010 photo)

I-House, Late 19th Century, Richmond Co. (2010 photo)

T-House, Late 19th Century, Richmond Co. (2010 photo)

American Four-Square House, ca. 1915, Westmoreland Co. (2010 photo)

Craftsman houses of the 1920s. While certainly not as ancient as most of the dwellings inventoried in this book, many of these houses are now well over a century old, and they are gradually disappearing due to neglect or development. In most instances the preservation of these dwellings, and the conservation of the farmland on which many of them stand, will only be possible through determined efforts of the kind outlined in Chapter 9.

Public education at the secondary level, with some degree of matching funds from the Commonwealth, was only introduced in Virginia after 1906 with the adoption of the Mann Act. In many counties, however, it took many years before full-fledged high schools were established. For example, the first two-year public high school in King George County was the *Shiloh School*, established in 1916. It would be 1923 before the first four-year high school was built in the county, on part of the old *Willow Hill* property.

Although a number of separate schools for blacks had been established in the years following the Civil War, these were devoted to primary education. Around the turn of the 20th century, and influenced in part by the examples of the Tuskegee and Hampton institutes, the black communities in the different counties sought to expand educational offerings into vocational and ultimately secondary education. In Essex County, the Southside Rappahannock Baptist Association spurred the establishment of the *Rappahannock Industrial Academy* in 1902. Across the river, in Richmond County, the Northern Neck Baptist Association founded in 1898 the *Northern Neck Industrial Academy*. To the southeast, the *Lancaster County Training School* was established about 1917, and within several years it had become a high school for blacks under its principal and leading educator, Albert Terry Wright, for whom the school was later named.

Also in 1917, the *Northumberland County Training School* was founded in Beverleyville, not far from Reedville. Although this school, like the others, was erected mostly with funds from the local

Rappahannock Industrial Academy (Mid-20th Century Photo, Courtesy of the Virginia Department of Historic Resources, Richmond, Va.)

African American community, it also was a recipient—along with a number of other schools in the region—of funding from the Rosenwald Fund, established by the wealthy philanthropist and benefactor of some 5,000 schools for blacks throughout the South between 1912 and his death in 1932. In the latter year, the Northumberland school was renamed the *Julius Rosenwald High School* in his memory.

But all was not just work or study in the Northern Neck region, and the early decades of the twentieth century saw the development of a number of beaches and associated entertainment centers, often including hotels and beach cottages. Popular shoreline recreation centers from that period included not only the well-known Colonial Beach in Westmoreland County, but also Belvedere Beach and Fairview Beach in King George County, White Stone Beach in Lancaster County, and Chesapeake Beach near Fleeton and Vir-Mar Beach in Northumberland County.

The end of this period, on the eve of World War II, was very much characterized, of course, by the hardships associated with the Great Depression. But perhaps more emblematic was the coming of the automobile and trucking in a major way. The first bridge to the Northern Neck was a drawbridge over the Rappahannock River dedicated in 1927, known as the *Downing Bridge* after the state senator who had pushed for its construction. This bridge ended more than $2^1/_2$ centuries of ferry service connecting Richmond County (and thus the rest of the Northern Neck) with Tappahannock in Essex County. It opened up the peninsula to a much wider world than even the steamboat had made possible, and much more directly. Now Richmond, by way of U.S. 360, came to replace Baltimore as the principal commercial center serving the Northern Neck.

Baltimore, however, was by no means completely removed from the picture. Even before the construction of a bridge spanning the Potomac, Thomas

Jennings Booth of Reedville had received an interstate commerce charter to transport, by ferry, several trucks every night carrying goods of various kinds between the Northern Neck and Baltimore commission houses. The ferry operated across the Potomac, from Potomac Beach in upper Westmoreland County to Morgantown in Charles County, Maryland.

The construction of the *Downing Bridge* was soon followed by the building of the *James Madison Memorial Bridge* (1934) over the Rappahannock River, connecting King George County with Caroline and Essex counties on the south side. The Potomac River Bridge, today known as the *Harry W. Nice Bridge*, was completed in 1940, finally creating a direct highway route between King George County and southern Maryland. U.S. Route 301, which crosses these two bridges, became a major highway linking Baltimore and Washington, D.C. to Richmond, but also it made it easier to reach both the Northern Neck and Essex County. This era of building bridges to the Northern Neck was completed somewhat later, with the construction of the *Robert O. Norris Bridge* connecting Lancaster County with the south side of the Rappahannock in 1957.

While making the Northern Neck region now more accessible to tourists as well as to trucks, the building of these bridges and the continued widening and improvement of the highways leading to the region has been a mixed blessing. This is because the increased traffic and the development it fosters also threatens the pristine nature of the region's landscape as well as the integrity of many of its historic structures.

1940 to the Present

Other than the wartime service of area youths, the most significant impact of World War II in the Northern Neck region was the expansion of the Dahlgren Naval Proving Ground in King George County along the Potomac. With further postwar growth, Dahlgren now covers a land area of 4,300 acres and includes a 20-mile down river range for projectile testing. It is the largest single employer in the Northern Neck region.

As noted in the introduction to this chapter, since World War II the region's population has grown more rapidly, at least by local standards, although the pattern across the counties making up the region has differed. But perhaps the most significant change, in the social sphere, has been the abolition of the legal separation of the races.

The 1954 U.S. Supreme Court decision in *Brown* v. *Board of Education* of course came as a huge shock to the South, including Virginia. In the Commonwealth, this was followed in 1958 by the "massive resistance" policy, whereby in some areas public schools were shut down rather than to allow their being integrated. Within about a decade, however, resistance to the integration of schools had passed, and in the Northern Neck region, while integration proceeded slowly in most counties, it occurred without major incident. Today the discussion—earlier in this chapter—of separate white and black schools, carries a peculiarly anachronistic ring. Segregation was certainly part of the history of this region, just as it was in much of the country, whether by law in the South or *de facto* elsewhere. But while the congregations of most churches in this region are still organized, as a matter of choice, along racial lines, the schools and society and the economy more generally were long ago integrated.

One thing that has not fundamentally changed is the predominantly rural nature of this region. The production of grain and corn has increased markedly, but this has been due mainly to the adoption of sophisticated machinery, hybrid seeds, and better fertilizers, which have led to large gains in productivity, and is not the result, as in earlier centuries, of the expansion of farm acreage. And as in most of the rest of the country, small family farms have gradually tended to give way to large commercial agricultural operations, either through purchase or lease. Today most farms follow a pattern of three-crop rotation (corn, winter wheat or other grain, and soybeans) over a two-year period.

The export of fresh or canned vegetables, and of fresh fish to nearby metropolitan centers, however, has declined precipitously. This has been caused mainly by the invention of refrigerated trucks and railroad cars, and the initiation of air freight shipments from far-off agricultural centers such as Florida and California, and competition from even overseas producers. Pollution and other environmental problems in the Chesapeake Bay and its tributaries have also contributed in a major way to the fall-off of local catches of oysters and a number of other types of seafood. Timber harvesting, on the other hand, has continued apace, in part because of growing demand from the pulp and paper plant at West Point on the Middle Peninsula, together with the maintenance of large wooded areas by their owners.

Overall, the economy of the region has held up, and even grown. This is not only due to increased grain and corn harvests, but also to the area's growing popularity as both a weekend retreat and a retirement community for residents of the rapidly growing metropolitan areas centered on Washington, D.C., Richmond and Baltimore. These "come heres" are attracted to the Northern Neck region by the possibilities for sailing, or for fishing, or for simply seeking out a quieter, still predominantly rural atmosphere. While they are perhaps sometimes oblivious of the customs of this still rural and somewhat isolated region, they are probably second-to-none in their appreciation of it. Indeed, many of them have also been attracted by the possibility of acquiring, stabilizing and restoring historic homes of the type that are discussed in this book.

Selected Bibliography

Axelson, Edith F. *Virginia Postmasters and Post Offices, 1789-1832*. Athens, Ga.: Iberian, 1991.

Baylor, Cherry. "'It Is Better To Light a Candle Than To Curse the Darkness': Henry Christopher, His Land, and the Founding of the Stebbins School During Reconstruction in Northumberland County," *The Bulletin of the Northumberland County Historical Society* 46 (2009): 5-17.

Billings, Warren M. *Sir William Berkeley and the Forging of Colonial Virginia*. Baton Rouge: Louisiana State University Press, 2004.

Brown, Katharine L. *Robert "King" Carter: Builder of Christ Church*. Irvington, Va.: The Foundation for Historic Christ Church, 2001.

Bush, Richard C. "Pillars of Liberty's Temple," *The Bulletin of the Northumberland County Historical Society* 40 (2003): 29-40.

Dabney, Virginius. *Virginia: The New Dominion*. Charlottesville: University Press of Virginia, 1971.

Davison, Doris M. "Chicacoan and Isle of Kent," *The Bulletin of the Northumberland County Historical Society* 35 (1998): 20-30.

Delano, Robert Barnes. "Northern Neck Farming in Historical Perspective," *Northern Neck of Virginia Historical Magazine* 50 (2000): 5941-5946.

Doran, Michael F. *Atlas of County Boundary Changes in Virginia, 1634-1895*. Athens, Ga.: Iberian, 1987.

Dunn, Susan. *Dominion of Memories: Jefferson, Madison and the Decline of Virginia*. New York: Basic Books, 2007.

Egloff, Keith and Deborah Woodward. *The Early Indians of Virginia*. Charlottesville: University of Virginia Press in association with the Virginia Department of Historic Resources, Second Edition, 2006.

Eubank, H. Ragland. *Touring Historyland: An Authentic Guide Book of the Historic Northern Neck of Virginia*. Colonial Beach, Va.: Northern Neck Assoc., 1934.

Evans, Emory G. A "Topping People:" *The Rise and Decline of Virginia's Old Political Elite, 1680-1790*. Charlottesville: University of Virginia Press, 2009.

Farr, R. R. *Virginia School Report, 1885: Fifteenth Annual Report of the Superintendent of Public Instruction for the Year Ending July 31, 1885*. Richmond: R. U. Derr, 1885.

Fischer, David Hackett and James C. Kelly. *Bound Away: Virginia and the Westward Movement*. Charlottesville: University Press of Virginia, 2000.

Fithian, Philip Vickers. *Journal and Letters of Philip Vickers Fithian: A Plantation Tutor of the Old Dominion, 1773-1774* (ed. by Hunter Dickinson Farish). Charlottesville: University Press of Virginia, 1943.

Gearhart, James E. "Northumberland County: Major Events Leading to the Formation of the County," *The Bulletin of the Northumberland County Historical Society* 37 (1995): 69-74.

Grigsby, Hugh Blair. *The History of the Virginia Federal Convention of 1788.* New York: Da Capo Press, 1969; first published in 1890-91.

Harper, Robert R. *Richmond County Virginia, 1692-1992: A Tricentennial Portrait.* Alexandria, Va.: O'Donnell Publications, 1992.

Harrison, Fairfax. *Virginia Land Grants: A Study of Conveyancing in Relation to Colonial Politics.* Richmond: Old Dominion Press, 1925.

Haynie, Miriam. *The Stronghold.* Richmond: Dietz Press, 1959.

Haynie, Miriam. *Reedville 1874-1974.* Reedville, Va.: The Men's Club of Bethany United Methodist Church, 1974.

Haynie, W. Preston. "Northumberland Academy—Its Rise and Decline," *The Bulletin of the Northumberland County Historical Society* 38 (2001): 31-48.

Heads of Families at the First Census of the United States Taken in the Year 1790 (Records of the State Enumerations: 1782 to 1785) Virginia. Wash., D.C.: Government Printing Office, 1908.

Hening, William Waller. *The Statutes at Large.* Richmond: Multiple vols., 1820s.

Horn, James. *Adapting to a New World.* Chapel Hill: University of North Carolina Press, 1994.

Howard, A. E. Dick. *Commentaries on the Constitution of Virginia.* Charlottesville: University Press of Virginia, 2 vols., 1974.

Jenkins, F. W. Jr. "The Lost Colonial Port Towns of the Northern Neck," *The Bulletin of the Northumberland County Historical Society* 38 (1991): 40-48.

Jett, Carolyn H. "Northumberland County, Virginia," *The Bulletin of the Northumberland County Historical Society* 34 (1997): 7-20.

Jett, Carolyn H. "Northumberland County 1700-1783," *The Bulletin of the Northumberland County Historical Society* 35 (1998): 31-39.

Jett, Carolyn H. "Northumberland County 1783-1860," *The Bulletin of the Northumberland County Historical Society* 36 (1999): 71-85.

Jett, Carolyn H. *Lancaster County, Virginia: Where the River Meets the Bay.* Lancaster, Va.: The Lancaster County Book Committee, 2003.

Jones, Elizabeth Headley. "Yesterday Along the Coan River," *The Bulletin of the Northumberland County Historical Society* 16 (1979): 50-52.

Kauffman, Michael W. *American Brutus: John Wilkes Booth and the Lincoln Conspiracies.* New York: Random House, 2004.

Kinsley, Ardyce and Don Kinsley. *Passage to Sharps: From Plantation to Village.* Sharps, Va.: Gazebo Books, 1996.

La Follette, Robert, Anita Harrower and Gordon Harrower. *Essex County Virginia: Historic Homes.* Lancaster, Va.: Anchor Communications for the Essex County Museum, 2002.

Lee, Elizabeth Nuckols and Jean Moore Graham. *King George County: A Pictorial History.* Virginia Beach, Va.: Donning, 2006.

Levy, Andrew. *The First Emancipator: The Forgotten Story of Robert Carter.* New York: Random House, 2005.

Lowe, Richard. *Republicans and Reconstruction in Virginia, 1856-70.* Charlottesville: University Press of Virginia, 1991.

McCarty, William M. and Thomas A. Wolf. "The Cox Cousins of Cherry Point: Divergent Geographical Paths and Different Allegiances During the Civil War," *The Bulletin of the Northumberland County Historical Society* 46 (2009): 79-95.

McClure, Phyllis. "Rosenwald Schools in the Northern Neck," *Virginia Magazine of History and Biography* 113 (2), 2005: 114-145.

McGuire, Lillian H. *Uprooted and Transplanted: From Africa to America.* New York: Vantage Press, 1999.

McKenney, Robert N. "The History of the Menhaden Industry in Virginia," *Northern Neck of Virginia Historical Magazine* 10 (1960): 910-928.

Maddox, William Arthur. *The Free School Idea in Virginia Before the Civil War.* New York: Teachers College, Columbia University, 1918.

Meade, Bishop William. *Old Churches Ministers and Families of Virginia.* Philadelphia, 2 vols. 1857.

Miller, Cynthia Leonard. *The General Assembly of Virginia: July 30, 1619-January 11, 1978.* Richmond: Virginia State Library, 1978.

Miller, Mary R. *Place Names of the Northern Neck of Virginia.* Richmond: Virginia State Library, 1983.

Morgan, Edmund S. *American Slavery—American Freedom: The Ordeal of Colonial Virginia.* New York: W. W. Norton, 1975.

Morrison, A. J. *The Beginnings of Public Education in Virginia, 1776-1860.* Richmond: Davis Bottom, 1917.

Morton, Louis. *Robert Carter of Nomini Hall.* Williamsburg, Va.: Colonial Williamsburg, Inc., 1945.

Nelson, John K. *A Blessed Company: Parishes, Parsons, and Parishioners in Anglican Virginia, 1690-1776.* Chapel Hill: University of North Carolina Press, 2001.

Norris, Walter Biscoe Jr., ed. *Westmoreland County Virginia: 1653-1983.* Montross, Va: Westmoreland County Board of Supervisors, 1983; 4th Edition, 2008.

Nugent, Nell Marion. *Cavaliers and Pioneers, Volume 1, 1623-1666.* Richmond: Dietz Press, 1934.

Parent, Anthony S. *Foul Means: The Formation of a Slave Society in Virginia: 1660-1740.* Chapel Hill: University of North Carolina Press, 2003.

Potter, Stephen R. *Commoners, Tribute, and Chiefs: The Development of Algonquian Culture in the Potomac Valley.* Charlottesville: University Press of Virginia, 1993.

Presnall, Clifford C. "Ferrys of the Northern Neck of Virginia," *Northern Neck of Virginia Historical Magazine* 29 (1979): 3258-3280.

Rice, James D. *Nature & History in the Potomac Country.* Baltimore: The Johns Hopkins University Press, 2009.

Rountree, Helen C., Wayne E. Clark and Kent Mountford. *John Smith's Chesapeake Voyages, 1607-1609.* Charlottesville: University of Virginia Press, 2007.

.

Ryland, Elizabeth Lowell, ed. *Richmond County: A Review Commemorating the Bicentennial.* Richmond: Whittet and Shepperson, 1976.

Scarborough, William Kauffman. *Masters of The Big House: Elite Slaveholders of the Mid-Nineteenth Century South.* Baton Rouge: Louisiana State University Press, 2003.

Simmons, C. Jackson. *Speaking of the Northern Neck of Virginia.* Self-published, 1998.

Slaughter, James B. "School Desegregation in the Northern Neck," *Northern Neck of Virginia Historical Magazine* 32 (1982): 3615-3651.

Slaughter, James B. *Settlers, Southerners, Americans: The History of Essex County, Virginia 1608-1984.* Salem, W.Va.: Walsworth Press, Inc., 1985.

Virginia Statistical Abstract. Charlottesville: Weldon Cooper Center for Public Service, University of Virginia, 1999.

Walsh, Lorena S. *Motives of Honor, Pleasure, & Profit: Plantation Management in the Colonial Chesapeake, 1607-1763.* Chapel Hill: University of North Carolina Press, 2010.

Warner, Thomas Hoskins. *History of Old Rappahannock County, Virginia, 1656-1692.* Tappahannock: Pauline Pearce Warner, 1965.

Welch, John W. II. "Tomato Canning on the Northern Neck of Virginia: History of Evenripe Brand Tomatoes and the Welch Canneries," *The Bulletin of the Northumberland County Historical Society* 41 (2004): 85-89.

Wells, Camille. "The Eighteenth-Century Landscape of Virginia's Northern Neck," *Northern Neck of Virginia Historical Magazine* 37 (1987): 4217-4255.

Wells, Camille. "The Planter's Prospect: Houses, Outbuildings, and Rural Landscapes in Eighteenth Century Virginia," *Winterthur Portfolio* 28(1), 1993: 1-31.

Wells, Camille. "The Multistoried House: Twentieth-Century Encounters with the Domestic Architecture of Colonial Virginia," *Virginia Magazine of History and Biography* 106(4), 1998: 353-418.

Wilson, John C. *Virginia's Northern Neck: A Pictorial History.* Virginia Beach, Va.: Donning, 1984.

Wolf, Thomas A. "The 1679 Tithables List for Northumberland County: Its Context and Significance," *The Bulletin of the Northumberland County Historical Society* 41 (2004): 24-39.

Wolf, Thomas A. "Another Place in Time: The Cherry Point 'Community' in the Late Colonial and Early Federal Periods, 1760-1810," *The Bulletin of the Northumberland County Historical Society* 43 (2006): 12-36.

Wolf, Thomas A. "Northumberland County Court Order Books in the Context of Judicial and Governmental Reform in Virginia, 1789-1904," *The Bulletin of the Northumberland County Historical Society* 45 (2008): 54-67.

Chapter 3
King George

King George County, named for King George I of Great Britain, was formally established as a county in 1721, although early English settlement here dates from the mid-17th century. The county lies between the Potomac and Rappahannock rivers at the northern end of the peninsula known as the Northern Neck. Since 1785, the county seat has been at the small town on Route 3 now known simply as King George.

The county is composed of 187.8 square miles, of which 180.0 square miles are land. The population of King George County in 1790 was 7,366, of which 44 percent was free. Although the county's population by 1940 had fallen to 5,431, by 2000 it had risen to 16,803, making it the most populous county in the Northern Neck region.

Historic Sites in King George County

Beginning at the intersection of Routes 301 and 205

Ralph Bunche High School (1) Named after the African American educator, diplomat and Nobel Peace Prize winner, this school was dedicated in 1949 as a result of a suit filed by black citizens of King George County in 1946 and a federal district court order of 1948 calling for the provision of "separate but equal" education for black students in the county. In

1954, the landmark U.S. Supreme Court decision in *Brown* v. *Board of Education* declared that "separate but equal" was still discriminatory, and with the completion of the new desegregated King George High School in 1968, the Ralph Bunche High School was closed and thereafter was used for various educational offices, programs and meetings. The alumni of the school formed a preservation committee in 1998 after plans for demolishing the building had been discussed. Later that year the county Board of Education approved a resolution to preserve the building. *VLR and NRHP. Visible from the road; owned by the county. (Map A)*

Ralph Bunche High School (1)

Hanover Baptist Church (2) This church was established in 1789, making it the oldest Baptist church in King George County. Nearly all Baptist churches in the county have been formed from this church or its offspring. In 1820, Ebenezer Baptist Church was established; it was later named Round Hill Baptist Church and moved to its present location. In 1856, Shiloh Baptist Church was formed. Both blacks and whites worshipped at many

King George County

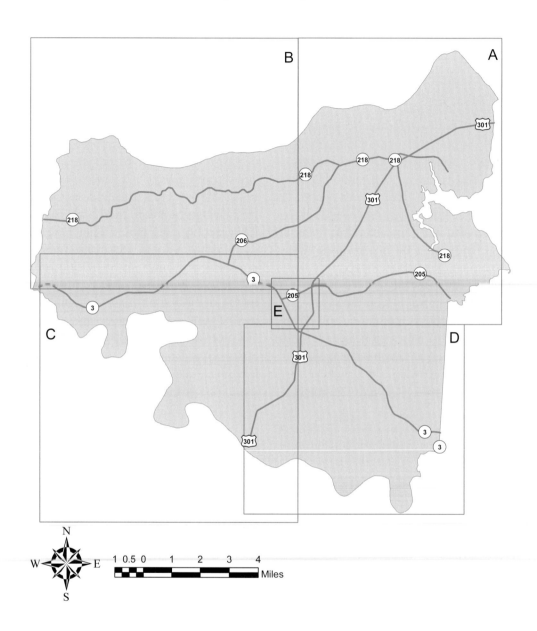

Hanover Baptist Church (2)

of these early churches, including Little Zion Baptist Church, whose trustees were deeded the former Hanover church building in 1868 when that congregation built a new church. The first Hanover meeting house was located at Shiloh, and the second was located at Allnut. The third and present church building was built in 1873 on land donated by James F. Jones. The church was enlarged in 1907, and the gallery was removed and the floor was inclined. Sunday school rooms were built in the basement and additional improvements were made in the 1950s. A fellowship hall was added later. *Visible from the road. (Map A)*

Ashland (3) The original part of this unusual two-story gable-roofed brick house, sitting atop an English basement, is thought to date from about 1800, and may have had a side-hall plan. It was laid in Flemish bond, but appears to have been partially destroyed by fire in the mid-19th

Ashland (3)

century. Both Union and Confederate troops rested here during the Civil War. The house was partially rebuilt in 1879, and that may be when the three-story addition on the right hand side was built. An old brick smokehouse, also laid in Flemish bond, is still standing on the property. It is uncertain who actually built the original house; over the past two centuries it has passed through many hands. *Visible from the road; privately owned. (Map A)*

Office Hall (4) What remains today of an earlier 18th century plantation of this name in the southeast section of King George County are these largely unaltered early 19th-century brick outbuildings—a two-story detached kitchen and a large, hip roof smokehouse. In the late 20th century, the buildings were moved to their present site in order to preserve them. Many believe that it was at Office Hall that William "Extra Billy" Smith (1797-1887), a U.S. congressman, Confederate congressman, and two-time Governor of Virginia, was born.

The kitchen, which dates from 1805-20, is one of the very few one-room, two-story brick plantation kitchens still

Office Hall (4)

extant in Virginia. It has several unusual features, including formal Federal detailing, a mixture of brickwork patterns, and a second-story room originally accessible only by an exterior stair. It is believed to have been used as a school by the mid-19th century.

King George County, Map A

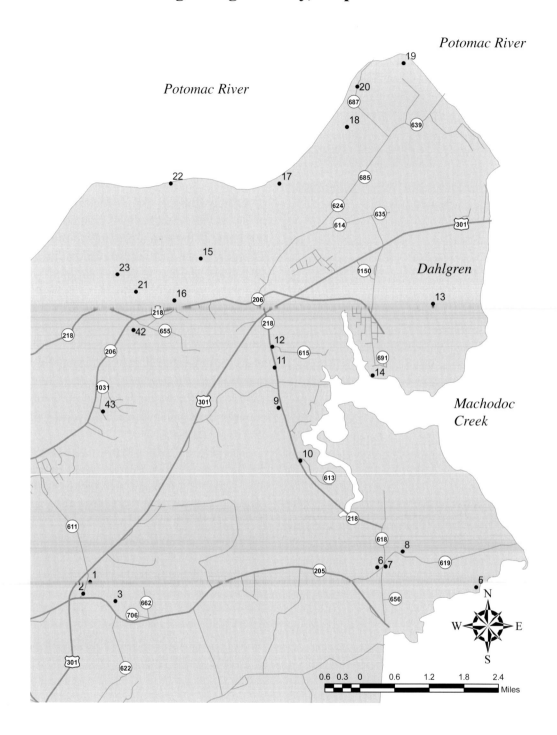

Potomac River

Potomac River

Dahlgren

Machodoc Creek

The builders of the smokehouse, which dates from the same period, dispensed with tie beams and instead used false joists fastened to outriggers resting atop the four walls, in order to create an unencumbered roof space for hanging meat. *VLR and NRHP. Visible from the road; privately owned. Endangered. (Map D)*

Marengo (5) This house, situated on Rozier's Creek with an excellent view of the Potomac River, is the competitor of Office Hall (4) as the likely birthplace of former Virginia governor William "Extra Billy" Smith. The original home here dated from the 18th century, and possibly earlier, the land on which it stands having belonged to both the paternal grandfather and great-grandfather of George Washington. The kitchen of the original house was in the English basement. After that house burned, the present frame structure was built in the early 19th century with lumber from the earlier dwelling. Additions were made in the first half of the 20th century. *Visible from the road; privately owned. (Map A)*

Marengo (5)

Good Hope Baptist Church (6) Good Hope, Antioch, Little Ark, Salem and St. Stephen's Baptist churches are all African American churches with roots from the Reconstruction period. Prior to the Civil War, there were no established black churches in King George County. After the War and with emancipation,

African Americans desired a place of worship of their own. The earliest known places of worship were brush arbors. At one of these, just below Spy Hill (8) at Ninde, the first recorded African American church in the county was established by former members of Ebenezer (now known as Round Hill) Baptist Church. This new church was recorded as Good Hope Baptist Church when one acre of land was donated to its members by Col. Thomas B. B. Baber in June 1868. The present church stands on this same site.

The second black Baptist church was originally known as Little Zion Church, whose trustees had received by donation, in July 1868, the former building of Hanover Baptist Church. Little Zion came to be known as Antioch Baptist Church, which stands on its original site at Edgehill. In 1869, a group of worshippers purchased land and built Salem Baptist Church near Welcome. This was the third African American church to be founded in King George County, and the present church stands on its original site. Two other churches were formed in the 1870s: Saint Stephen's Baptist Church and Little Ark Baptist Church. Both were established by Antioch's ministerial sons. The Rev. John Dunlop and the Rev. Woodson Hickerson founded St. Stephen's at Comorn in 1873. Rev. Hickerson then moved on and founded the Little Ark Baptist Church at Owens in 1876. Both churches today stand on their original sites. *All are visible from the road. (Map A)*

Good Hope Baptist Church (6)

Round Hill/Tetotem (7) These are the two names that are used to describe this historic area of King George County running from Machodoc Creek to Rozier's Creek and on to Route 205 in Westmoreland County. Until 1778, when the county lines were redrawn, this was part of Westmoreland. Round Hill was a large estate of over 2,000 acres owned by one of George Washington's great-grandfathers. The Washington family built Round Hill Anglican Church in 1720-22, which replaced a log building dating from the last quarter of the 17th century. Tetotum was a plantation of 1,076 acres owned here by Nathaniel H. Hooe until his death in 1844. It was in this area that Good Hope Baptist Church (6), the first black Baptist church in King George County, was established in 1868. *Visible from the road; private/public property. (Map A)*

Round Hill/Tetotem (7)

Spy Hill site (8) This site, so named because the large hill to the north was used during the War of 1812 to watch for British ships on the Potomac River, once contained a large frame house. The original structure, believed to have been built in 1734, was a 16-foot square, two-story home over a basement, with a wide-paneled winder stairway. A large chimney at one end served two fireplaces, and the opposite wall was constructed of brick nogging. The property passed from the Washington family to Col. Thomas B. B. Baber in the early 1800s, and Baber is thought to have added a large two-story addition with two chimneys at both ends, with a wing connecting with the original house. The Garnett family and their Taliaferro descendants have owned this property since 1828. Time and termites took their toll on the structure, however, and having been vacant from 1967, it had collapsed by 2009. Much of the woodwork and other old items have been saved, however, and the original colonial section is now in the process of restoration. *Site not visible from the road; privately owned. (Map A)*

Spy Hill site (8)

Society Hill site (9) A two-story, five-bay brick Georgian style home, with a gable roof and interior end chimneys, was built here by Col. Francis Thornton in the mid-18th century. Thornton built his dock at the foot of the property on the Potomac River, and it was visited by ocean-going ships. He was also a well-known owner of race horses. Several generations of the Thornton family lived here, and later it became the property of the Hooe family. In the late 19th century the house was struck by lightning and was in ruins for many years until it was dismantled and the bricks were sold in the early 20th century to the Mount Vernon Ladies Association, which had them transported by barge to Mount Vernon where they were used to repair the walls between the manor house and the servants' quarters. *Site not visible from the road; privately owned. (Map A)*

Society Hill site (9)

Rokeby (north) site (10) One of two houses by this name, Rokeby (north) was originally part of the Society Hill tract overlooking the Potomac River. The house was built by George D. Ashton Jr. in 1848, and a local post office was located here for many years. The original house has been remodeled several times and is now twice its original size. On the property is an old brick well, some 90 feet deep, which had to be filled in. The farm's old wharf can still be seen to the left of the present house. *Visible from the road; privately owned. (Map A)*

Rokeby (north) site (10)

Windsor (11) Also once part of the Society Hill plantation, this two-story three-bay, side-hall house was built in the Federal style about 1830 by Henry Thacker Washington Jr., a cousin of the president. The frame house, on a high basement, has a gable roof and two chimneys at one end of the original portion. The shed-like addition was probably made sometime later. *Visible from the road; privately owned. (Map A)*

Windsor (11)

Buena Vista (12) This rambling house is thought to have been built in the mid-to late-19th century by John Peyton Washington, a relative of the Washingtons of Windsor (11). The rear of the house appears to have been originally the front. The dwelling is a $2^1/_2$ story frame farmhouse with a hip roof, and overlooks the Potomac River valley. Together with its surrounding early 20th century outbuildings, the house represents a vernacular farm complex. *Visible from the road; privately owned. (Map A)*

Buena Vista (12)

Dahlgren (13) Named in 1921 for Rear Admiral John Adolphus Dahlgren, usually viewed as the father of modern ordnance

Dahlgren (13)

and gunnery, this proving ground was commissioned during World War I as the safety hazards of the traditional proving ground at Indian Head, Maryland—farther up the Potomac—became more apparent. On the eve of and during World War II, the facility was expanded, taking in much of Pumpkin Neck, which had been included in Tetotem (7) and Spy Hill (8) and other properties. Although mainly a testing area, Dahlgren personnel also were involved to a small degree with the Manhattan and Elsie projects to develop the atomic bomb. With the advent of computers, Dahlgren became a major research and development center in the late 1950s. Dahlgren now has a land area of 4,300 acres that include several miles of Potomac shoreline, and a 20-mile down river range for projectile testing. *Owned by the federal government. (Map A)*

Quesenberry House (14) On the Machodoc Creek, in Dahlgren, the Cottage, as it is frequently called, is the first house where Abraham Lincoln's assassin, John Wilkes Booth, stopped for aid after he had crossed the Potomac River into Virginia.

Quesenberry House (14)

Mrs. Rose Quesenberry, a widow with small children, was later arrested for allegedly assisting Booth. This old photograph shows a $1^1/_2$ story frame house with a chimney at one end, and probably a later addition on the chimney side. Today the house bears little resemblance to the 19th century cottage due to multiple additions. *Visible from the road; privately owned. (Map A)*

Beginning at the intersection of Routes 301 and 218

Panorama site (15) The Panorama property, also known as Green Hill, was originally part of the Bedford estate owned by the Fitzhugh family, and was known for its very scenic view. About 1830, Richard Henry Stuart Jr. of Cedar Grove (22) bought the property for his daughter and her husband, Thomas Lomax, who had the house built about 1835. It was a two-story three-bay brick house with chimneys at both ends, set atop an English basement. By the 1930s, when it was visited by WPA photographers, the house had already been abandoned. It burned in the 1960s and is now a lost site. *Site not visible from the road; privately owned. (Map A)*

Panorama site (15)

Hylton site (16) This was an old seat of the Washington family. John Washington,

King George County, Map B

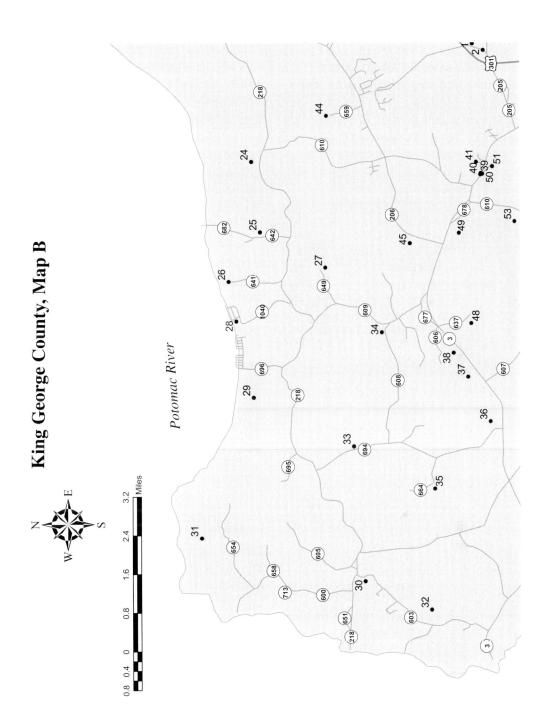

Potomac River

a great uncle of the president, purchased Hylton in 1690. According to a diary, George Washington dined with his brothers and cousins at Hylton in 1768. Little is known about the architecture of the original dwelling. By the early 1970s, the house, by then a two-story three-bay gable-roofed house with a frontal wing extending from the left hand side bay, was in poor condition, but it is still standing. *Not visible from the road; privately owned. (Map A)*

Hylton site (16)

Waterloo site (17) Originally called Chotank, this property stood in Stafford County until 1778, when the county lines were redrawn. George Washington's father, Augustine Washington, spent his childhood here as a ward of a cousin, after being orphaned in 1697/98. The name was changed to Waterloo much later. The president visited here often, both as a youth and an adult. The house passed out of the Washington family in 1842, and

Waterloo site (17)

was later destroyed, although its ruins still exist. Lewis Alexander Ashton II built this two-story frame house on the property about 1905. His father is said to be the one who shot and killed the Union soldier who had killed Capt. William Latané during Stuart's daring ride around Gen. McClellan's army in October 1862 (see The Meadow site (29) in Essex County), and whose burial became one of the symbols of The Lost Cause. Waterloo is a "Century Farm." *Site not visible from the road; privately owned. (Map A)*

Liberty (18) This deep two-story five-bay frame house, with three interior chimneys and an asymmetrical hip roof, stands on an eminence overlooking the Potomac River about a mile upriver from Mathias Point. The house was built by Col. John Stuart in 1824-25, and consists of four large rooms on each floor with a center hall with a fine curving stairway. It has recently been subject to considerable restoration. *Not visible from the road; privately owned. (Map A)*

Liberty (18)

Mathias Point area (19) This point of land, often referred to as the Great Eastern Bend, is located at a tortuous turn on the Potomac River upstream from what is now called the Dahlgren (13) area. It was named for Mathias Hooe in 1713, about the same time the first regularly scheduled ferry across the river was established by Col. William Hooe. Barnesfield, evidently a large brick house on Mathias Point, was the home of the Hooe family. George Washington often referred to the house in his diary as the place where he stayed before crossing the Potomac on his travels north.

Barnesfield was destroyed during the Civil War, when the Union gunboat *Resolute* shelled the house after Confederate militia had burned a grounded Union ship. The Ruggles Confederate camp was located at Mathias Point in early 1861, but a Union gunboat was also assigned to remain near the point for the war's duration to catch spies and disrupt smuggling. The first naval officer to die in the Civil War, Comdr. James Ward of the Federal navy, was killed in a skirmish at Mathias Point. *Historical Marker EP-6. Visible from the road. (Map A)*

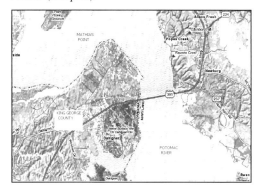

Mathias Point area (19)

Woodstock (20) A large brick home on this property, which was situated in Stafford County before the county lines were redrawn in 1778, was probably built by a member of the Stuart family in the late 18th or early 19th century. It was burned by Union troops in 1862. The original part of the present frame house, which is a two-story three-bay frame dwelling with a gable roof and two interior chimneys, with a frontal gable centered over the porch that runs the width of the front façade, was built ca. 1865 by George Washington Park Custis Grymes as the replacement to his destroyed home. *Not visible from the road; privately owned. (Map A)*

Woodstock (20)

Litchfield (21) This two-story two-bay frame house has a side-hall plan and tall exterior chimneys at each end of a gable roof. It was built about 1802 by Langhorne Dade, and the Dade family owned the house until 1852 when it was sold to James Arnold. *Visible from the road; privately owned. (Map A)*

Litchfield (21)

Cedar Grove (22) This property came into the Stuart family through marriage in 1750. The present house, which replaced an earlier one on the property, was built in late Georgian style about 1840 as a two-story, five-bay hip roof brick building with two large external end chimneys. Almost certainly added later are three-story wings to either side, each with its own interior end chimney ranging out of a semi-hip roof. *Not visible from the road; privately owned. (Map A)*

Cedar Grove (22)

Caledon Natural Area (23) Once a 17th century estate belonging to the Alexander family, and the site of an early 18th century ferry as well as an early tobacco inspection station known as Boyd's Hole, this property is now known as the Caledon Natural Area. Col. William Fitzgerald operated a ferry here beginning in 1705, and this later became the southern terminal of a ferry to Nalley's Landing across the Potomac River on the Maryland shore. Boyd's Hole developed from a tobacco inspection station in 1742 to a commercial hub on the eve of the Revolution. This included *inter alia* an ordinary (tavern), ferry, and storehouse. A century later, steamboats stopped at Boyd's Hole almost daily.

Today's Caledon Natural Area, a gift by Ann Hopewell Smoot to the county in 1973 in the memory of her husband, Lewis Egerton Smoot (also see King George Courthouse complex (39)), includes a large population of eagles, a $3\frac{1}{2}$ mile

Caledon Natural Area (23)

long nature trail leading to the Potomac River, and demonstrations of early farming techniques. *Visible from the road; open to the public. (Map A)*

Mount Stuart (24) Built about 1780 by John J. Stuart, this two-story, five-bay predominantly frame gable-roofed manor house has several additions and a total of fourteen bedrooms. The principal façade is accented by a two-story four-columned Greek Revival portico extending the length of the three center bays. It was later acquired by the Grymes family and in the late 20th century was the property of Lewis Egerton Smoot and his family. *Visible from the road; privately owned. (Map B)*

Mount Stuart (24)

Eagle's Nest complex (25) Eagle's Nest was the family seat established by William Fitzhugh (1651-1701), who emigrated to Virginia in the early 1670s. It came to be the core of a plantation that is said to have included more than 54,000 acres in the late 17th century. The family cemetery on the grounds includes many very early Fitzhugh family graves, including that of the immigrant. His son, also named William, married Ann Lee, the only daughter of Richard Lee II of Machodoc (66) in Westmoreland County, thereby joining two very influential families, and she and her first husband are buried at Eagle's Nest as well. (It remains highly debated to this day whether William Fitzhugh I first built the lost site Bedford as

Eagle's Nest (25)

his home, or whether Eagle's Nest was actually his first house of consequence.)

The house suffered severe damage from a fire in the late 18th century, and several additions were made in the first half of the 19th century. The main part of the present house is a two-story frame structure with a gable roof and two very tall interior chimneys that serve eight working fireplaces. Inside, the house has two end stair halls which are connected by a central transverse hall.

Also at the Eagle's Nest complex are two very old houses that were rescued from possible destruction by the late 20th- and early 21st-century owner of Eagle's Nest and were moved to that property. One is the Indian Town house, a 1½ story dormered house with tall end chimneys, and which by local tradition may have been built in the 17th century, and later, in the 18th century, became the office of Thomas, Lord Fairfax (1693-1781). The proprietor of the Northern Neck Proprietary through inheritance, Fairfax later moved to Greenway in the Shenandoah Valley. A second building moved onto this property is the Richard Henry Hudson house. This log dwelling has been dated to the period 1780-1820. *VLR and NRHP. Historical Marker J-103. Visible from the road; privately owned. (Map B)*

Chatterton (26) This house, situated on a bluff near the Great Eastern Bend, is believed to have been built by John Tayloe

several decades prior to the Civil War, after a land exchange with Henry Thacker Washington Jr., who built Windsor (11). During the War, Chatterton Landing was an important shipping point for the Confederacy, and the house is said to have been occupied by a Confederate officer. Much of the original plantation remains in the Tayloe family. As it stands today, the house is a two-story, five-bay brick dwelling with a gable roof and interior end chimneys. At each end there is also an addition. *Visible from the road; privately owned. (Map B)*

Chatterton (26)

Marmion (27) Built in the second quarter of the 18th century, for John Fitzhugh or his son Philip, this home remained in that family until purchased in 1785 by George Lewis, a nephew of George Washington and son of Col. Fielding Lewis and Betty Washington, who built Kenmore in Fredericksburg. The house remained in the Lewis family until 1977, and has since undergone restoration. The two-story, five-bay frame dwelling has a gable roof and interior end chimneys built with all-glazed header brickwork flush with the frame siding. The wood paneling in the largest room on the first floor was purchased in the early 20th century by the Metropolitan Museum of Art in New York, where it is presently displayed. Tradition has it that during the Revolutionary War, a Hessian mercenary soldier found ill on the banks of the Potomac River was cared for by the

Marmion (27)

family until restored to health, and in gratitude he painted the elaborate scenes on the woodwork, in the manner then prevailing in Europe. *VLR and NRHP. Historical Marker J-63. Visible from the road; privately owned. (Map B and Map C)*

Fowkes site (28) This was the ancestral seat of the Fowkes family, one of whom was the grandmother of the 18th century statesman George Mason IV of Gunston Hall. The core of the house—a simple 1½ story frame dwelling with narrow chimneys at each end—appeared to date from the 18th century and was still standing in the 1930s when photographed by WPA researchers. *Site not visible from the road; privately owned. (Map B)*

Fowkes site (28)

Friendly Cottage (29) The original section of this 1½ story frame dormered house with exterior end chimneys is believed to date from the early 18th century. At some point, a rear addition and shed-like side additions were built. Originally located near Fairview Beach

at Smith's Wharf, the house was moved to higher ground and renovated after the hurricane of 1932 nearly took it into the Potomac River. *Visible from the road; privately owned. (Map B)*

Friendly Cottage (29)

Fletcher's Chapel (30) An early Methodist congregation constructed a church across the street from the present building in 1851. During the Civil War, the church was seized by Union troops and used as a hospital to treat smallpox victims. The building was then burned by these soldiers. Following the War, land was deeded on the present site for construction of a new church. The present edifice, with Gothic Revival features, was built between 1894 and 1909. *Visible from the road. (Map B and Map C)*

Fletcher's Chapel (30)

Passapatanzy Indian site (31) This was one of the many towns inhabited by members of the Patawomeck (anglicized to Potomac) Indian tribe in the area where the upper Potomac River begins to take another turn to the north. While it is known that Capt. John Smith came in contact with the Patawomecks during his exploratory expedition up the Potomac in June/July 1608, there is no written record of his having stopped at this village. It was in this area that Pocohantas was kidnapped by Samuel Argall and his men in 1613 and taken off to Jamestown, from whence she later met and married John Rolfe. *Exact location unknown. (Map B)*

Friedland (32) During the Civil War, Union troops occupied this house, but allowed various members of the Hooe family to continue living in an addition on the rear. The house—a two-story, five-bay frame structure with a gable roof and two external end chimneys—was probably built in the late 18th or early 19th century. The addition projecting from the center of the front façade was added much later. *Visible from the road; privately owned. Endangered. (Map B and Map C)*

Friedland (32)

Green Heights (33) The original portion of this frame house, built about 1820 by Addison Hansford, possibly consisted of just the two-story, three-bay gable-roofed section to the left, with a side-hall plan. This is uncertain, however, because before its restoration in the late 20th century, the house had fallen into very poor condition and was used as a chicken coop. *Visible from the road; privately owned. (Map B and Map C)*

Green Heights (33)

Strawberry Hill (34) The construction date of this house is uncertain, although its original aspects—including the English basement—would appear to date from at least the early-19th century, when it was owned by the Wallace family. It was later Victorianized, probably by Dr. John Thomas Minor, and an eight-foot deep porch now encompasses the body of the house. The entryway features interior stained glass doors, and the fireplace hearths exhibit different designs of Italian marble. *Visible from the road; privately owned. (Map B and Map C)*

Strawberry Hill (34)

White Hall (35) White Hall is a gracious but unpretentious two-story, five-bay Federal style brick house with a standing seam gable roof and exterior end chimneys. While the property, and probably an earlier house standing on it, belonged to the Rev. James Wishart (d. 1774) of nearby Lambs Creek Church (36), this house likely dates from the very late 18th or possibly the early 19th century. Later it

King George County, Map C

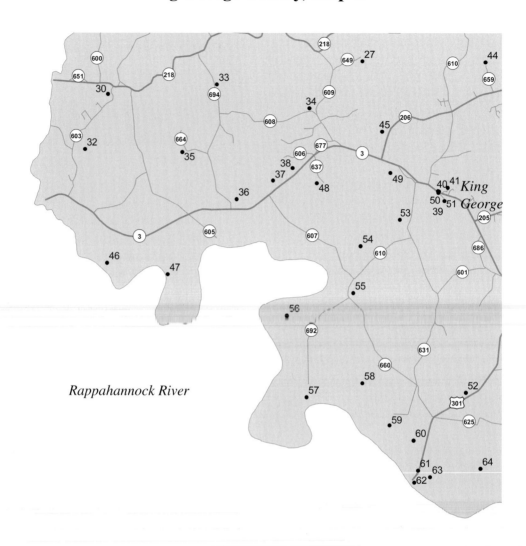

Rappahannock River

Miles

was owned by Gustavus Brown Wallace, who left the Rokeby (37) property to his son Robert. *Visible from the road; privately owned. (Map B and Map C)*

White Hall (35)

Lambs Creek Church (36) This Anglican congregation was founded in 1732, and the present church was built about 1769-77, having probably been designed by John Ariss (Ayres). The church, with its rectangular plan, hip roof and side entrance, is viewed as a classic example of a rural Anglican church. Following disestablishment, and as with most Episcopal churches of the time, this building was abandoned and fell into disrepair. It was refurbished in 1816, and services were held here regularly until St. John's Church was built at King George Courthouse in 1840-42 (it being later torn down after the Civil War and replaced by a smaller church of the same name). During the Civil War, Lamb's Church served as a stable for Union troops. Today it is used just once a year, in late August, on "Lamb's Creek Day." The building houses

Lambs Creek Church (36)

one of only seven known existing bibles printed in 1716 and known as the Vinegar Bible because the word "vineyard" was misprinted. *VLR and NRHP. Historical Marker J-62. Visible from the road. (Map B and Map C)*

Rokeby (37) Situated on a hill overlooking the Rappahannock, this house is thought to have been built about 1845 by Robert Wallace, the son of Gustavus Wallace of White Hall (35). One of the grandest extant homes in King George County, the main part is a two-story, three-bay brick edifice with a hip roof and end chimneys, and a large central portico. It is flanked by two wings—later additions—one of which has its own chimney. During the Fredericksburg campaign of December 1862, Union Maj. Gen. Ambrose E. Burnside used Rokeby as his headquarters. *VLR and NRHP. Visible from the road; privately owned. (Map B and Map C)*

Rokeby (37)

Shelbourne (38) This two-story, three-bay frame house with a gable roof was built in the mid-19th century and served as the home of Judge John E. Mason. The house was likely added onto later, but it is unclear whether the front gable is original to the house or an addition. The house served as the residence for several years for the novelist Paul Kester (1870-1933), who wrote *His Own Country* while living here. *Not visible from the road; privately owned. (Map B and Map C)*

Shelbourne (38)

King George Courthouse complex (39) The present courthouse building, with its massive white columns holding up a broad Classical Revival portico, was erected in 1922-23. It was built on the site of an earlier courthouse, erected about 1785 after the county seat was moved here from Canning. That building was a two-story, three-bay Georgian style brick structure with a hip roof and interior chimneys at each end. A series of old jails stood near here beginning in 1790, the most recent of which—used from 1895 to 1949—has housed the King George Museum and Research Center since 1997. In 1969, the Lewis Egerton Smoot Library was added to this complex of judicial and county administrative buildings, as the result of the donation from his widow of the land, the building and its contents to King George County, as well as of an endowment to support the library (also see Caledon Natural Area (23)). *Visible from the road; owned by the county. (Map C and Map E)*

King George Courthouse complex (39)

Confederate Monument (40) This 24-foot high granite obelisk was erected through the efforts of the Ladies Memorial Association of King George County, and was dedicated in 1869. It is believed to be the earliest Confederate monument to be built in Virginia. The obelisk was initially a memorial to those King George soldiers who had lost their lives in the Civil War, but in 1912, the Camp of Confederate Veterans of the county decided to add the names of all those county citizens who had served the Confederate military. Changes in the roadway and enlargement of the courthouse necessitated the movement of the monument twice, and it now stands in front of today's courthouse. *Visible from the road; owned by the county. Endangered. (Maps B, C and E)*

Confederate Monument (40)

St. John's Rectory (41) This frame structure was originally a plantation house built about 1752 by Daniel Riding and known as Woodlawn. That property also housed a tavern, the Surf and Twig, which business was moved, about 1800, across the road from the courthouse (see the King George Tavern/Hotel (51)). In 1859 this house, along with 200 acres, was sold to St. John's Church, and since that time Hanover Episcopal Parish has used the building as its rectory.

Originally it was a 1¹/₂ story side-hall plan house with a shake hip roof with dormers, but a full second story was added later. The wide hall has old, hand-carved woodwork and a stairway to the second floor. The old kitchen, which stands in the yard to the right of the house along with the old smokehouse, is a two-story building with two very large fireplaces that separate the two downstairs rooms. Both outbuildings have unusual slanted wood plank doors. *Visible from the road; privately owned. (Maps B, C and E)*

St. John's Rectory (41)

St. Paul's Episcopal Church (42) One of two extant Virginia churches with a true Greek-cross plan and two tiers of windows, St. Paul's was built in 1766-67. Despite its fine brickwork and medallion cornice, the exterior of the church is simple and in this sense quite different from the more elaborate Georgian churches of that general period, In his diaries, George Washington mentioned worshipping at St. Paul's.

After the Revolution and disestablishment, the building fell into disuse and most of its 18th century woodwork was destroyed or vandalized. The building was renovated to serve as a school in

1808, and was returned to the Episcopalian vestry in 1830. Communion service dating from 1721 and a 1762 bible have survived as treasures of the church. *VLR and NRHP. Historical Marker J-65. Visible from the road. (Map A)*

St. Paul's Episcopal Church (42)

Cleydael (43) This two-story, five-bay gable-roofed frame house with interior chimneys at both ends was built about 1859 by Dr. Richard Stuart, who had purchased the land on which it stands in 1845. It is said that Stuart named the 3,000 acre plantation after the ancestral castle of his mother in Belgium. During the Civil War, he considered that his family would be safer at Cleydael than at the family home at Cedar Grove (22), since Union gunboats were patrolling the Potomac River in that area. Two of Gen. Robert E. Lee's daughters lived with their Stuart cousins at Cleydael during the summer of 1861.

After Lincoln's assassin, John Wilkes Booth, had stopped at the Quesenberry House (14) during his escape southwards, he then stopped at Cleydael with his accomplice. Dr. Stuart fed them supper, but

Cleydael (43)

being suspicious, declined to give them lodging. Dr. Stuart was not implicated in aiding Booth's attempted escape. While the house is now more or less surrounded by a housing development, since 2002 Cleydael and twelve acres have belonged to a resident interested in maintaining the house as a living history site. *VLR and NRHP, and BHR easement. Historical Marker EP-9. Visible from the road; privately owned. (Map A)*

Hobson (44) Built about 1790, this Federal style two-story, three-bay gable-roofed house with a side-hall plan was originally a simple clapboard structure but was bricked in the 1960s with bricks from the Panorama site (15). It is thought that possibly two old mulberry trees near the house predate its construction, as the British Crown encouraged Virginia land-owners to plant mulberries, hoping to establish a silk industry in Virginia. *Visible from the road; privately owned. (Map B and Map C)*

Hobson (44)

Waverley site (45) The original home here was built about 1850 by William Saunders Brown. It was a large two-story frame house over an English basement, and one of his daughters, Nannie Brown Doherty, wrote her memoirs of life here during the Civil War and provided detailed descriptions of the numerous Union raids on the farm. This house was destroyed by fire in 1896. It was rebuilt, and Doherty's

daughter Marie and her husband Thomas Lomax Hunter (1875-1948), poet laureate of Virginia, lived here. Their home incorporated old millstones in the front walkway. In 1970, while the home was being remodeled by its new owners, it was totally destroyed by fire. The millstones continue to mark out what was once the entrance way. Some old outbuildings still survive on the property. *Not visible from the road; privately owned. (Map B and Map C)*

Waverley site (45)

King George County, Map D

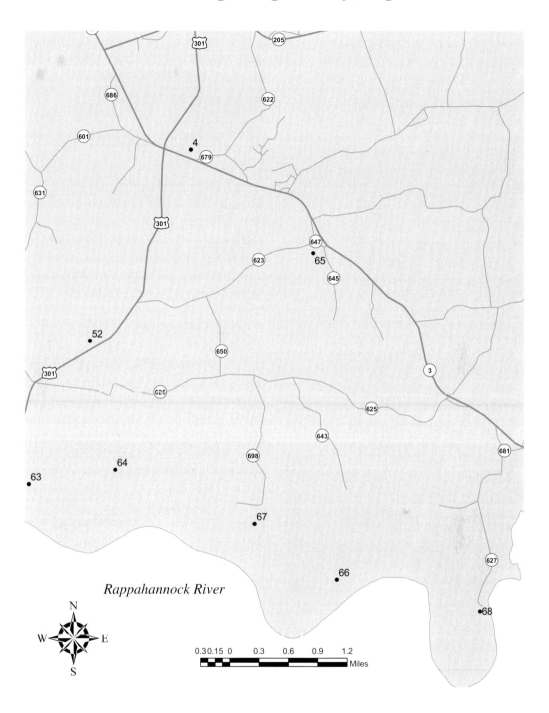

Between Route 3 and the Rappahannock River

Spring Hill (46) Spring Hill farm is thought to have been the home of Joseph Jones (1726-1805), an uncle and the guardian of President James Monroe (see James Monroe Birthplace site (7) in Westmoreland County) and in his own right, a delegate to all five of the Virginia State Conventions at the time of the Revolutionary War. He was one of the members of the committee advising George Mason in his drafting of the Virginia Declaration of Rights, a member of the Continental Congress and a delegate to the Virginia State Convention that ratified the U.S. Constitution. During the Civil War, Fanny Byrd Turner Dade, a widow, lived at Spring Hill and was suspected of spying for the North and helping escaped Union prisoners find their way home. The frame house is a two-story, five-bay hip roof structure with end chimneys, sitting atop an English basement. *Visible from the road; privately owned. (Map C)*

Spring Hill (46)

Farley Vale (47) Built about 1862, this simple two-story, three-bay frame house with a standing seam gable roof and two interior end chimneys was inherited by Spotswood Corbin—a son of James Parke Corbin who had built the mansion known as Moss Neck Manor in Caroline County—in 1864. Spotswood Corbin was known as an outstanding

Farley Vale (47)

farmer, and established the Virginia Farm Bureau. The house originally consisted of a wide central hall with two rooms on each side. It was restored in the second half of the 20th century, and it now has a large kitchen addition. *Not visible from the road; privately owned. (Map C)*

Bleak Hill (48) This house, on a high hill overlooking the Rappahannock River, was built about 1790. It is a two-story, three-bay frame dwelling with the front door off to the right side of the principal façade, suggesting that it might have begun as a smaller, side-hall house. During the Civil War, the property was visited by both Union and Confederate soldiers. *Visible from the road; privately owned. (Map B and Map C)*

Bleak Hill (48)

Willow Hill site (49) Thought to have been built in 1756, this house had almost certainly been altered somewhat before it was burned down to make way for a subdivision development in 2004. As shown, the dwelling was a two-story, five-bay house with a gable roof and exterior end chimneys, and had a two-story colonnaded front porch. It is now a totally lost site. *Not visible from the road; privately owned. (Map B and Map C)*

Willow Hill site (49)

Hunter House (50) The Hunter home appears on the 1805 plat of the King George courthouse area, described however as the "Store Home." The house is a two-story, three-bay frame dwelling, with a gable roof and two very distinctive double chimneys on its east side which are unique in King George County. It was the home of Thomas Lomax Hunter, grandfather of the poet laureate (see Waverley site (45)), and the front yard was the initial site of the Confederate Monument (40). *Visible from the road; privately owned. (Maps B, C and E)*

Hunter House (50)

King George Tavern/Hotel (51) Along with St. John's Rectory (41), across the street, this building stands on what was once known as Woodlawn plantation.

Now a two-story, three-bay gable-roofed frame house over an English basement, it has one chimney on its left side. The tavern/hotel was built about 1800 soon after the county seat was moved from Canning to King George Courthouse, and at that time the Surf and Twig tavern business moved from what later became St. John's Rectory to this building. The tavern is long gone, but the building remains with its original flooring, woodwork and chimneys. Its large center hall has two rooms on each side, and the second floor contains five bedrooms. A large fireplace is in the basement. *Visible from the road; privately owned. (Maps B, C and E)*

King George Tavern/Hotel (51)

White Plains (52) White Plains was built about 1825, probably by the Thornley family who also built Mount Pleasant, a house of similar design which burned in 1999. The two-story, three-bay frame house with a gable roof and exterior end chimneys, sits on a hill overlooking the Rappahannock River. *Not visible from the road; privately owned. (Map C and Map D)*

White Plains (52)

Mt. Ida (53) This 1¹/₂ story, five-bay frame house sits atop an English basement and is believed to date from the 18th century. It has a shingled gable roof flanked by exterior chimneys. Its original owner is unknown. *Not visible from the road; privately owned. (Map C)*

Mt. Ida (53)

Powhatan (54) Built in the second quarter of the 19th century, Powhatan is sited prominently on a ridge overlooking the Rappahannock River valley. The main part of the house is a hip-roofed two-story, three-bay brick structure atop an English basement, with three tall chimneys. Single-story hyphens on either side connect it with symmetrical one-story wings. This manor house was built by Edward Thornton Tayloe (1803-1876), a grandson of the builder of Mount Airy (42) in Richmond County, and a private secretary to several U.S. diplomats serving abroad, before he settled in to becoming a planter at Powhatan.

During the Civil War, the estate was used as a headquarters for Union troops, and much of the furniture was destroyed, paintings slashed and silver stolen. While the Tayloe descendants sold off parcels of the Powhatan estate in the late 19th and early 20th centuries, Raymond R. Guest, former Ambassador to Ireland, began to reassemble them as a whole in 1955. *The Powhatan Rural Historic District is listed on the NRHP. Visible from the road; privately owned. (Map C)*

Powhatan (54)

Dogue House/Celtwood/Grantswood (55) Each of these properties, in the Dogue area of King George County, was once part of the William Rollins (1833-1901) estate. Dogue House, a two-story, five-bay gable-roofed frame house, was his home site. Celtwood, also a two-story, five-bay house with a gable roof and a central front gable, was given by Rollins to his daughter, and was part of the Cherry Point estate that had earlier belonged to Daniel McCarty Fitzhugh. Grantswood, built in the 17th century, originally belonged to Alexander Rose but is now a lost site. *Visible from the road; privately owned. (Map C)*

Celtwood (55)

Berry Plain (56) This property remained in the Berry family from 1665 to 1845. Part of the present house is thought to have its origins in the first half of the 18th century. It is now a two-story, five-bay gable-roof frame structure, with two large interior end chimneys. Thomas Berry married a first cousin of George Washington in

Berry Plain (56)

1758 and made the two-story, three-bay addition to the main section, with its own large interior end chimney, and it was he who named the plantation Berry Plain. The smaller addition to the left hand side of the house was put on somewhat later. *Not visible from the road; privately owned. (Map C)*

Cleve (57) Built in the mid-18th century for Charles Carter, a son of Robert "King" Carter of Corotoman (5) in Lancaster County, the exterior of Cleve may have been inspired by the designs of the English architect James Gibbs. A classic Georgian structure, with its two stories, seven bays on its south side, hip roof and tall interior chimneys, Cleve was long noted for its distinct symmetry. The dark brick walls were contrasted with the light stone quoins from the Aquia quarry, the stone water table, and the bold rusticated door and windows. It is not known for certain who actually built the house; it may have been William Walker, who later reconstructed the Capitol in Williamsburg.

The house remained in the extended Carter family until 1852.

The original house was greatly damaged by fire in 1790, although the thick masonry walls of the exterior appear to have survived. In the extensive renovations that followed, the hip roof was replaced by a gable roof. A second fire nearly destroyed the house in 1917, and although it was rebuilt in 1923, little of the original structure may be seen today. *Not visible from the road; privately owned. Endangered. (Map C)*

Canning site (58) The original King George County seat was located here, and it was only moved to its present site—the village of King George—about 1785 following the boundary changes with Stafford County to the northwest and Westmoreland County to the southeast. The manor house here was built in 1839 by William Taylor Smith and his wife, Columbia Turner, a daughter of Richard Turner of Walsingham (63). The house burned in 1889. It was rebuilt in 1932, but that dwelling later burned as well. *Site visible from the road; privately owned. (Map C)*

Millbank (59) At least three houses have been built on this site over the past three centuries. The first house, built about 1725 by Samuel Skinker, is thought to have been early Georgian in style. A second house was erected about 1800, but this burned about 1900. The present house incorporated one of the original chimneys

Cleve (57)

Millbank (59)

King George County, Map E

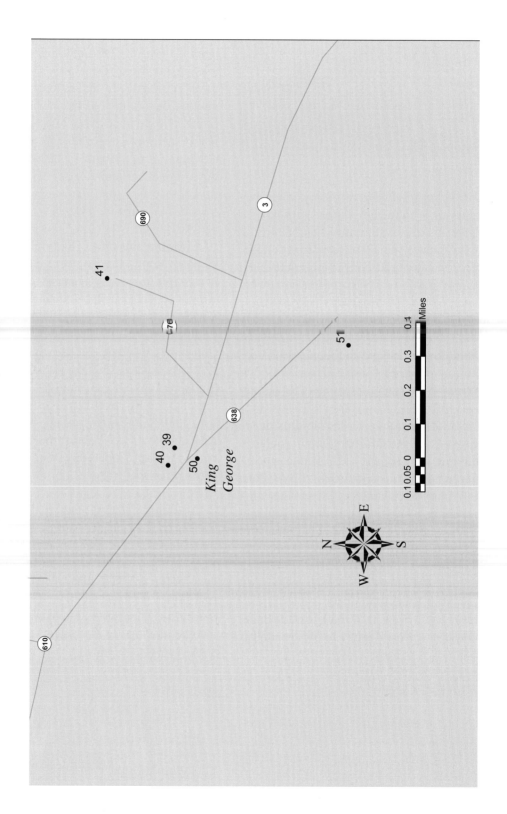

and portions of the 18th century basement. The property also contains evidence of an 18th century warehouse and remnants of an early millrace. *VLR and NRHP. Not visible from the road; privately owned. (Map C)*

Belle Grove (60) James Madison (1751-1836), the fourth president of the United States, was probably born a few hundred yards east of Belle Grove. Although his parents lived in Orange County, in the Piedmont, his mother Nelly (Conway) Madison had come back to have her child at her mother's home near what later became known as Port Conway (62) on the Rappahannock River just a few miles south of Fredericksburg. The present Belle Grove house, built in 1792 on what had once been Conway property, was probably designed by Richard and Yelverton Stern for John Hipkins, who gave it to his only child, Fannie, wife of William Bernard. The two-story house was built with projecting entrance halls. In 1839, Carolinus Turner bought Belle Grove, and in addition to modifying the interior, he had the porticoes and end-wings added. *VLR and NRHP. Historical Marker EP-8. Not visible from the road; privately owned. (Map C)*

Belle Grove (60)

Emmanuel Church (61) Built on land given to the church trustees by Carolinus Turner of nearby Belle Grove (60) in 1859, tiny Emmanuel Church is the third Anglican/Episcopal church built in the Port Conway area. The first such church, known as Strother's Church, was the site of the baptism of James Madison, who was born nearby. Today, Emmanuel Church, an example of country Gothic Revival, but with an Italianate tower, is one of three Episcopal churches comprising Hanover Parish, which was established in 1713. During the Civil War, the church was damaged, although tradition has it that a Union soldier who sat and played the church organ was able to persuade his fellow troops not to destroy the building. After the War, the church was restored with funds collected by the Friends of the Episcopal Church in the North. *VLR and NRHP. Visible from the road. (Map C)*

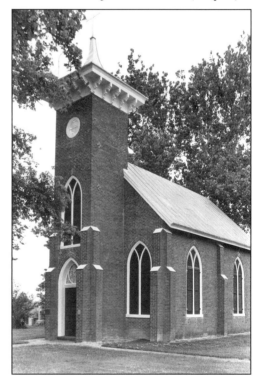

Emmanuel Church (61)

Port Conway site (62) Francis Conway, the maternal grandfather of President James Madison, laid out this town in 1783, and a year later the General Assembly passed an act establishing the town. Some twenty years later, the King George

Port Conway site (62)

County court again produced a specific plan for a town, but the plan did not materialize and lots were simply sold off to individual owners. A small, but thriving town did develop, and its wharf reached out into the deepest waters of the Rappahannock River where barrels could be rolled onto ships. Later, push carts and rails were used.

During the Civil War, Union Army engineers built a floating wharf here for Federal gunboats. On September 1, 1863, Federal cavalry actually shelled two Union gunboats here that had been captured by the Confederates. This is where John Wilkes Booth, Lincoln's assassin, after his visits to the Quesenberry House (14) and Cleydael (43), was ferried across the river into Caroline County, where he was finally cornered and killed by federal troops at the Garrett farm. Port Conway continued as a town well into the 20th century, but the last remaining houses disappeared in 1963 when Route 301 was widened. *Historical Marker J-66. Site visible from the road; private property. (Map C)*

Side trips off of Route 301 and Route 3 in the southeast

Walsingham site (63) A lost site, the only extant image of this huge home is as a distant shot in a photograph taken of troop movements at Port Royal, in Caroline County across the Rappahannock River from Port Conway (62). Walsingham was the estate of the prominent Turner family of King George County. In 1829, upon the death of Richard Turner, the property was divided between his eldest son, Albert, who inherited this house, and his younger son, Richard Jr., who inherited the eastern portion of the plantation and its house, known as Woodlawn (64). *Site visible from the road; privately owned. (Map C and Map D)*

Walsingham site (63)

Woodlawn (64) The original portion of this house was built for the Turner family about 1790. In 1829 it passed to Richard Turner Jr. The house has undergone several additions over time, and today it

Woodlawn (64)

is a two-story, five-bay frame house with a hip roof and two interior chimneys at each end, combining several architectural styles. Woodlawn actually constitutes an historic and archaeological district, for in addition to the manor house, it includes five Indian archaeological sites, several outbuildings, a plantation ditch network, and a field system and farm road network. *VLR and NRHP, and BHR easement. Not visible from the road; privately owned. (Map C and Map D)*

Johnston House (65) One of only a few old log cabins remaining in the area (although now covered by a frame house), and most likely the only old log cabin in the county that is still occupied today, the Johnston House was the home of Philip Potts Johnston. His son, Philip Preston Johnston, Adjutant General of Kentucky from 1907 to 1911, was born in this house. *Visible from the road; privately owned. (Map D)*

Johnston House (65)

Nanzatico Archaeological Area (66) During Capt. John Smith's August 1608 exploratory expedition up the Rappahannock River, he visited with the Nand-taughtacund (later anglicized to Nanzatico) Indians, evidently a friendly people who maintained one of the largest settlements in the Rappahannock River valley at that time. They are thought to have had ten towns with a total of 640 people, including some 150 warriors, although these totals may have included some

Pissasecks (see Pissaseck Indian Village (13) in Westmoreland County). Although the Nanzatico Indians pledged loyalty to the Virginia colony in 1677, following Bacon's Rebellion, their population dwindled over time and by 1722 they had ceased to exist as a tribe. *VLR. Visible from the road; privately owned. (Map D)*

Nanzatico (67) The date of construction of this house, located just west of the Nanzatico Indian archaeological site, and directly on that part of the Rappahannock River known as Nanzatico Bay, has long been in dispute. Often attributed a date of about 1770 and ownership of Charles Carter Jr., a grandson of Robert "King" Carter of Corotoman (5) in Lancaster County, more recent research suggests that this formal two-story hip-roofed frame house with high end interior chimneys was probably built by Thomas Turner sometime between 1780 and 1800. The center of the seven-bay façade overlooking the river has four fluted pilasters with Ionic capitals, which in turn support a highly decorative entablature and a classical pediment. On the land side, an extended and wide passage—from which the staircase has been removed to a little-noticed hall—constitutes a large welcoming room.

As with Belle Grove (60), it is believed that Nanzatico was designed and built by Richard and Yelverton Stern. Indeed, Nanzatico is very similar to Belle Grove before the latter's 1839 alterations. Although renovated in the mid-20th century,

Nanzatico (67)

several of the outbuildings at Nanzatico still retain much of their original exterior character. *VLR and NRHP, and BHR easement. Visible from the road; privately owned. (Map D)*

Wilmont (68) In the early 20th century, this site on Toby's Point was one of more than 30 steamboat landings along the Rappahannock River. This area once boasted the Bristol Ironworks, one of the 18th-century investments of John Tayloe of Mount Airy (42) in Richmond County. Nearby, on Bristol Mine Run, there was also a glassworks.

Near the end of the 19th century, a company based in West Virginia leased much of this land in order to mine and mill fireproofing materials from the diatomaceous earth found in the high cliffs at Toby's Point. This brick was shipped by steamboat to Baltimore, Washington, D. C., and Norfolk, and to New England. A hotel was built at this site to accommodate travelers and laborers, and there were other commercial establishments. Mining of this material, by this company and its successor, and the making of brick, continued until 1934.

Today, the 365 acres of this point include only a dock, a public ramp for small boats and canoes, and a parking area. The rest of this property is part of the Rappahannock River Valley National Wildlife Refuge. *Visible from the road; publicly owned. (Map D)*

Wilmont (68)

Selected Bibliography

Arnold, Scott David. *A Guidebook to Virginia's Historical Markers*. Charlottesville: University of Virginia Press, 2007.

Kauffman, Michael W. *American Brutus: John Wilkes Booth and the Lincoln Conspiracies*. New York: Random House, 2004.

Ketchum, Ralph. *James Madison: A Biography*. Charlottesville: University Press of Virginia, 1971.

Lee, Edmund Jennings. *Lee of Virginia*. Baltimore: Genealogical Publishing Co., 1974; orig. published in 1895.

Lee, Elizabeth Nuckols and Jean Moore Graham. *King George County: A Pictorial History*. Virginia Beach, Va.: Donning, 2006.

Loth, Calder. *The Virginia Landmarks Register*. Charlottesville: University Press of Virginia, Fourth Edition, 1999.

Lounsbury, Carl R. *An Illustrated Glossary of Early Southern Architecture and Landscape*. Charlottesville: University Press of Virginia, 1994.

McClure, Phyllis. "Rosenwald Schools in the Northern Neck," *Virginia Magazine of History and Biography* 113 (2), 2005: 114-145.

Nagel, Paul C. *The Lees of Virginia: Seven Generations of an American Family*. New York: Oxford University Press, 1990.

Potter, Stephen R. *Commoners, Tribute, and Chiefs: The Development of Algonquian Culture in the Potomac Valley*. Charlottesville: University Press of Virginia, 1993.

Rountree, Helen C., Wayne E. Clark and Kent Mountford. *John Smith's Chesapeake Voyages, 1607-1609*. Charlottesville: University of Virginia Press, 2007.

Wells, Camille. *Cultural Landscapes of the Northern Neck: Virginia's Colonial Mansions*. Stratford, Va.: Stratford Hall Symposium, 2008.

Chapter 4
Westmoreland

Westmoreland County was formally established in 1653 out of Northumberland County. The county borders the Potomac River on the north, and the Rappahannock River to the southwest. The county seat is believed to have been at Montross, on Route 3, ever since the 1680s.

The port town of Kinsale, just off the Potomac River, is listed on both the Virginia Landmarks Register and the National Register of Historic Places as an historic district.

The county covers an area of 252.6 square miles, of which 229.2 square miles are land. The population of Westmoreland County in 1790 was 7,722, of which 43 percent was free. By 1940, the county's population had increased to 9,512, and by 2000 totaled 16,718, just behind King George County in the Northern Neck region.

Historic Sites in Westmoreland County

Colonial Beach and Oak Grove south

Pomona (1) This home, which has undergone many alterations over the past two centuries, is thought to date from the late 18th century, and may have been originally built by the Reverend Archibald Campbell, who acquired the property in 1760. Although the basement is laid in five-course American bond, suggesting later construction, late 20th-century excavations of the area immediately to the

Pomona (1)

north of the house uncovered a basement wall laid in English bond, typical of the 18th century. *Visible from the road; privately owned. (Map A)*

Treakle House (2) Built about 1855-60, this house has an unusual configuration, with the original one-story wing set forward from the façade of a two-story, two-bay main block, and it has gable roofs without lofts. The interior side hall leads to the stairs. While the downstairs openings have a simple Greek architrave trim, a simple beaded trim is found upstairs. Additions to the house were made in the 19th century. *Visible from the road; privately owned. (Map A)*

Treakle House (2)

Westmoreland County

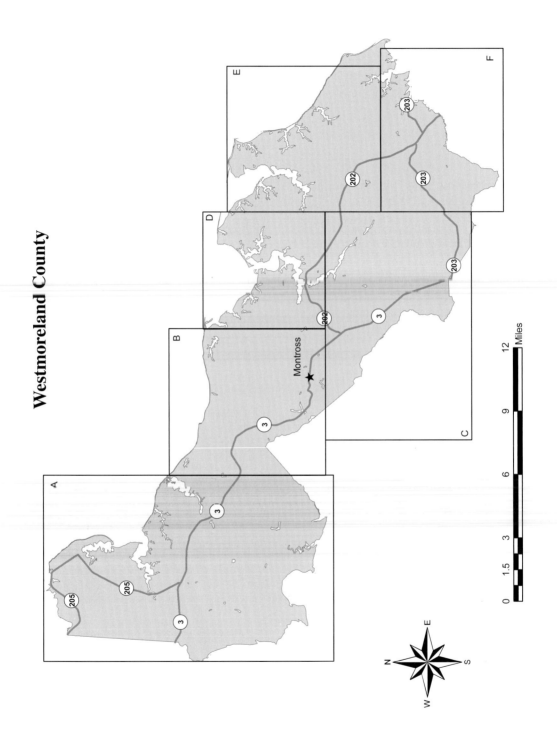

Hill Farm (3) Also known as Holly Tree Farm, this was originally a two-story, two-bay, side passage vernacular house, built about 1850. Later additions of wings on both sides reconfigured this house into a two-story, four-bay dwelling with an off-center passage. The standing seam metal roof has decorative snow birds at the roof edge, and the porch has scrolled sawn brackets and is skirted with lattice. *Visible from the road; privately owned. (Map A)*

Hill Farm (3)

Bluff Point (4) This Federal style home, at 3000 Riverview Avenue, appears to date from about 1790. It stands upon land that was once owned by Henry ("Light Horse Harry") Lee, the father of General Robert E. Lee (see Stratford Hall (26)). The house has a traditional center-hall, double-pile plan, and has a full basement. The nine-light windows on the first floor, complemented by the nine-over-six sashes on the second, are very characteristic of the Federal style. The wing on the south side of the house was added sometime later. *Visible from the road; privately owned. (Map A)*

Bluff Point (4)

Colonial Beach (5) This town was platted and named in 1882 by Henry J. Kintz, on a 650-acre farm he had recently purchased, and much of which had once belonged a century earlier to Henry ("Light Horse Harry") Lee, father of Robert E. Lee (see Stratford Hall (26)). The land was sub-divided into lots for the purpose of developing a commercial center as well as a summer resort. The town — now the largest single jurisdiction in Westmoreland County — was incorporated in 1892, and included both large resort hotels and many modest houses, mostly summer cottages. Steamboats ran daily to and from Washington, D.C., some 70 miles up the Potomac River.

When the Maryland Proprietary was established during the reign of Charles I, its boundary was established as far as the low water mark on the southern (i.e., Virginia) shore of the Potomac. After slot machines were legalized in Charles County, Maryland in 1949, enterprising souls in Colonial Beach — reacting to the prohibition of slot machines in Virginia — saw the advantage of building a pier out into the Potomac, and constructing on it such restaurants as "Little Reno," "Monte Carlo," and "Jackpot," beyond a small gap in the pier with a sign welcoming patrons to Maryland. Needless to say, this led to a new spurt of activity in Colonial Beach. In 1958, however, Maryland repealed its slot machine law, and the growth of Colonial Beach stagnated until recent years, when there has been a new wave of development. *(Map A)*

The Bell House (6) Owned by Alexander Graham Bell, the inventor of the telephone, from 1907 to 1918, this summer cottage, located at 821 South Irving Avenue in Colonial Beach, had been bought by Bell's father, Alexander Melville Bell, in 1886. Although Alexander Graham Bell usually summered to the north of Washington, D.C., he did use this house as well.

The frame dwelling was built about 1883 by Col. J. O. P. Burnside, and is an example of Stick-style Victorian architecture, frequently seen in the North but seldom in the South. In addition to its many Victorian details, such as polychromed glass overlights, its architectural complexity is reflected in its combination of gable roofs, cross-gables and projecting balconies on the third floor. Architecturally, the house is virtually unchanged since its late 19th-century construction. *VLR and NRHP. Visible from the road; privately owned. (Map A)*

The Bell House (6)

James Monroe Birthplace site (7) James Monroe (1758-1831), the fifth president of the United States, was born here. The son of a carpenter or joiner, Monroe grew up in a modest house but one which was probably above-average in size for the times. The rough-cut wooden house was situated on 500 acres filled with wetlands. Monroe inherited the house but sold it in 1781, at the end of the Revolutionary War. The house was abandoned about 1820, and later fell into ruin. Long thought to be a lost site, in 1976 an archaeological team from the College of William and Mary uncovered a 20-by-58 foot foundation that coincided with this 1845 etching.

The James Monroe Foundation, founded in 1928, plans to have a reproduction of the house built, using period materials

and building techniques. *VLR and NRHP. Historical Marker JP-6. Open to the public with a Visitor's Center. Located on Rt. 205, about two miles south of Colonial Beach. Visible from the road. (Map A)*

James Monroe Birthplace site (7)

St. Peter's Episcopal Church (8) Built at Oak Grove in 1849, this church has a highly regular plan. Gothic Revival elements on the exterior include point-arch doors with sidelights, a bipartite window above the entry and arched windows within square masonry openings. *VLR and NRHP. Visible from the road. (Map A)*

St. Peter's Episcopal Church (8)

Sweet Briar (9) The original part of this house dates from about 1797, although three separate 19th-century additions, each from a different period, have given it a rather mixed overall architectural style. It is now a two-story, four-bay, center passage vernacular dwelling, with basically a late 19th-century visage. Some further remodeling was carried out in the late 20th century. A smokehouse said to date from ca. 1830 stands on the property. *Visible from the road; privately owned. (Map A)*

Sweet Briar (9)

West on Route 3 to Claymont Road (Rt. 634)

Claymont (10) Built by Daniel Carmichael ca. 1810, the two-story rectangular portion of this house is original. The shed wings, as well as the room off the rear, were added later. The house has had at least two extensive renovations. In the yard are to be found a detached kitchen and two smokehouses. Around the turn of the 20th century, front columns were added as part of a renovation in the Classical Revival style. Extensive renovations were also undertaken at mid-century. Little visible evidence of the original house remains.

Claymont (10)

It is said that Claymont was used as a clandestine headquarters by sympathetic southern Marylanders who ran the Potomac River blockade to bring supplies to the Confederacy during the Civil War. *Visible from the road; privately owned. (Map A)*

Cherry Row (11) Although clearly very old, this frame house is attributed to different builders. Some think it was built in the 18th century, and this is suggested by the $1^1/_2$ story central part of the house, with its flanking chimneys. Others believe it was built somewhat later, ca. 1810, by Daniel Carmichael, the builder of nearby Claymont (10). The side additions, the cross-gable and the front porch are, in any event, clearly 19th-century features. The house is said to have once been a tavern. A detached kitchen stands in the yard. *Visible from the road; privately owned. Endangered. (Map A)*

Cherry Row (11)

Continue on Rt. 634 to Rt. 637

Liberty (12) This brick side-hall plan house is considered to have been built ca. 1820 by a Dr. Robb. Its Federal style is highlighted by the nine-over-nine light windows and walls laid in Flemish bond, co-existing with flat arches over the windows. In addition to the entrance stair hall, the house has two large rooms on each floor, each with a fireplace. It was on this property that Lawrence Washington, the immigrant and brother of John Washington, great-grandfather of the first president, settled by patenting a 650-acre tract in 1659. *Visible from the road; privately owned. (Map A)*

Liberty (12)

Pissaseck Indian village/Leedstown (13) Located on what is today Rt. 637, where the road bends to the Rappahannock River shoreline, this was perhaps the largest of several towns of the Pissaseck Indians, and Capt. John Smith visited here in the second half of August, 1608. Given the relative narrowness of the Northern Neck in this area, it is believed that the Pissasecks also claimed some territory on the Potomac River as well. The Indian village of Pissasec is mentioned in Westmoreland County records from 1662. Whereas perhaps some 280 Indians lived here in 1608, by 1705 only about twenty remained. A large cache of glass trade beads was found here in the early 1900s. *Historical Marker J-98.*

Richard Bray is credited with establishing Bray's Church here in 1655, and there was also a small colonial port. In 1742, the General Assembly decreed that a town be built at Bray's Church where "great numbers of people, of late, have settled themselves." Sixty-five acres were designated for a town, a plat was laid out, and it was ordered that the town be named Leeds (at that time, this site actually was in King George County). The town hosted at least three taverns, and in 1763 George Washington stayed in one of them.

In 1765, the British Parliament passed the Stamp Act. When Archibald Ritchie, a prominent Tappahannock merchant, announced that he intended to adhere to the Act, Thomas Ludwell Lee called together 115 men at Leedstown, and they signed a resolution drafted by his brother Richard Henry Lee (see Stratford Hall (26)), pledging to resist the new British legislation. Ritchie, when faced with an angry crowd supporting the Leedstown Resolves, ended his support for the Act.

Following the Revolutionary War, the town declined and by 1830 the tax records show only one family owning property. Only a brick fragment of Bray's Church remains. *Historical Marker JT 15. Site visible from the road; privately owned. (Map A)*

Leedstown House (14) This one-story four-bay center passage house, built about 1850, once had two large–shouldered brick chimneys and gable ends. The front gable is an addition. The house may actually be older than it appears, as the left hand wing of the house was found to have log walls, and the first floor joists are of mortise and tenon construction and were hand hewn. Several additions have been made, and recently there has been substantial modernization of the house. Only one chimney remains. *Visible from the road; privately owned. (Map A)*

Leedstown House (14)

Wirtland (15) This house is an excellent example of Gothic Revival architecture, and one of the few examples of this architectural movement on the Northern Neck. It was completed in 1850 by Dr. William Wirt Jr., a son of William Wirt, Attorney General of the United States under presidents James Monroe and John Quincy Adams. The house has a cruciform plan, with three finished floors above a full basement. Set on carefully landscaped grounds, it is said to conform to, and likely was inspired by, Andrew Jackson Downing's mid-19th century ideal of an American villa. As its architect is unknown, the house was likely based on published illustrations of the time. It housed a female academy after Dr. Wirt's death. He was the brother of Dabney Carr Wirt, who built Roxbury (16). *VLR and NRHP. Not visible from the road; privately owned. (Map A)*

Wirtland (15)

Roxbury (16) Completed in 1861, on the eve of the Civil War, Roxbury was probably inspired—as was Wirtland (15)—by the mid-19th century architectural designs of Andrew Jackson Downing, although period houses of this design are much more likely to be found in the North than in Virginia. With its asymmetrical plan, gable and cross-gable roofs, finely detailed chimneys and extensive Victorian trim, the house is a sophisticated work in both concept and execution. Roxbury

was built for Dabney Carr Wirt, another son of William Wirt Sr. A log cabin, said to predate the main house, sits in the yard at Roxbury. The cabin has recently undergone renovation as a residence, after having served as the model for the construction of the Log Lodge at Washington's Birthplace. *VLR and NRHP. Not visible from the road; privately owned. (Map A)*

Roxbury (16)

Twiford (17) Thought to date from the first half of the 18th century, this house stands at the crest of the ridge dividing the Potomac and Rappahannock river valleys. A good example of a frame Georgian plantation house, the entire dwelling was likely built at the same time, without later additions, despite the very different chimney designs on either end of the house.

The house has a traditional center hall plan. On the east side of the house are two rooms served by a connected double chimney, the mass of which forms a major part of that end of the house and which is a unique feature in surviving Westmoreland County houses. In 1935, the original paneling from the main room to the west of the center hall was considered to be of such high quality that it was removed and installed in the Westmoreland County Museum in Montross.

A major renovation of Twiford was carried out in the latter part of the 20th century, and in addition to rebuilding two flue stacks, using the original brick, several

Westmoreland County, Map A

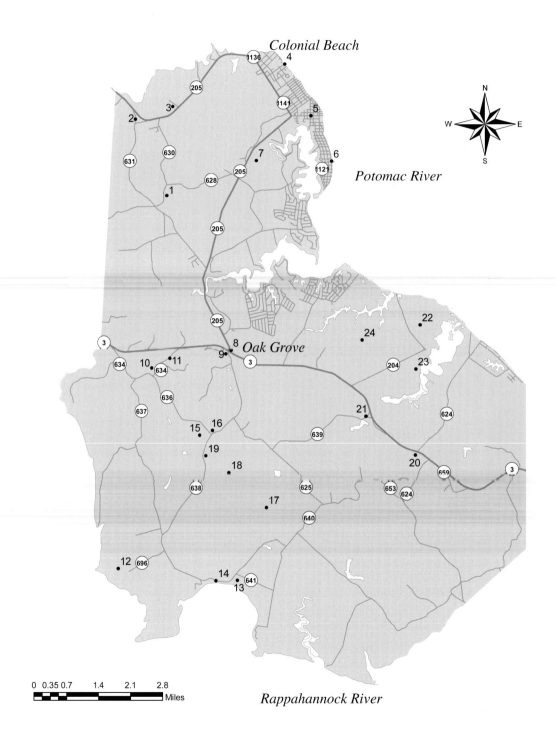

Colonial Beach

Potomac River

Oak Grove

Rappahannock River

0   0.35 0.7   1.4   2.1   2.8
Miles

Twiford (17)

Walnut Hill (18)

discoveries were made that enabled the gables and dormers to be restored to their earlier appearance. Although the builder of Twiford is unknown, this house has been inhabited by some of the most distinguished families of the region, including the Latanes, Fitzhughs, Beverleys, Hungerfords and Griffiths. *Not visible from the road; privately owned. (Map A)*

Walnut Hill (18) Facing the Rappahannock River, this 1½ story house is thought to have been built in the first half of the 18th century. The center hall, with double doors at either end, divides the main block into four rooms of different sizes. Of the four chimneys, that on the east end of the house is considered to be original, as it has smooth shoulders and is laid in Flemish bond. This chimney once had a twin, standing just beside it, but during the 20th century it was decided to pull it down due to structural deterioration.

The interior contains a great deal of original Georgian paneling and this, together with the numerous sets of HL hinges and the English bond foundation, suggest that the main block of the house was built by 1750. The two single-room wings off each side of this block also have foundations laid in English bond and their chimneys are of Flemish bond, suggesting that they were built at the same time as the central part of the house or soon thereafter. *Not visible from the road; privately owned. (Map A)*

Ingleside (19) Built in 1834, Ingleside is one of the finest Classical Revival structures in the Northern Neck region. It was initially constructed as the main building of the Washington Academy, a private preparatory school for the sons of plantation owners. According to tradition, the school's founders modeled the academy architecturally on Jefferson's Capitol in Richmond. Beneath the unique six-columned portico, the façade is distinguished by handsome overlights above the eight-over-eight windows, changed to the present six-over-six windows at the turn of the 20th century.

The floor containing the principal rooms, or *piano nobile*, of the house is built over a basement floor even with the ground rather than below it (also see Stratford Hall (26)). It has been conjectured that this base floor was used for dining and other domestic needs of the school, the main floor for instruction, and the second floor for sleeping. After the academy was closed in 1844, the building became a private residence. It was acquired in 1890,

Ingleside (19)

along with some 400 acres, by Carl Henry Flemer of Washington, D.C., and has remained in the family ever since. *VLR and NRHP. Not visible from the road; privately owned. (Map A)*

From Leedstown on Rt. 637 and Rt. 640 (Grant's Hill Road) to Rt. 3

Appomattox (Mattox) & Pope's Creek Churches, & the Mattox home-site (20) Two 17th-century churches named Appomattox (Mattox) were successively located at the mouth of Mattox Creek. The second church was 24-by-60 feet in size, and contained a gallery, and this is where George Washington was baptized. Both of these sites are now under water, and the church congregation had to keep moving.

Nearby was Mattox, the first home of the Washingtons in America. It was here that Col. Nathaniel Pope, a great-great-grandfather of George Washington, first settled, and about 1648 established the first wharf and warehouse in Westmoreland County. John Washington, the immigrant, came to Virginia in 1656, dropped anchor at Mattox, married Pope's daughter in 1658 and was given 700 acres of land (on both sides of today's Rt. 3) as a wedding gift. Their son, Lawrence, grandfather of the president, was born in the Mattox Creek house in 1659.

After disestablishment of the Anglican Church in Virginia following the Revolutionary War, Bishop Meade recalled a visit he made to the Mattox Church in 1812, noting that despite decay in the roof, there was a large congregation, including 28 children brought to be baptized, it being the first service performed in the church for a long time. The building continued to decay, however, and it was burned down to prevent injury prior to the publication of Meade's book in 1857.

The third Mattox church since 1662 was named "Mattox new Church" and is today referred to as Pope's Creek Church. Located at Flat Iron, on Route 3, Pope's Creek Church was under construction by 1746 and by 1751 it was finished enough to be used for worship. It was probably a brick church. *All lost sites. (Map A)*

George Washington's Birthplace to Montross

Potomac (Washington's) Mill (21) There was a mill here at least as early as 1728, when Nathaniel Pope sold the property to Augustine Washington, the father of the president. The present tin-clad structure is the only remaining mill structure in Westmoreland County that still has its old interior equipment and has not been thoroughly renovated (For a renovated, working mill, see Stratford Hall (26)). *Visible from the road; privately owned. (Map A)*

Potomac (Washington's) Mill (21)

George Washington Birthplace National Monument (22) The house in which George Washington (1732-1799) was born, later called "Wakefield," burned on Christmas Day, 1779. Excavated in 1930 and again in 1936, the archaeological site yielded some remains of this house, most notably of the foundations. These were roughly in accord with the evidence of the house in which Washington's half brother Augustine Washington

II's estate inventory was taken in 1762. Crushed oyster shells on the ground now mark the location of the home and the size and shape of the foundations.

In 1931, in the run-up to the 200th anniversary of Washington's birth, a Memorial House had been built to mark the approximate site of his birthplace. As sufficient evidence of the general plan of the original house was not then available, the Memorial House is not a replica, but it is typical of a Virginia plantation house of the 18th century. The memorial house was constructed out of bricks hand-made from local clay.

Washington's great-grandfather, John Washington (see Mattox (20)) settled this plantation at the original site on Bridges Creek in 1657. The family acquired additional land located on Pope's Creek, and this was where the house in which Washington was born was built before 1718, and later enlarged by his father between 1722 and 1726. In the 1770s, the house was further enlarged, becoming the ten-room house known as "Wakefield."

Thirty-two graves of Washington family members have been found at the Bridges Creek cemetery plot, including those of George Washington's father, grandfather and great-grandfather. *VLR and NRHP. Historical Marker J-69. Open to the public, and administered by the National Park Service. Located at 1732 Pope's Creek Road (Rt. 204, to the north off of Rt. 3). (Map A)*

George Washington Birthplace National Monument (22)

Wakefield Farm (23) This house, not to be confused with the home of Washington's birth and known as "Wakefield" when it burned in 1779, sits on property sold out of the Washington family in 1813, as was the property surrounding the Pope's Creek house in which the president was born. Part of the present house was built in 1849 by John E. Wilson of Maryland, and when he married a Washington descendant in 1856, the property in this sense returned to the Washington family. All architectural trim and mantels are plain, typical of the Greek Revival architectural style just prior to the Civil War. The original part of the house, of uncertain construction date, had an entry side-hall with stairway at the rear. Two large rooms, each with fireplaces, were on each of the two floors, and the attic was also finished as a room and had two fireplaces. *Not visible from the road; privately owned. (Map A)*

Wakefield Farm (23)

Blenheim (24) This relatively simple Georgian house succeeded Pope's Creek (Wakefield) as the Washington family's principal residence, after the burning of Washington's birthplace in 1779. It was built in 1780 by William Augustine Washington, son of George Washington's half brother, Augustine Washington II. He chose to build the new house inland, given active British naval activity on the Potomac River. Nevertheless, according to tradition, brick from the destroyed house

Westmoreland County, Map B

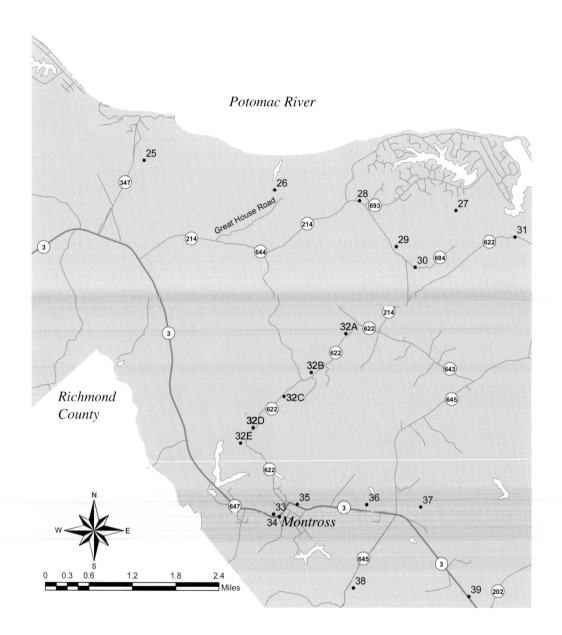

Potomac River

25

347

26

28
693

27

Great House Road

214

214

3

644

214

29

30   684

31
622

214

32A   622

622

32B

3

643

32C

622

645

32D

32E

*Richmond
County*

622

N

W   E

S

0   0.3   0.6   1.2   1.8   2.4
Miles

647

622

35

33

36

37

3

34 *Montross*

645

3

38

39   202

was used in the construction of Blenheim. Except for one period, ownership of Blenheim has remained with the descendants of the Washington family to the present day. One of these descendants restored the house from an advanced state of deterioration, in the 1970s.

Blenheim is a traditional two-story center hall structure, with a stairway running up the left side of the center hall to a landing, before doubling back to reach the second floor. The center hall is flanked on either side by a formal room, and this floor plan is repeated on the second level. The frame wing was originally an overseer's house on the Washington estate, and may date from 1720. *VLR and NRHP. Not visible from the road; privately owned. (Map A)*

Blenheim (24)

Westmoreland State Park (25) This park, which runs for about 1½ miles along the south side of the Potomac River and includes spectacular river views from Horsehead Cliffs, covers approximately 1,300 acres. It was built by the Civilian Conservation Corps (CCC) in the 1930s and is one of the six original state parks opened in Virginia in 1936. Most of its roads and trails were originally dug by hand. The land was part of "Clifts Plantation" patented by Nathaniel Pope about 1650, and it later became part of the nearby Stratford estate of Thomas Lee. It is open for hiking, camping, fishing and kayaking, and includes the Helen & Tayloe Murphy Center for meetings and conferences. *VLR and NRHP. Historical Marker J-75. (Map B)*

Stratford Hall (26) This National Historic Landmark on the banks of the Potomac River consists of a great colonial manor house, a number of well-preserved outbuildings, a working grist mill, archaeological sites, a museum, a research library and 1,900 acres of farmland. The manor house itself was built in the 1730s by Thomas Lee, a grandson of Col. Richard Lee the immigrant (1618-1664). Although it passed out of possession of the Lee family in 1822, it was acquired in 1929 by the Robert E. Lee Memorial Association for its preservation and restoration. Stratford is now used for programs and activities meant to aid in the interpretation of colonial plantation life in the Tidewater area, as well as of various members of the Lee family.

The original tract on which Thomas Lee built Stratford contained some 1,050 acres, but over time this property came to encompass 6,600 acres. Lee named his new home for his grandfather's purchased estate (once thought to be a Lee ancestral home) near London, called Stratford-Langthorne. The brick manor house, whose architect or even precise architectural inspiration in England is unknown, has an H-plan with each leg of this plan capped by a hip roof crowned with a square cluster of four chimneys, joined in such a way as to form observation decks. This house was placed in the center of a parterre, at the four corners of which stand dependencies, including an office, a kitchen/laundry, a schoolhouse and a garden house. All these buildings are original.

Stratford Hall (26)

Other restored plantation buildings include a stable, a smokehouse and a working grist mill. A coach house, store, and two slave cabins have been rebuilt from foundations discovered by archaeologists.

One of the most distinctive features of the Stratford house is the arrangement of the rooms. Unlike most other Tidewater plantation houses, the principal rooms—including the Great Hall, which connects the two legs of the H-plan—are to be found on the second floor, whereas virtually all the sleeping rooms are located on the west side of the first floor. The separate east side of this first floor, built directly on the ground, is a vaulted cellar used as a service area.

Stratford is one of the most historic houses in the United States. Thomas Lee, its builder, was a member of the Royal Governor's Council and served as acting Governor of the colony of Virginia during the last year of his life. Two of his sons — Richard Henry Lee (see Chantilly (27)) and Francis Lightfoot Lee (see Menokin (30) in Richmond County)—were the only brothers to sign the Declaration of Independence.

Their niece, who inherited Stratford, married their first cousin once-removed, Henry ("Light Horse Harry") Lee, who was a governor of Virginia in the 1790s and gave the famous funeral oration for George Washington ("First in war, first in peace..."). One of Henry's sons by his second wife was Robert E. Lee, who was born at Stratford. After West Point and long service in the U.S. Army, and after turning down the overall command of the Union army at the outset of the Civil War, Robert E. Lee joined the forces of his native state and later became commander of the Army of Northern Virginia. *VLR and NRHP. Historical Marker J-76. Open to the public; admission charge for non-members. Located on Great House Road, off of Route 214, about one mile east of Rt. 3. (Map B)*

Chantilly site (27) This archaeological site is where Richard Henry Lee (1732-1794), author of the Leedstown Resolves (see Leedstown (13)) lived. As a delegate to the Continental Congress in 1776, Lee also moved the resolution for independence from Great Britain, and he was a signer of the Declaration of Independence.

Leasing this property from his elder brother, Philip Ludwell Lee, in 1763, Richard Henry Lee may have already built what was probably a frame house over an English basement which had fourteen-inch thick walls, with a central block measuring 31 feet square. Accounts differ as to the degree of architectural elegance of the house.

The house stood on a promontory formed by deep ravines facing lowlands stretching to the Potomac River. It had almost entirely disappeared by the mid-19th century, but the causes of its destruction are still debated. An archaeological investigation in 1972 determined that while the house was most likely damaged by shelling from British gunboats during the War of 1812, the house was probably not destroyed by fire. Rather, the shelling may have made the house uninhabitable, and this was followed by a period of gradual deterioration of the remaining structure. *VLR and NRHP. Historical Marker J-76. Site not visible from the road; privately owned. (Map B)*

From Stratford Hall northeast on Route 214 (Stratford Hall Road)

Delaware Cottage (28) Also known as the Drover's Cottage, this house was built in 1852 by Robert Polk of Delaware as a summer cottage for the owners, who lived outside the area. The house, a single-pile, five-bay, $2^{1}/_{2}$ story dwelling, has spectacular period trim. It was reported in a local newspaper, in 1890, that the house had been newly renovated and at that time belonged to the Mt. Airey Stock Company.

Delaware Cottage (28)

Visible from the road; privately owned. (Map B)

Reed-Jenkins House (29) Also known as Chantilly Acres, the original part of this house may have been constructed by Joseph Reed in the early 19th century, or possibly already in the early 1790s. The original dwelling was a small 1¹/₂ story house with front and back porches. The chimney was built primarily of native sandstone.

Around the turn of the 20th century, a single-story, one-room house was moved against the south wall, where the chimney is, and converted into a kitchen. Further additions were made in the 1930s, and the main part of the house was raised to a full two stories at that time. The house has remained in the Reed and Jenkins families since it was built. *Visible from the road; privately owned. (Map B)*

Reed-Jenkins House (29)

Log Cabin Doleman Road (30) This small structure is one of the last, if not the last, of the old log cabins in Westmoreland

County which have not been encapsulated with other siding. The front section appears to have two rooms. The large sandstone chimney would seem to date the cabin from before the Civil War. Much more recently, it was used as a woodworking shop. *Visible from the road; privately owned. Endangered. (Map B)*

Log Cabin Doleman Road (30)

From Stratford Hall Road left on to Currioman Road (Rt. 622)

Currioman House (31) The original part of this house is thought to date from the early 18th century. A millstone, bearing a 17th century date, and possibly from what was once Speake's Mill, has been preserved on the property. Modern additions have considerably enlarged what was once a very small house, which contained an enclosed stairway and rooms on both floors served by a single chimney. The

Currioman House (31)

house and its 2,000 acres were purchased from the Chilton family by William H. Sanford in 1824. Sanford had served in the artillery division of the American garrison guarding the U.S. gunboat *Scorpion* at the naval engagement off Kinsale, on July 14, 1813. *Visible from the road; privately owned. Endangered. (Map B)*

Back down Rt. 622, which becomes Panorama Road

Panorama Road houses (32A-E) This old road connecting Montross and the hamlet of Chiltons, contains several interesting pre-Civil War houses that were inhabited by families of modest means. The northern part of this area was part of the Lee holdings at Stratford and Chantilly. All of the extant modest houses have a large exterior sandstone chimney, with a brick flue, which was typical of the Chiltons area, which contains native sandstone in the fields. *All these structures are visible from the road, but privately owned. All but the Balderson House are endangered. (Map B)*

The **Johnson House** dates from just before the Civil War. With a side-hall, single-pile plan, this house originally had a verandah across its two floors, a door to which can still be seen boarded over on the second floor of the main façade. Each of the two major rooms has a fireplace. The decorative fascia board on the eave

appears to have been added in the late 19th century, probably at the same time the verandah was replaced by a single-story porch. As of publication, the house will soon be lost unless rescued. *(Map B)*

The **Double House** is a unique structure consisting of a pair of two-story, two-bay houses joined by a small one-story addition. The front house probably dates from ca. 1900, with a front porch and interior chimney at one end. The rear house dates from about 1870 or earlier; the pitch of its roof is dramatically steeper than the later house. *(Map B)*

Double House (32b)

The **Uriah Balderson House** appears to have been originally a two-bay, single-pile house with a side entrance and sandstone chimney, and was quite possibly built before the Civil War. The right hand side of the house was built later, possibly in the mid-1870s. A very old frame outbuilding stands in the yard. *(Map B)*

Johnson House (32a)

Uriah Balderson House (32c)

The **Hennage House**, with its sandstone chimney and brick flue, was probably built before the Civil War. The house has hand-hewn beams and log posts, and a balloon construction. The rear kitchen wing may also be antebellum. The house has no hall, and a winder stair connects the two floors. *(Map B)*

Hennage House (32d)

The **Balderson House** is said to have been built in 1856. It is a 1¹/₂ story, single-pile vernacular frame house, which has been modernized. Of most interest is its large sandstone exterior chimney. *(Map B)*

Balderson House (32e)

Continuing on to Montross on Rt. 622

Mont Calm (33) The original part of this house—a two-story, side-hall, double-pile structure—was built ca. 1810 by Dr. William A. Spence of Woodbury (36) for his son. In 1818, the Westmoreland County court recommended to the governor that the court meet here (referred to as "Thomas Spence's Brick House") until a new courthouse could be built. In 1878, an addition was constructed on the north side of the original house, creating a T-plan. Both the original house and the addition had two rooms on each floor. *Visible from the road; privately owned. (Map B and Map C)*

Mont Calm (33)

Brick House (34) Built ca. 1820, this Federal style house has a center-hall plan, and sits on a full English basement with a fireplace at one end. There are five fireplaces in the house, all being served by flush chimneys at the center of the north- and south-end walls. The house gained a

Brick House (34)

Westmoreland County, Map C

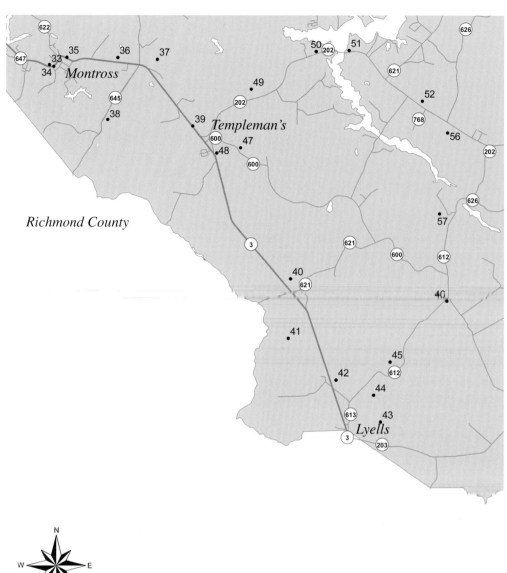

622

647
35
33
34
Montross
36
37

645
38

50 202
51

621

626

52

768

56

202

49

202

39
Templeman's
600
48
47
600

Richmond County

626

57

3

621

600

612

40
621

40

41

45
612

42

44

613
43
Lyells
3
203

N
W   E
S

0   0.5   1   2   3   4
Miles

frame addition in the 1890s and the present front porch early in the 20th century. *Visible from the road; privately owned. (Map B and Map C)*

Hutt House (35) Located on the north side of Rt. 3 near the center of Montross, this dwelling was built ca. 1830 by William Hutt, then the clerk of the Westmoreland County Court. The house was built on a two-story side-hall single-pile plan over an English basement. Fireplaces on each floor were served by a large chimney on the west end.

This simple house was converted into a double-pile dwelling prior to the Civil War, by a frame addition off the rear, with its own chimney. A further addition to the side in the late 19th century gave the house a center-hall plan, and a columned porch was erected in order to tie together the two sides of the house. It was about this time that the earlier windows were replaced with the two-over-two light sashes typical of that period. *Visible from the road; privately owned. (Map B and Map C)*

Hutt House (35)

Woodbury (36) This was the home of Dr. William A. Spence, who also built Mont Calm (33). The original house burned ca. 1845 and the present structure, with an L-shaped plan, was built about 1848. All major rooms, on both floors, are provided with fireplaces served by two interior chimneys. While Greek Revival plaster ceiling medallions are in the downstairs hall and parlor, the exterior trim reflects the Gothic

Revival style. *Visible from the road; privately owned. (Map B and Map C)*

Woodbury (36)

Springfield (37) Located east of Montross, Springfield appears to date from the first half of the 19th century. This $2^1/_2$ story house has a center-hall plan, and it appears to have been built all at the same time. The entrance doors, with their transoms and side-lights, and the verandah columns, are all in the Greek Revival style. All four major rooms have fireplaces, and both sides of the house have chimneys laid in Flemish bond brickwork. One downstairs room has wainscot paneling. *Visible from the road; privately owned. (Map B and Map C)*

Springfield (37)

Tate House (38) The original portion of the house, likely dating from the first half of the 19th century, consisted only of the center hall and the rooms to its south. After the Civil War, an asymmetrical addition was built on the north side, and the large front porch with scroll-saw work

Tate House (38)

was probably added at this time. *Visible from the road; privately owned. (Map B and Map C)*

Montross to Lyells and back to Templeman's

A. T. Johnson High School (39) Built in 1937 in the Colonial Revival style, this was the first public high school for African Americans in Westmoreland County. The school was named for Armstead Tasker Johnson (1857-1944), a black educator and community leader. After teaching in the Westmoreland public schools for many years, he later taught at the Northern Neck Industrial Academy (8) in Richmond County. Following complete integration of the Westmoreland schools in 1967, the Johnson school became a junior high school and then a middle school until 1998. Since enlarged and converted into a county office building, the original part now contains a museum. *VLR and NRHP. Historical Marker JT-19. Visible from the road; open to the public. (Map B and Map C)*

A.T. Johnson High School (39)

Nomini Grove Farm (40) This home is difficult to date, having been altered a number of times. In all likelihood the original part of the house was a side-hall, single-pile plan, and was built ca. 1800, and the front rooms date from that period. The west chimney was built with double shoulders. Later, but probably before the Civil War, a single pile was added to the other side of the stair hall, enlarging the house into a center-hall structure. *Visible from the road; privately owned. (Map C)*

Nomini Grove Farm (40)

Oak Farm (41) Likely built in the early 19th century, Oak Farm is a $1^1/2$ story center-hall home, with principal façades that are identical. Fine paneled double doors with transom lights are at each end of the center hall. The house is constructed on an English basement with large window openings; all brickwork is five-course American bond. Each of three floors has two rooms, each containing a

Oak Farm (41)

Westmoreland County, Map D

Potomac River

Nomini Creek

fireplace. The basement level contains the original kitchen and dining room; on the first floor is the parlor and master bedroom; and two sleeping rooms are on the second floor. *Not visible from the road; privately owned. Endangered. (Map C)*

Level Grove (42) was quite clearly built in two phases. The oldest part—a $1^1/_2$ story side-hall, single-pile plan, with a stair hall with double doors at both the front and rear, and built over an English basement—appears to date from the mid-18th century. The wide, beaded weatherboard on the rear of the house is original. The two dormers, with semi-circular ornament and keystone, were probably added later. The two-story single-pile addition to the south is thought to date from the first quarter of the 19th century. *Visible from the road; privately owned. (Map C)*

Level Grove (42)

Rochester House (43) This 20-by-16 foot hall-plan dwelling would appear to be the smallest surviving house from the 18th century in the Northern Neck region. Thought to have been built in the 1740s, it may still have been larger-than-average for that time and place. The sturdy braced-frame structure, with mortise-and-tenon construction, has but one main room, and a sleeping loft upstairs, but is built over a full basement. Two small original board-and-batten doors in the attic kneewalls have survived, and the two small windows flanking the fireplace downstairs may be original. The large exterior chimney, with its T-shaped stack, suggests that for its time the house was probably of above-average quality.

The house was built by William Rochester, son of the immigrant. His grandnephew, Nathaniel Rochester (1752-1831), is believed to have founded the city of Rochester, New York in the early 19th century. The dwelling has been modified several times, initially around 1800 when remodeling added some Federal style elements. *VLR and NRHP. Not visible from road; privately owned. Endangered. (Map C)*

Rochester House (43)

Clear Spring (44) is believed to date from the first half of the 18th century. The original part of the house is the $2^1/_2$ story brick section on the left side of the main structure. An unusual fireplace mantel with herringbone scoring is in the single first-floor room of this part of the house. An original stairway, less than two feet wide, connects the second and third floors.

The addition to the right of the front door was likely added in the first quarter of the 19th century. Unlike the original house, this addition contains just $1^1/_2$ stories, although it is of the same overall height. Clear Spring is thus one of the earliest "split level" houses in the United States. *Visible from the road; privately owned. (Map C)*

Clear Spring (44)

Carville Farm (45) The oldest part of this house, containing a single room on each floor, is thought to date from the late 18th century. It has split lathing and beaded trim, and a tiny enclosed stairway. The present house, which incorporates the original, is twice its size, and includes the large sandstone and brick chimney on the new west end of the house. It has been conjectured that the door to the original house became the southeast window of the enlarged dwelling, and that the west addition replaced an original stick chimney. The structure is currently in a state of disrepair and is used for farm storage. *Visible from the road; privately owned. Endangered. (Map C)*

Carville Farm (45)

Kremlin School (46) This school was established about 1870, one of five private schools founded to serve Westmoreland County's African American community during Reconstruction. It later became a public school, but in 1958 it was sold to Jerusalem Baptist Church. *Visible from the road. (Map C)*

Kremlin School (46)

West on Rt. 600 to Templeman's X Roads

Twinmore Farm (47) Built about 1780 and lying well off the road, this is a 1½ story, three-bay, single-pile house with a saltbox roof. The construction is of pegged posts and wrought nails. *Visible from the road; privately owned. (Map C)*

Twinmore Farm (47)

Nomini Baptist Church (48) was organized in 1786 and is the oldest Baptist congregation in the Northern Neck after Morattico Baptist Church (1) in Lancaster County. Capt. Joseph Pierce is considered the founder of the church. The present church was built between 1858 and 1860, at Templeman's Crossroads.

This Classical Revival church has a highly regular, rectangular plan. The façade is three bays across, with large double doors under a pilastered Doric entablature. The sides of the church are four bays, and there is a single door near each end of the church with two windows in between. Each opening on the first floor is echoed by a window on the second. Above these windows, a wide corbelled brick cornice with brick dentils runs under the eaves. *Historical Marker J-79. Visible from the road. (Map C)*

Nomini Baptist Church (48)

Templeman's X Roads to Hague, along Rt. 202

Oakville Farm (49) This frame $1\frac{1}{2}$ story center-hall single-pile plan house with double-shouldered chimneys at each end is believed to date from the late 18th century. The rear addition was built later. Particularly notable are the dormer windows that rise flush with the façade, the only known instance of this architectural

Oakville Farm (49)

feature in the Northern Neck region. The cornice under the eaves was continued around the faces of the three dormers. *Visible from the road; privately owned. Endangered. (Map C and Map D)*

Ferry Hill (50) Also known as Thompson's Hill, this house overlooks Nomini Creek from a hilltop just west of the Nomini Creek bridge. The oldest part of the house, thought to date from the first half of the 18th century, is a $1\frac{1}{2}$ story structure with one room on each floor, each with a fireplace with original mantels. The chimney is largely made of sandstone.

By 1750, Dr. Thomas Thompson had built a large dwelling on this site, with the original house incorporated as a wing. Philip Vickers Fithian (see Nomini Hall (57)), in his famous diary, recorded visiting Dr. Thompson in 1774. Although the larger Thompson house has disappeared, the original small house survives today as the core of the present, 20th century house. *Not visible from the road; privately owned. (Map C and Map D)*

Ferry Hill (50)

Nomini Church (51) Originally built in 1757, the church was burned by the British during the War of 1812. The land on which that church and its present successor were built, was deeded to Cople Parish by Thomas Youell in 1703, and the original church was built over the graves of Youell and his wife, who was a daughter of Richard Lee the immigrant (see Cobbs Hall (81) in Northumberland County). Descriptions of services at the original church appear in Philip Vickers Fithian's diary of 1773-74.

The present church was built in 1852, and by some is thought to contain one wall surviving from the original structure. The Flemish-bond brickwork of the façade of the present building probably also came from the ruins of the earlier church. The façade combines both Classical Revival doorways, with single-panel doors hinged in the center and to one side, and a Gothic Revival pointed-arch window with polychromed lights. Each of the side walls contains three large Classical Revival sash windows with semi-circular brick heads. *Historical Marker JT-2. Visible from the road. (Map C and Map D)*

Nomini Church (51)

Spring Grove (52) This Federal period Classical Revival style house was built in 1834 by Robert Murphy, and is one of a relatively small group of formal brick dwellings built in Westmoreland County in the early 19th century. The façade is laid in Flemish bond, whereas the other sides are in three-course American bond. At the main entrance, the portico features finely detailed Ionic columns based directly on the pattern books of Boston architect Asher Benjamin.

The floor plan of Spring Grove is unique to Westmoreland County. Although the house has a basic center-hall plan, the house is not a true double-pile

as the first floor contains only two major rooms. The four symmetrical chimneys are built flush with the walls. Much of the first floor interior, notably the principal rooms, contains woodwork and decorative plasterwork also based on Benjamin's pattern books.

A separate kitchen and a smokehouse survive as dependencies in the yard. *VLR and NRHP. Visible from the road; privately owned. (Map C and Map D)*

Spring Grove (52)

Side trip on Mt. Holly Road (Rt. 621)

Bushfield (53) The exact construction date of the original two-story, single-pile, center passage four room brick manor house, laid up in Flemish bond, is unknown, but its scale and massing suggest it was built in the 18th century. Bushfield was in the Washington family for many years, and in 1799 it was passed on to Bushrod Washington (1762-1829), a nephew of the president and an Associate Justice of the United States Supreme Court from 1798 until his death. The house was shelled by the British in 1814 during a raid into Nomini Creek. After this, Bushrod Washington took up residence at Mount Vernon, which he had also inherited. Renovations to Bushfield appear to have been carried out in 1843 and again in 1857.

In 1916, the house was extensively renovated and doubled in size by the noted architect Waddy Butler Wood. The addition was linked with the original structure through existing door and window openings, and the original building's interior spaces and architectural elements, such as crown moldings, baseboards and fireplace surrounds were retained. These elements were then reflected in the interior of the new addition. Further renovations were made between 1995 and 2000. *VLR and NRHP. Historical Marker JT-5. Visible from the road; privately owned. (Map D)*

Bushfield (53)

Morgan Jones Pottery Kiln Archaeological Site (54) At least as early as 1669, Morgan Jones, a Welsh potter, was making pottery in Westmoreland County. In 1677, Jones signed an agreement with Dennis White to operate a pottery kiln near Glebe Creek, a tributary of Lower Machodoc Creek. Within months, however, White had died. Since Jones could not satisfy his own creditors, he left Westmoreland County for Maryland. The foundations of this site lay hidden for nearly 300 years. In the winter of 1973, archaeologists from the Virginia Historic Landmarks Commission (now the Virginia Department of Historic Resources) discovered a concentration of pottery fragments and an almost perfectly preserved kiln, the first such early kiln found in the commonwealth.

The archaeologists described the kiln as cross-shaped with a large doughnut hole at the junction of the two arms of the cross. Inside the doughnut, about five feet in circumference, were two raised, half-moon sections separated by a canal. The kiln is significant both because of its early date, and because of its design, which is distinctive from other excavated colonial kilns.

As the Lords of Trade in London did not permit manufacturing in Virginia at that time, the Jones-White venture was actually illegal. Nonetheless, remnants of Morgan Jones pottery have been found on other archaeological sites in Westmoreland County, such as at Washington's Birthplace (22), Stratford Hall (26) and Nomini Hall (57). Samples of Morgan Jones pottery are on display in the county office building. *VLR and NRHP. Historical Marker JT-14. Site not visible from the road; privately owned. (Map E)*

The Glebe (55) This glebe house, built for the rector of Cople Parish, is the only remaining glebe house in the Northern Neck (but in Essex County, see St. Anne's Parish Glebe (9)), and it is said to be the oldest extant example of a glebe house in the entire commonwealth of Virginia. All major social figures in pre-revolutionary Westmoreland County would have been entertained here.

Substantial renovations were made to this house in the 20th century, and the present house is in the style of an Edwardian resort house. Nevertheless, elements of the

The Glebe (55)

original structure, possibly dating from the late 1600s, remain, although largely hidden from view. The oldest part of the house, that to the east of the front door, is laid in over-sized Flemish-bond bricks with glazed headers. Running about two-thirds the length of the present house, the original glebe house had chimneys flush with the end walls. The windows were long and narrow with segmentally-arched heads.

The addition to the west of the entrance is thought to date from about 1720, and it has a third chimney at its end. While also laid in Flemish bond, this brickwork was done without glazed headers.

Because the 20th century renovations removed any vestiges of the original interior, the legacy of the past is only to be seen in this exterior brickwork. *Historical Marker JT-3. Visible from the road; privately owned. (Map E)*

Rt. 202 to Hague

Boscobel (56) This Greek Revival house was built by Dr. Franklin Brown ca. 1850. The house has exceptional trim, and is probably the finest example of the Greek Revival style in Westmoreland County. The front doors and six-over-nine light parlor windows are set out in fine entablatures supported by pilasters and plinth blocks on the exterior, and this approach is taken on the interior as well. The several wings

Boscobel (56)

were added in the 20th century. *Visible from the road; privately owned. (Map C and Map D)*

Side trip on Beale's Mill Road (Rt. 626) and Rt. 612

Nomini Hall (57) This was one of the largest mansions built in Virginia during the colonial period, erected under the direction of Robert ("King") Carter (see Corotoman site (5) in Lancaster County) for his son, Robert Carter II. The property was inherited by Robert ("Councillor") Carter III, so named for his relatively short tenure on the colonial Council of the commonwealth. The younger Carter rebelled against the political leadership role into which he was born, and is perhaps best known for his controversial emancipation, begun in 1791, of some 450 slaves.

Despite its size and importance, relatively little is known about the original Nomini Hall, which burned in 1850. The main sources of information about the house are the diary of Philip Vickers Fithian, tutor to the children of Robert ("Councillor") Carter during 1773-74, and the somewhat primitive 19th century sketch by E. Maund. The brick mansion was of rectangular shape, but the brick was covered with a strong lime mortar, giving the appearance of a stucco finish. In the Northern Neck only Menokin (30), in Richmond County, had a similar stucco finish.

Nomini Hall (57)

The house had several Palladian features, including the porticos on both principal facades, which may have been added in 1771, and the windows flanking the double doors on the south elevation. It is unclear when these windows were rendered in this style, but if they were present on the original house of ca. 1730, that may have been the first use of such an element in American architecture.

The principal façade of Nomini Hall faced north towards the Nomini Creek, but was approached from its east side along a line of poplars beginning at the road connecting the Westmoreland and Richmond county courthouses. It sat in the center of a landscaped square, similar to the layout described for Stratford Hall (26). *Historical Marker J-72.*

A second dwelling by the name of Nomini Hall was erected near the foundations of the original house, following the fire of 1850. The traditional center-hall plan is modified in this Late Greek Revival house, the hall being truncated in its rear half, which become rooms. The front porch was added ca. 1920. *Visible from the road; privately owned. (Map C)*

Rt. 202 at Hague

Drum Bay (58) Tradition has it that this house was erected in 1698 for Col. Richard Lee II, son of the immigrant. It is one of the oldest, but also one of the smallest, surviving houses in the Northern Neck. This survivor from early colonial times sits on a ridge of the Potomac River flood plain not far from the neighboring Lee estates of Lee Hall (60), Mount Pleasant and Machodoc (66). Although a complete renovation in 1963 eliminated all traces of the original interior plan, the placement of the end chimneys and fireplaces suggests that this house had two rooms downstairs of unequal size as well as two above.

Drum Bay (58)

Although the exterior is simple, its solid Flemish-bond walls and simple corbelled brick cornice beneath the eave reflect superior craftsmanship. *Not visible from the road; privately owned. (Map E and Map F)*

Buena Vista (59) Thomas Brown built this house between 1835 and 1839, using timber cut and dressed on the property. The two chimneys incorporated into the body of the house made it possible to heat all eight rooms with fireplaces using only two flues. The house is little changed from the original, except for two side porches and an attached kitchen. The interior trim, mantels and cornices reflect Greek Revival influences. An elegant curving stairway at the rear of the house connects the two floors. The house also has an unusual protruding entrance vestibule.

During the Civil War, Thomas Brown and his wife, a cousin of General Robert E. Lee, hosted here British emissaries who had been sent to Richmond to evaluate the wisdom of recognizing the Confederacy. A raiding party of Union troops

Buena Vista (59)

at one point captured a blockade runner hidden in the attic at Buena Vista. *Visible from the road; privately owned. (Map E and Map F)*

Lee Hall site (60) This lost site was located at Hague. Little is known about the architecture of this large brick house built in 1720 by Thomas Lee for his brother, Henry Lee. Philip Vickers Fithian (see Nomini Hall (57)) wrote of a three-day ball hosted here in 1774 for 70 guests by the eldest son of Henry Lee, known as "Squire" Richard Lee. Squire Lee remained a bachelor, with an estate of nearly 10,000 acres (including over 1,000 acres in Cherry Point in Northumberland County), until he married, at age sixty, a 16-year old cousin known for her beauty. She gave him four children before he died in 1795. His younger brother, Henry Lee, settled in Prince William County and Henry's family became known as the "Leesylvania" Lees, which included his own son Henry ("Light Horse Harry") Lee and grandson General Robert E. Lee. *Historical Marker erected by The Society of the Lees of Virginia. (Map E and Map F)*

Hague House (61) Evidently the only 18th century gambrel-roofed house in Westmoreland County, this 1½ story frame dwelling is said to have been built by a family named Hague, which also gave its name to the nearby post office. It has a center-hall plan, with both first floor rooms having fireplaces served by large double-

Hague House (61)

shouldered chimneys. Curiously, while the front door and dormers are centered on the house, the major windows are asymmetrically placed. *Visible from the road; privately owned. (Map E and Map F)*

Linden (62) This house was probably built before 1830 by Willoughby Newton Sr., who had married the young widow of "Squire" Richard Lee of Lee Hall (60). Linden was said to have been architecturally similar to Spring Grove (52), which was built for Newton's son-in-law. During the mid-19th century, Linden was the home of Willoughby Newton Jr. (1802-1874), a U.S. congressman and later president of the Virginia Agricultural Society. The property was actually attributed a higher taxable value than Stratford, before it burned in 1884.

The present frame house was built in 1929, but several outbuildings from the original plantation, including an office to the east of the main house and a kitchen/laundry to the west, are said to have been built prior to the original mansion. *Visible from the road; privately owned. Endangered. (Map E and Map F)*

South at Hague on Tavern Run Road (Rt. 616) and back to Rt. 202

Afton (63) A Greek Revival two-story side-hall plan house, Afton was built ca. 1840. The house is entered through a classical portico of square ornamented posts. The stair hall has double doors on both the east and west sides of the house, and the first floor has two large rooms of equal size, each with a fireplace. The two sleeping rooms above also have fireplaces. An addition on the south side of the house was added later in the 19th century. *Visible from the road; privately owned. (Map E and Map F)*

Westmoreland County, Map E

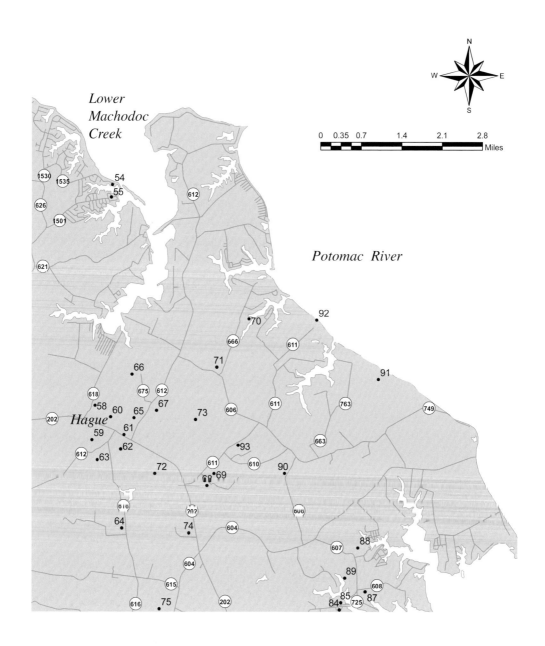

Lower
Machodoc
Creek

Potomac River

Hague

Afton (63)

Goldberne (64) Sitting on a knoll, this frame house was built ca. 1825. Originally a side-hall, single-pile structure, it was built over a high basement. A wing consisting of four bedrooms was built in 1920, and the original chimney is enclosed in the body of the larger house. The entrance now has a vernacular Classical Revival portico, which assists in carefully tying the addition to the original part of the house. *Visible from the road; privately owned. (Map E and Map F)*

Goldberne (64)

Rt. 612 (Coles Point Road)

Mt. Pleasant (65) Located near Hague, this is a three-story, 17-room Queen Anne style house built in 1887 by John E. R. Crabbe of Baltimore, who had decided to return to his boyhood home. It is one of the few examples of Queen Anne style residential architecture in Westmoreland County. Based on published illustrations of Late Victorian architecture, the house was assembled from prefabricated parts. After some 30 years of neglect, it was purchased and thoroughly restored in the late 1990s.

The house is framed in cypress, stands on a brick basement, and has floors of Virginia pine. It has a gable roof, four brick chimneys, and a single-story verandah that runs along its north and west sides. Mt. Pleasant has a number of notable Late Victorian decorative features, including six faux grained slate mantels, a stained glass skylight, and ten gasoliers. A smokehouse, carriage barn and wellhouse stand to the rear of the home. *VLR and NRHP. Visible from the road; privately owned. (Map E and Map F)*

Mt. Pleasant (65)

Machodoc and Burnt House Field (66) Machodoc was the first Lee house on the 2,000 acre tract patented by Richard Lee the immigrant in 1658, and was the seat of his son, Richard Lee II, a member of the Governor's Council. This pre-Georgian house burned about 1729, and its site is known as "Burnt House Field." This site is marked today by a family cemetery containing the graves of, among others, Thomas Lee, builder of Stratford (26), and his son Richard Henry Lee (see Leedstown

(13) and Chantilly (27)). *Historical Marker erected by The Society of the Lees of Virginia. On Rt. 675 off of Rt. 612. Visible from the road; open to the public. (Map E and Map F)*

Fort Hill site (67) Close to the intersection of routes 675 and 612 on the east side of Rt. 612 is a hill which local legend claims was one of the last Native American fortifications in the area. The Indians were alleged to have fired from here on European settlers clearing their land. During both the War of 1812 and the Civil War this site was used as an observation point. *Site visible from the road; privately owned. (Map E and Map F)*

Hague to Kinsale along Rt. 202

Centreville (68) Also known as "Carey's Corner," this house was built by William Carey in 1849. The Greek Revival house is located on a knoll that is one of the highest points in Westmoreland County. The façade is laid in Flemish-bond brickwork, and the other sides are in five course American bond. The openings through the 20-inch thick walls are all headed by flat arches.

Although the house appears from the outside to have a center-hall plan, there is but a small triangular vestibule behind the double front doors. This vestibule opens

Centreville (68)

into two large rooms. The interior woodwork is an excellent example of the Greek Revival style.

During the Civil War, Centreville was the site of a skirmish between a detachment of Mosby's Rangers and foraging Union troops who had located a storehouse of wheat on the premises. During the fight, the storehouse burned and carbonized wheat can still be found on the site today. Long after the skirmish, bullet holes could still be detected in the façade of the house. It was renovated for the first time in 1977. *Not visible from the road; privately owned. (Map E and Map F)*

Kirnan (69) The original house, which may date from the early 18th century, was a $1^1/_2$ story side-hall plan home with two rooms of equal size on the ground floor, each having a corner fireplace. Toward the end of the 18th century it was expanded to a center-hall structure. The addition included a large room with a fireplace, with a paneled overmantel and shelf, and a small unheated room to the rear. A great deal of 18th century detail is preserved inside the house. In 1852, an enclosed Classical Revival porch was added to the front, and a detached kitchen with a large cooking fireplace, located behind the house, was joined to it by a breezeway. Currently under renovation. *Not visible from the road; privately owned. (Map E and Map F)*

Kirnan (69)

Wilton (70) The present house, a two-story center-hall plan laid in Flemish bond with glazed headers, is typical of the Early Georgian period. Recent dendrochronological work indicates that it may have been built about 1742, probably by Robert Jackson, who had bought the property from Robert Eskridge four years earlier. Prior to its ownership by Eskridge, the property had belonged to John Gerard II, whose family had owned it since the 1660s. During its ownership by the Gerard family, this site had contained a much more modest 17th-century house. After the Civil War, it passed into the Arnest family, which carried out extensive renovations. The original, modest house may have occupied what is now the center hall and the two rooms on the west side, both of which have corner fireplaces. *Visible from the road; privately owned. Endangered. (Map E)*

Wilton (70)

Banqueting Hall site (71) The Banqueting Hall, viewed as the first clubhouse in the English colonies in America, stood in "Peckatown's Field," at the entrance to Wilton (70), on the northwest corner of the intersection of routes 606 and 666. It was built in 1670 by four planters whose lands adjoined: Henry Corbin, John Lee (the eldest son of Richard Lee the immigrant), Isaac Allerton (who had migrated from Massachusetts, and whose father and mother—the daughter of William Brewster—had come over on the *May-*

flower), and Thomas Gerard of Wilton. According to their written agreement of record, they established the hall "for the continuance of good neighbourhood," as a convenient meeting place for processioning the bounds of their properties, and "to make an honorable treatment, fit to entertain the undertakers thereof, their men, masters and friends, yearly and every year thereafter; to begin upon the 29th of May, 1671." *Site visible from the road; privately owned. (Map E and Map F)*

La Grange (72) Built in 1850 by Robert H. Chowning, the house shows Greek Revival influences, but follows no traditional floor plan of that period. The house features a modified side-hall plan, in which the entry hall contains the stairway but does not cross through the house. This reflects the changes in architectural design occurring just prior to the Civil War which would become common in many of the houses of the Victorian era. *Not visible from the road; privately owned. (Map E and Map F)*

La Grange (72)

Auburn (73) Considered to have been built about 1830, Auburn began as a side-hall plan house, although the later addition of a Classical Revival portico on the west gable end of the house gives the impression that the house is organized according to a center-hall plan. In actuality, the principal entrances were the double-door openings on the south and north side of

Auburn (73)

the original structure. The stair hall is considered one of the most outstanding architectural spaces in Westmoreland County. Although a long and narrow addition was made to the rear of the house later in the 19th century, little of significance has been changed since it was built, and Auburn remains an admirable example of careful preservation. *Not visible from the road; privately owned. (Map E and Map F)*

Woodbourne (74) Although this house was built ca. 1840, during the Classical Revival period, its plan actually reflects 18th century architectural design. The house is a two-story, center-hall, single-pile plan, with flush chimneys on either gable end. The front is laid in Flemish-bond, while the other three sides are in four-course American bond. The center hall is entered through double doors at both the front and rear. Classical Revival ornamentation, however, is seen throughout the interior. The frame addition on the north side dates from the late 19th century. *Visible from the road; privately owned. (Map E and Map F)*

Woodburne (74)

Kinsale Area
(Route 203 west)

Elba (75) This house, considered to have been built by Charnock Cox who patented this property in 1667, may date from about 1690 and if so would be the oldest surviving structure in Westmoreland County. The $1^1/_2$ story dwelling has a center-hall, single-pile plan. The brick walls are Flemish bond, and the chimneys on each end, also laid in Flemish bond, each have three shoulders. The chimney on the east end is original but that on the west was rebuilt in the 20th century.

The center hall is flanked by two rooms of equal size, and contains an enclosed stairway to the second floor, which contains two bedrooms. All four rooms have fireplaces. The very few windows in the house have undergone considerable change, but their small number contributes to the feeling of age of this simple house. The house was sold by the last Cox descendant about 1960, and was renovated at that time. *Visible from the road; privately owned. (Map E and Map F)*

Elba (75)

Elba Schoolhouse (76) Built in 1890, this one-room vernacular style schoolhouse is one of the very few remaining in Westmoreland County. *Visible from the road; privately owned. (Map F)*

Elba Schoolhouse (76)

Back to the east on Rt. 203

Locust Farm (77) This 1¹/₂ story single-pile brick house was built for the Cox family, probably by John Heath in 1717, as his name, this date, and "Liverpool, England" are carved on a rough-hewn beam beneath the first floor. The walls and foundation are laid out in over-size brick, an indication of great age. The walls are laid in Flemish bond, and rest on an English basement in English bond. At each end of the house are double-shouldered chimneys laid in Flemish bond.

The house has two front doors, just two feet apart in the center of the façade. The first floor is bisected by an original wall that rests on the inscribed oak beam. The front door on the east side leads into a small entry hall from which the basement stairs and one of the first floor rooms are reached. The east room contains a six-foot wide fireplace with a segmental arch and

Locust Farm (77)

a mantel shelf 6¹/₂ feet above the floor. The other first floor room may be entered either from this entry hall or through its own front door. It contains an even larger fireplace, eight feet wide, and an original mantel shelf over six feet above the floor. An enclosed stairway off this room connects with the upstairs. A wing was added to the house in the 1930s. *Visible from the road; privately owned. (Map F)*

Gilbert's (78) This house has been added to many times over the centuries, but the original 1¹/₂ story side-hall house is thought to have been built about 1800. This original section was raised to a full two stories in 1899. *Visible from the road; privately owned. (Map F)*

Gilbert's (78)

Ebenezer Methodist Church (79) Organized in 1838, the congregation constructed this Classical Revival church in 1859. A two-story brick rectangular

Ebenezer Methodist Church (79)

Westmoreland County, Map F

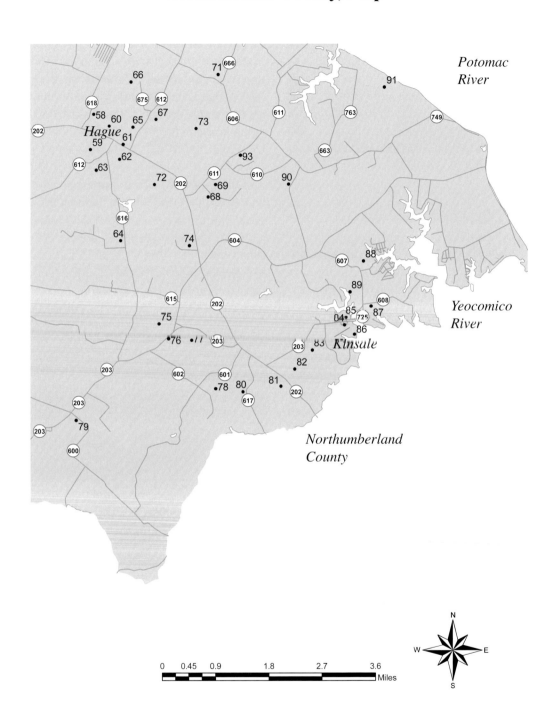

Potomac River

Yeocomico River

Northumberland County

Hague

Kinsale

0   0.45   0.9   1.8   2.7   3.6
Miles

structure, the principal façade is laid in Flemish bond, while the other three sides are in four-course American bond. A wooden tower was added to the façade in 1900 and was bricked over in the mid-20th century. Two symmetric stairways ascend to the church gallery within this tower. The interior contains a mixture of Classical and Gothic Revival detail. *Visible from the road. (Map F)*

Back on Rt. 202 headed south

Headley House (80) This was originally a small yeoman's house with a second story of only one-half height and windows with only one sash. The double-shouldered chimney on the south end suggests the house was built in the first half of the 19th century. The longer side of the house, to the north of the entrance, was probably erected after the Civil War. *Visible from the road; privately owned. Endangered. (Map F)*

Headley House (80)

Lampkin (81) Thought to have been built by the Murphy family, the architectural detail of this two-story dwelling suggests it was erected ca. 1800-40. The house has a side-hall, single-pile plan. The stairway has a walnut balustrade and rises to a large room over the principal room of the first floor, both with fireplaces. A detached kitchen was moved against the rear of the house in the late 19th century.

Plainview Cottage at Lampkin is a one-room structure built in the mid-19th century. It originally formed part of a larger house located at Plainview (87), across the creek from the village of Kinsale. A stairway rises from the ground floor room to a second floor, covered by a steeply pitched roof, and which has two small windows in the north gable flanking the chimney. After having been moved once, this little cottage was moved again to Lampkin in the late 1920s. *Both visible from the road; privately owned. (Map F)*

Lampkin (81)

*Back north on Rt. 202
to Rt. 203 east*

Jeffries House (82) The original house, probably built ca. 1750 by a member of the Bennett family who owned the land

Jeffries House (82)

which may later have become Jeffries, forms the core of the present structure, which incorporates renovations carried out about 1970. The original structure was a small frame house with a side-hall and room plan, and with another very small chamber off this room in a shed addition against the north of the house. The hall contained stairs to the English basement and to the second floor. There were three fireplaces, one on each of the three levels, all served by one chimney. The dormers and front stoop were added during ca. 1970 renovations. *Not visible from the road; privately owned. (Map F)*

Federal Hill (83) This house, which is situated on a hill near Kinsale with an outstanding view of the Yeocomico River and the Southern Maryland shore of the Potomac beyond, was rebuilt just prior to the Civil War. The original house appears on an 1836 survey of that area. During the Civil War, Federal Hill was Station Number 1 in the line of Confederate signal stations along the lower Potomac River.

The house is a mixture of late Greek Revival features and some Victorian-era detail. Set out in the traditional T-plan, the house is assured cross-ventilation in all rooms on both floors. After many years of neglect, the house was renovated in the first decade of the 21st century. *Visible from the road; privately owned. (Map F)*

Federal Hill (83)

Kinsale Historic District (84) The Kinsale Historic District—so designated by the Virginia Department of Historic Resources and the U.S. Department of the Interior in 2005—is located in the village of Kinsale, on Rt. 203 in Westmoreland County.

Kinsale grew up around the wharves established very early in its history. It has both a deepwater port and an extremely sheltered harbor, and it benefited from the trade of both the deep-drafting ships of colonial times, and the shallow draft schooners of the Chesapeake Bay and the Atlantic Coast.

Although designated as a town by the General Assembly in 1705, and again in 1784, Kinsale did not really prosper until the early 19th century with the advent of the Steamboat Era. The village was burned by the British during the War of 1812, and most of the surviving buildings therefore date from the late 19th and early 20th centuries. By the end of the 19th and the turn of the 20th century, the village had several hotels, taverns and barrooms, stores, and canneries, in addition to the post office that was first established there in 1792. Substantial commercial activity continued until the early 1950s, when the last of the canneries closed. Since that time, Kinsale has been primarily a residential community.

The historic district includes several examples of popular architectural styles of the first quarter of the 20th century, including Queen Anne, American Foursquare, Colonial Revival and the Craftsman Bungalow. To drive or walk through Kinsale is to experience a fairly intact collection of buildings that capture the village's character during the late 19th and early 20th centuries.

The Kinsale Museum, open on Fridays, Saturdays and Sundays, has a walking tour brochure of the village and many artifacts and exhibits. *VLR and NRHP. Historical Marker JT-8. (Map E and Map F)*

The Little House (85) This dwelling was built early in the 19th century, probably by the locally prominent Bailey family. The 1½ story house reflects the transition from the Federal style of the early 19th century to a new fashion in design, the Gothic Cottage. With the burning of Kinsale during the War of 1812, this small house is one of the oldest remaining structures in the village. Tradition has it that the yard of the house was used as an abattoir for cattle confiscated by Union forces during the Civil War, and for this reason the house was spared destruction.

The parlor with fireplace and the master bedroom above, on the east side of the present house, are believed to have constituted the original house. The present entrance hall and dining room with fireplace were added ca. 1850, and have ceilings several feet higher than the earlier section. *Visible from the road; privately owned. (Map E and Map F)*

The Little House (85)

The Great House (86) is located on a bluff overlooking the Yeocomico River with a view across the Potomac to the Southern Maryland shore. A house was built on this site in the 17th century, but it may have been partially or totally destroyed as a result of the burning of Kinsale during the War of 1812. Major Robert Bailey, whose family had long owned adjoining property, acquired this land in 1827 and built the present house. Tradition has it that he had this house, or a portion of it, constructed over the brick and sandstone cellar of the original house.

The owners have traditionally kept a light lit at night in the upstairs hall with a dormer, as a nautical gauge to mark the channel of the Yeocomico River into Kinsale. The yard of this estate contains several outbuildings that may predate the War of 1812. The family cemetery contains the grave of Midshipman James Butler Sigourney, commander of the *USS Asp*, who was killed defending Kinsale on July 14, 1813. His remains were removed by his family in the 1990s. The Great House is inhabited by the 11th and 12th generations of direct descendants of the very early emigrant to Westmoreland County, Stephen Bailey I. *Not visible from the road, but visible from the Yeocomico River; privately owned. (Map F)*

The Great House (86)

*Across the Yeocomico River
at Kinsale*

Plainview (87) Built ca. 1860 by John Bailey, this 2½ story center-hall, single-pile house has an 18th-century plan but windows and interior detail found in the Greek Revival style of the early to mid-19th century. The two equal-sized first floor rooms can be entered from the square hall, but the stairway to the second floor is located off another square hall at

Plainview (87)

the rear of the house. The third floor has two rooms, each having dormer windows facing both east and west. *Visible from the road; privately owned. (Map E and Map F)*

Arlington (88) The original part of this house, built about 1800 by Jeremiah Murdock, is the center section with two rooms on both floors, all with fireplaces. The front porch is original to the house, and exhibits a typical feature of many farmhouses of its time with its roof extending from the house roof at a reduced pitch. The two dormers were added during the early 20th century. The two wings were built in the mid-19th century. *Visible from the road; privately owned. (Map E and Map F)*

Arlington (88)

The Grove (89) Sitting on a high bank across from the village of Kinsale, this dwelling was built in 1832 by David Taylor. The Federal style house has a center-hall, single-pile plan, and an English basement. With walls laid in Flemish bond, its doors and windows have flat arches made of painted wood. The portico on the façade is original, and features four Tuscan columns

and rope molding. The area between the two columns engaged against the house wall was stuccoed and scored to resemble ashlar in order to highlight the front doorway. *Not visible from the road; privately owned. (Map E and Map F)*

The Grove (89)

Kinsale Bridge Road to a left at Sandy Point Road (Rt. 604), then right on to Old Yeocomico Road (Rt. 606)

Yeocomico Church (90) This National Historic Landmark—the fourth oldest extant church in Virginia—was built in 1706 on the site of, and possibly even encapsulated a portion of, a wooden church dating from 1655. The present form of the church reflects the addition of a T-wing ca. 1730-40, and this probably accounts for the entrance and south side being laid in Flemish bond, while the rest of what is thought to be the original church is laid in English bond. The structure may be

Yeocomico Church (90)

viewed as a transition piece between the Gothic style of the Middle Ages and the emerging classical style manifested by Georgian architecture in England.

Among the Gothic features of the church are the tracery motif of the semi-circles and the diapering above the porch entrance, the battened doors, the stepped gables, and the splayed eave. The wicket door inside the principal door may have come from the original 1655 church. Reconstructed pilasters reflect the classical architectural additions.

The church has survived numerous threats to its structural integrity. During the Revolutionary War it was used as a barracks. Following that War and disestablishment of the Anglican church, the building was used by Methodists who later disputed the Episcopal claim to the church. It then entered a period of desertion and decay, and during the War of 1812 it was used by both British and American troops. Yeocomico Church became a barracks for yet a third time when it was occupied by the Confederate Home Guard during the Civil War. Not surprisingly, the church has undergone frequent renovations over the past three centuries.

Notable additions to the church include the installation of elaborate Georgian chancel paneling during the renovation of 1906, and the movement of the pulpit against the south wall, probably during the late 19th century, when the slip pews were instituted. *VLR and NRHP. Visible from the road. Tours available. (Map E and Map F)*

Spence's Point (91) A Federal style house with two full floors over a raised basement, Spence's Point was built ca. 1806 by John Critcher. The exterior walls are laid in common bond. A wide side hall with a straight-run staircase runs through the house, providing a view of the Potomac River at the rear. On both the first and second floors, the hallway opens onto two large rooms with fireplaces. The

house was purchased by the father of the novelist John Dos Passos in the late 19th century, and the author renovated the house in 1949, including the adding of a wing to the west side of the house. Dos Passos did much of his writing at this country home. *Not visible from the road; privately owned. (Map E and Map F)*

Spence's Point (91)

Side trip to Rt. 611 east to the Potomac River

Peckatone site (92) Gawen Corbin built an early Georgian mansion here, beside the Potomac River, in 1750. The plantation had originally been named for a local Indian chief by Nicholas Journeau, the original patentee of the 900-acre tract in 1650 who assigned his patent to Henry Corbin in 1660.

In 1886, Peckatone was gutted by a mysterious fire, and its site later eroded into the Potomac. The only photograph of the ruins, dating from about 1888, shows

Peckatone site (92)

an imposing brick structure seven bays wide, with the first floor windows taller than those above. The water table was of molded brick, and the house had a full basement. Two tall chimneys within the body of the house suggested that it had had a hip roof. A visitor to the house prior to the fire observed that a wall extended from a corner of the manor house to a brick kitchen and servants' quarters. This is suggestive of an enclosed villa-style forecourt popular in England in the early 18th century. *Site visible from the road; privately owned. (Map E)*

Zion Baptist Church (93) This church is home to one of the oldest African American congregations in Westmoreland County. Tradition has it that before the end of slavery, services were held under a brush arbor on a farm, close to nearby Tucker Hill. Zion was formally organized in 1867, when the congregation built a log structure. This early building, and two later structures from the late 19th century, were replaced by the present church in 1932. Other early black Baptist congregations that were formed during the five years following the Civil War included Old Monrovia and Macedonia, near Colonial Beach; Little Zion, Siloam, Galilee, Salem and Shiloh Baptist, in or near Montross; Potomac near Hague; and Jerusalem at Oldhams. *Historical Marker JT-18. Visible from the road. (Map E and Map F)*

Zion Baptist Church (93)

Selected Bibliography

Arnold, Scott David. *A Guidebook to Virginia's Historical Markers.* Charlottesville: University of Virginia Press, 2007.

Beale, George William. "Chantilly: The Home of Richard Henry Lee," *Northern Neck of Virginia Historical Magazine* 23 (1973): 2409-2412.

Davison, Bertha. "A History of Washington Parish," *Northern Neck of Virginia Historical Magazine* 13 (1963): 1195-1211.

Davison, Treadwell. "The Old Pope's Creek Church Site," *Northern Neck of Virginia Historical Magazine* 10 (1960): 869-871.

Davison, Treadwell. "St. Peter's Episcopal Church," *Northern Neck of Virginia Historical Magazine* 12 (1962): 1058-1059.

Depratt, Harden V. "Yeocomico Church, Westmoreland County," *Northern Neck of Virginia Historical Magazine* 4 (1954): 299-301.

Dos Passos, Elizabeth H. "Peckatone: Then and Now," *Northern Neck of Virginia Historical Magazine* 23 (1973): 2427-2436.

Egloff, Keith and Martha McCartney. "Excavations at James Monroe Birthplace," *Northern Neck of Virginia Historical Magazine* 31 (1981): 3483-3496.

Fithian, Philip Vickers. *Journal and Letters of Philip Vickers Fithian: A Plantation Tutor of the Old Dominion, 1773-1774* (ed. by Hunter Dickinson Farish). Charlottesville: University Press of Virginia, 1943.

Flemer, Carl F. Jr. "History of Ingleside," *Northern Neck of Virginia Historical Magazine* 3 (1963): 1214-1215.

Hatch, Charles E. Jr. "The Washington Pope Creek Plantation was a Living Farm," *Northern Neck of Virginia Historical Magazine* 8 (1968): 1686-1701.

Healy, Elton C. "History of Nomini Baptist Church," *Northern Neck of Virginia Historical Magazine* 9 (1969): 1855-1858.

Historic & Architectural Resources. *Survey of Architectural Resources in Westmoreland County, Virginia.* Richmond: Department of Historic Resources Archives, File WM-39, 2001.

Hoge, William Aylet. "Notes on Leedstown," *Northern Neck of Virginia Historical Magazine* 14 (1974): 2664-2668.

Latane, Lawrence Washington. "Blenheim," *Northern Neck of Virginia Historical Magazine* 15 (1975): 2706-2707.

Lee, Edmund Jennings. *Lee of Virginia.* Baltimore: Genealogical Publishing Co., 1974; orig. published in 1895.

Loth, Calder. *The Virginia Landmarks Register.* Charlottesville: University Press of Virginia, Fourth Edition, 1999.

Lounsbury, Carl R. *An Illustrated Glossary of Early Southern Architecture and Landscape.* Charlottesville: University Press of Virginia, 1994.

Mcade, Bishop William. *Old Churches Ministers and Families of Virginia.* Philadelphia, 2 vols., 1857.

Nagel, Paul C. *The Lees of Virginia: Seven Generations of an American Family.* New York: Oxford University Press, 1990.

Norris, Walter Biscoe Jr. *Westmoreland County Virginia: 1653-1983.* Montross, Va.: Westmoreland County Board of Supervisors, 1983; Fourth Edition, 2008.

O'Dell, Jeffrey M. "1972 Excavation at the Chantilly Manor House Site," *Northern Neck of Virginia Historical Magazine* 23 (1973): 2413-2426.

Rountree, Helen C., Wayne E. Clark and Kent Mountford. *John Smith's Chesapeake Voyages, 1607-1609.* Charlottesville: University of Virginia Press, 2007.

Tidwell, Brig. Gen. W. A. "Virginia's Forgotten Anchorage; Machodoc Creek and the Origins of Kinsale," *Northern Neck of Virginia Historical Magazine* (in four parts) 26 (1976): 2913-2926; 27 (1977): 2996-3004; 28 (1988): 3156-3177; and 29 (1979): 3310-3332.

Virginia Historic Landmarks Commission. "Morgan Jones Kiln Site," *Northern Neck of Virginia Historical Magazine* 23 (1973): 2435-2436.

White, Edward J. "Kinsale—The Middle Period," *Northern Neck of Virginia Historical Magazine*, 53 (2003): 6453-6463.

Chapter 5
Northumberland

Known as the "mother county" of the Northern Neck, Northumberland County was formally established in 1648, having earlier been known as the Chickakoan Indian District. The county borders the Potomac River to the northeast, and the Chesapeake Bay to the east. Since 1681, the county seat has been located at what today is known as Heathsville.

Both Heathsville, which lies near the center of the county, and Reedville, situated just off the Chesapeake Bay, are listed on both the Virginia Landmarks Register and the National Register of Historic Places as historic districts.

Northumberland County includes an area of 285.7 square miles, and thus is technically the second largest county in the region, after Essex County. But only 192.3 square miles of Northumberland's territory are composed of land. The population of the county in 1790 was 9,163 (making it the most populous in the region at that time), of which 51 percent was free. By 1940, the county's population had risen to 10,463, and by 2000 amounted to 12,259.

Historic Sites in Northumberland County

Rt. 360 east towards Callao

Burnt Chimneys (1) According to local tradition, this $1^1/_2$ story three-bay frame house with a high-pitched gable roof and dormers was built between the chimneys that remained after British troops burned the original dwelling in August 1814. The house that was burned belonged to the heirs of Rodham Davis, but was at that time occupied by the family of Capt. William Henderson. He and his militia company had tried unsuccessfully to prevent the British from landing at nearby Mundy Point on the Potomac River. After burning Henderson's home, store and other buildings at Mundy Point, the British troops marched inland and burned the Davis home and other buildings. The present house has two chimneys on its north end but only one on the south side. A later addition extends off the back. *Visible from the road; privately owned. (Map A)*

Burnt Chimneys (1)

Northumberland County

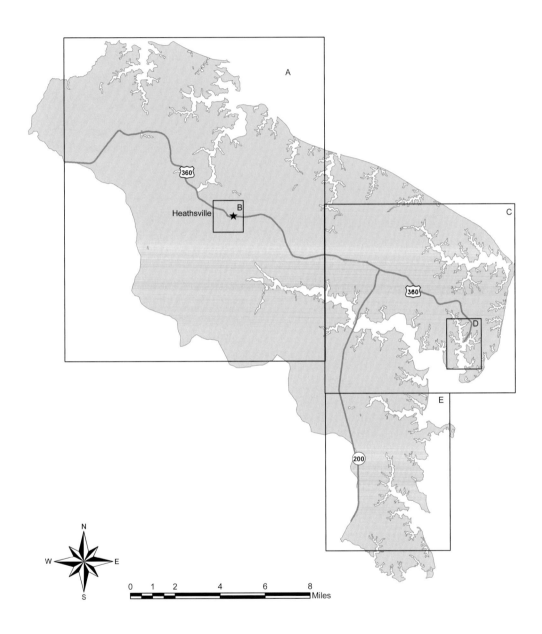

Heathsville

Callao bank building (2) The earliest bank in the upper Northumberland town of Callao (Citizens Bank), erected in 1919, this structure is a good surviving example of a well-built early 20th-century commercial building on the Northern Neck. Its exterior walls consist of ornamental concrete blocks, likely produced in White Stone, in Lancaster County. Closed in 1933, during the nationwide bank run, this bank reopened and operated until 1964. Later it was the home of the Northern Neck Planning District Commission. It is now a commercial establishment. *Visible from the road. (Map A)*

Callao bank building (2)

From Rt. 360 north on Lewisetta Road (Rt. 624) to Cherry Point

Mt. Zion (3) From the mid-18th century, this property had belonged to the locally prominent Jones family, two of whom played major military roles in the War of 1812 and another, from the next generation, being the commander of the *Merrimac* in its Civil War naval battle with the *Monitor*. Their old brick home—dating from the 1760s—was torn down about 1860 by Dr. Andrew J. Henderson, whose wife was a daughter of Capt. Dandridge Cox of Cherry Point, who had given the plantation to the couple. The Hendersons erected a large frame dwelling with four rooms on each of two stories,

Mt. Zion (3)

and topped it off with a cupola, reflecting Henderson's interest in astronomy. Since that time the house has passed through many hands, but is in good condition today. The Jones's frame schoolhouse from the 18th century, with large chimneys at both ends, was later abandoned and left to deteriorate, and was torn down in the late 20th century. *Visible from the road; privately owned. (Map A)*

Texas (4) This two-story, five-bay frame house stands on a part of a tract once known as South Texas, which earlier had been part of the plantation known as Texas, one of five plantations consolidated by Dr. William H. Harding into his Wheatland (7) plantation in the late 1840s and early 1850s. During the 18th century, much of the land making up the Texas tract was owned by the Opie family, and it then passed through several families in the early 19th century before being acquired by Dr. Harding in 1852.

There was probably an earlier house here, but the most evident early part of the

Texas (4)

present house is antebellum in style and was almost certainly built prior to the sale of the Texas tract to Harding. It is a single pile gable-roofed structure with interior brick chimneys at either end, and sits atop an English basement which has been partially filled in due to the high water table. From the central hall, a stairwell with a fine banister and interspersed with several landings climbs three floors all the way to the spacious attic level. The two-storied portico on the front and the large addition to the rear were built in the mid-20th century. The origin of the "Texas" name for the larger property is debated. The house is undergoing restoration. *Visible from the road; privately owned. (Map A)*

Claughton-Wright House (5) This $1^{1}/_{2}$ story, 24-foot square braced-frame plantation house was built by William Claughton about 1787. At his death in 1808 he was among the upper three percent of Northumberland householders in terms of taxable wealth, which suggests that the vast majority of local residents at that time lived in much more modest dwellings. This sturdy house with a steeply pitched gable roof was built on a six-foot deep English-bond brick foundation that once contained a cellar. Its $11^{1}/_{2}$ foot wide chimney is laid in glazed-header Flemish bond, and serves three fireplaces, including two corner fireplaces on the first floor.

Despite internal renovations in the 1820s, which introduced some Federal elements, from the 1840s this was used simply as a tenant house for neighboring Wheatland (7), into which it had become incorporated. Very few of such tiny dwellings from the 18th century have survived the ravages of time (but also see the Rochester House (43) in Westmoreland County) or, as was very often the case, later inclusion within a much larger and more pretentious structure. After standing abandoned and rapidly deteriorating for a

Claughton-Wright House (5)

quarter century, restoration of the house was completed in 2006. *VLR and NRHP, and BHR easement. Visible from the road; privately owned. (Map A)*

Lindsay/Opie Gravesite (6) These graves are on the property known as North Texas, a portion of the larger tract once known as the Texas tract (see Texas (4)). The grave of the Reverend David Lindsay (d. April 3, 1667), one of the earliest Anglican ministers in Northumberland County, is believed to be the oldest marked tomb in the Northern Neck. The stone notes that the body of his grandson, Thomas Opie Jr. of Bristol, England (d. 1702), is also buried right here. Not far from this site was the home where Mary Ball, the mother of the first president, spent part of her girlhood, having been born several years earlier at what later came to be called Epping Forest (62) in Lancaster County. *Not visible from the road; privately owned. (Map A)*

Wheatland (7) Built by Dr. William Hopkins Harding in the late 1840s, this was the manor house for his 1,250-acre plantation, which included several large recently purchased neighboring tracts. Harding, a member of one of the most prominent 19th century families in Northumberland County, was a physician, and while still a relatively young man was elected to the Virginia House of Delegates. In January 1856, during his first session, Harding

Northumberland County, Map A

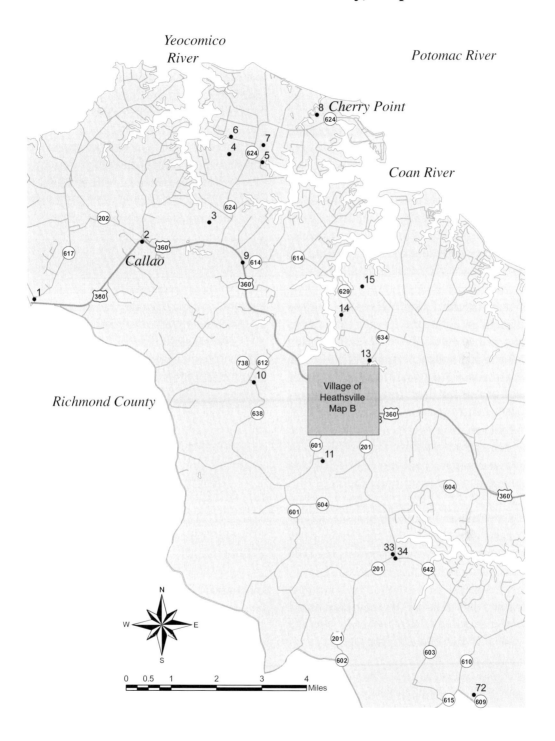

Yeocomico River

Potomac River

8 Cherry Point
624

Coan River

6
4   7
624   5

624

3

202

2
360
Callao

617

9
614   614

360

15
629

14

634

13

738   612
10

638

Village of
Heathsville
Map B

Richmond County

3   360

601   201

601   11

604

604   360

601

33   34
201   642

603   610

201

602

72
615   609

N
W   E
S

0   0.5   1   2   3   4
Miles

Wheatland (7)

died in Richmond of an accidental overdose of medicine. As it was an unusually cold winter, his body was returned from the capital to Wheatland partly on a sledge pulled across the thick ice then sealing the Rappahannock River at Tappahannock.

Wheatland is very similar to a house that a cousin of Harding's was building at about the same time in the southeastern part of the county by the Chesapeake Bay (Clover Dale, which in the course of the 20th century was neglected, abandoned and finally fell into ruin), and it seems likely that they used the same architect. Wheatland is a five-bay, $2^1/_2$ story home with nearly identical two-story Doric porticos on both the land and river sides, and a number of original outbuildings. Single-story wings had been added by 1856. The interior includes both provincial Federal and Greek Revival style woodwork and sophisticated ceiling medallions. The house and much of the surrounding property remained in the hands of Harding's widow, and then one of their sons, until 1916. *VLR and NRHP. Visible from the road; privately owned. (Map A)*

Cypress Farm (8) The main dwelling, once a combined $2^1/_2$ and $1^1/_2$ story frame structure measuring 60 by 32 feet, stands on a slight elevation on Cherry Point Neck, looking out over the Potomac River about half a mile to the north. It was built in the first quarter of the 19th century by wealthy lawyer and planter Baldwin Mathews Leland on the English bond

foundation of his earlier home, which had been burned by the British as they made raids on the Potomac in August 1814.

The farm, which once included more than 800 acres of land, also contains the remnants of a cemetery with two of the oldest still intact, and legible, tombstones on the Northern Neck. These mark the grave sites of William Keene (d. 1684) and Thomas Banks (d. 1697), successive husbands of Elizabeth Rogers, the daughter of Capt. John Rogers who resided on Cherry Point by the early 1650s. *Visible from the road; privately owned. (Map A)*

Cypress Farm (8)

Route 360 corridor east towards Heathsville

Holley Graded School (9) Established in 1869 by Sallie Holley (1818-1893) and her companion Caroline Putnam, the Holley Graded School was one of several such schools built in Northumberland County during the early Reconstruction period by ardent northern proponents of abolition, women's rights and education for the newly freed African American population. The original one-room schoolhouse was rebuilt in 1878 and again in 1886-87. About 1914, construction was begun on a larger structure, financed largely by the local black community. The present building was not completed until about 1933.

The present one-story weatherboarded and shingled building, built on piers,

Holley Graded School (9)

measures roughly 62-by-41 feet, and is a cross-shaped plan with four identically-sized classrooms off of a central hall. The ceilings are $11^{1}/_{4}$ feet high. In contrast to most other early rural schools in the region, this building has a number of architectural refinements, including decorative gables and a semi-circular fanlight over the wide front entrance. The Holley School was the largest black elementary school in Northumberland County. It closed in 1959 when a larger, public school was built in Lottsburg. *VLR and NRHP. Historical Marker O-48. Visible from the road; owned by the school trustees. (Map A)*

Coan Baptist Church (10) Built to serve the growing congregation of what was originally Wicomico Baptist Church, formed in 1804, Coan Baptist Church replaced the Coan Meeting House that had been moved to this site in 1811. The present building was dedicated in 1847. A Classical Revival structure with a seventy-foot long sanctuary and a U-shaped

Coan Baptist Church (10)

gallery that likely was for the congregation's large number of black members, the church was the largest in the Northern Neck at the time it was completed. *VLR and NRHP. Historical Marker O-56. Visible from the road. (Map A)*

Kirkland Grove Campground (11) Named for Dr. William Heath Kirk, a local Baptist preacher who served almost fifty years in the mid-19th century, Kirkland Grove is notable for its massive tabernacle and is one of the few remaining 19th century religious campgrounds in Virginia. The wooden tabernacle was designed and constructed by William Dandridge Cockrill, a local craftsman, in 1892. It is the only campground in the region that continues to hold annual revivals. *VLR and NRHP. Visible from the road. (Map A)*

Kirkland Grove Campground (11)

Roanoke (12) The oldest part of this dwelling complex is a $1^{1}/_{2}$ story brick house with an end interior chimney, built in 1828. The $2^{1}/_{2}$ story frame addition to the south was erected by 1851 by A. J. Brent, who served as county clerk in the 1850s and again during part of the 1860s. This addition has one end interior chimney, and sits on a large English basement, once probably used as a kitchen. The property contains several outbuildings. Various renovations, including a second addition, were made around the turn of the 21st century. *Visible from the road; privately owned. (Map B)*

Roanoke (12)

Clark's Mill (13) This mid-19th century 2$\frac{1}{2}$ story wooden grist mill, together with a ca. 1850s frame miller's house, is one of the very few old mills in the region which, together with much of its equipment, is still intact. The site has been the location of a succession of mills since the late 17th century, and is situated on a very large millpond. *Visible from the road; privately owned. (Map A)*

Clark's Mill (13)

Chicacoan Indian settlement (14) In his exploratory expedition up the Potomac River in June of 1608, Capt. John Smith is not thought to have directly encountered the Sekakawons, who resided on the south side of the Potomac at a point where it is seven miles wide. As he recorded their existence on his 1612 map, however, it is evident that Smith was made aware of them and possibly visited their villages during his expedition's return down the Potomac in July of that year. This Indian group's name was later anglicized to Chicacoan (or Chicacone) and their settlement, situated on the protected eastern bank of what is now called the Coan River and thought to include about 130 people at that time, was thoroughly surveyed archaeologically in the 1970s. This relatively protected area around the Coan, not incidentally, is where one of the earliest English settlements was made on the Northern Neck, in the 1640s. *(Map A)*

Mantua (15) A 2$\frac{1}{2}$ story brick manor house situated on a hill south of the Coan River, Mantua overlooks both that waterway and the Potomac River. The home, with its huge chimneys at either end of the main house, sits atop an English basement with a brick floor in a herring-bone design and a seven-foot wide fireplace. The original house was built about 1785 by James Smith, a wealthy merchant who had immigrated from Ireland by way of Baltimore. Smith purchased several thousand acres of land, which included part of the Coan Hall estate that had been the home of Col. John Mottrom, one of the early European settlers in Northumberland County and its first representative in the House of Burgesses. It is said that Smith's house was partially erected with bricks from the Presly family's old Northumberland House, which burned as the result of a British shelling in 1814.

James M. Smith, the immigrant's son, was one of the two largest antebellum landowners (along with William Harding) in

Mantua (15)

Northumberland County. It is believed that he renovated and expanded the house about 1820. This may have been when the two-story wings on either side of the house were added. *Historical Marker JT-12. Not visible from the road; privately owned. (Map A)*

Heathsville Historic District

(All sites visible from the street unless otherwise indicated.)

Entering Heathsville on Rt. 360 from the north, continue down the east side of the highway, and then—at the junction with Rt. 201—around the corner on the north side of Rt. 360

Springfield (16) This imposing brick mansion was built on property formerly owned by John Heath (1758-1810), one of the founders of Phi Beta Kappa in 1776 while a student at the College of William and Mary, later a U.S. congressman, and a member of the Governor's Council, and the man for whom Heathsville was named.

After the property passed through several hands, the central portion of the present $2^1/_2$ story house with an English basement was built in 1828 by the wealthy merchant and very large landowner William Harding. The double front doors open into a large foyer with a spiral staircase to the second floor, and the ornamental medallions on the ceilings of the generally Federal style first floor rooms add a Greek Revival stylistic feature. About 1850, brick wings with parapets were added and further refinements were made to the two-story portico. *VLR and NRHP. Historical Marker O-65. Privately owned. (Map B)*

The Academy & Chicacoan Cottage (17) The Academy is a $1^1/_2$ story three-bay gable-roofed brick house with an English basement. It was built well before 1850, and possibly as early as the turn of the 19th century, as a rental house, by John Heath, the then owner of what later became known as Springfield (16) plantation. The brickwork, laid in Flemish bond on the principal façade and the west side facing the main road, with the other elevations laid in American bond, is considered to be of particularly fine quality. The house is a vernacular structure with some Federal style details. Built with a center-hall plan, there are two rooms on each floor. Much of the original interior woodwork, including the original stairway, has been preserved.

Renovations in the 1920s had involved the addition of dormers and the installation of Doric-columned porches, but the porches were replaced by simpler 19th-century style porches during restoration work in the 1990s. An old smokehouse (ca. 1830-50) still stands on the property; the frame barn dates to the late 1920s. *VLR and NRHP. Privately owned. (Map B)*

The Academy (17)

Springfield (16)

Northumberland County, Map B
Village of Heathsville

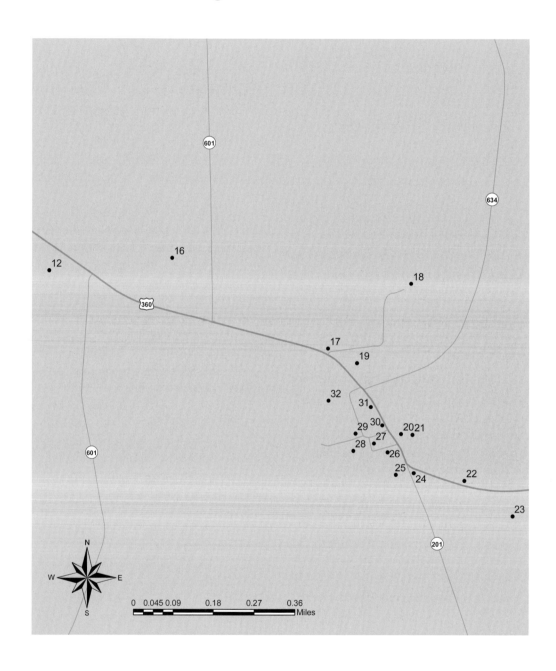

Just down the lane stands **Chicacoan Cottage**, a painted brick house architecturally quite similar to the Academy. It was almost certainly built at about the same time as the Academy, for the same purpose, by the then owner of Springfield plantation. *Privately owned.*

Belleville (18) The original part of this home, consisting of a brick cellar with an earthen floor, an unusual brick platform and exposed hand-hewn beams, one-over-one rooms upstairs, and a kitchen house in the backyard, may date from the mid-18th century. Beginning in 1782, Thomas Edwards, the first clerk of the District Court for the four counties of the lower Northern Neck, lived here with his family. In the mid-19th century, the house was enlarged into a two-story frame five-bay structure with exterior end chimneys. *Not visible from the street; privately owned. (Map B)*

Belleville (18)

St. Stephen's Church (19) Designed by T. Buckler Ghequiere, a young Baltimore architect, and consecrated in 1881, this church was built in the wooden Carpenter's Gothic style which by that time had already passed its peak of popularity in the United States. The church was built on land purchased in 1874 by the trustees of the Protestant Episcopal church, and was constructed as the successor parish church—a century after the disestablishment of the Church of England—of Upper St. Stephen's parish for which a church and glebe had been erected in Cherry Point in upper Northumberland County in

St. Stephen's Church (19)

the early 1650s. *VLR and NRHP. Historical Marker O-49. (Map B)*

Lawson-Headley, Lawson, & Harding-Elmore Houses (20) These three houses all date from roughly the same time period and are located very close to one another. The **Lawson-Headley House** was built between 1820 and 1860. It was possibly moved, after 1848, to its present site. It is a frame, 1^1/$_2$ story, three-bay, full brick basement dwelling, the original portion of which was just 16-by-24 feet. *Privately owned. Endangered. (Map B)*

The **Lawson House** is thought to have been built prior to 1848 as a 1^1/$_2$ story house. While it has subsequently been dramatically enlarged and changed in appearance (including with three two-story porch columns), considerable evidence of the earlier dwelling exists in the interior. *Privately owned. (Map B)*

The **Harding-Elmore House** (aka Mothershead House), pictured here, is located behind the two foregoing homes,

Harding-Elmore House (20)

and was built prior to 1826. The original house, which was 18-by-24 feet, consisted of a large room on the first floor and an attic upstairs, and sat atop an English basement. The Victorian verandah and rear shed now in evidence are later additions. *Not easily visible from the street; privately owned. (Map B)*

Haynie (et al) cemetery (21) This is a very old graveyard, the oldest marker being a stone slab for Elizabeth Haynie with a death date of 1697. One of the oldest extant gravestones on the Northern Neck, it is inscribed with fleur-de-lis and skull motifs. *Not visible from the street; privately owned. (Map B)*

Wall-Lackey-Rowe House (22) Built ca. 1830-35, this is a vernacular frame 1½ story house with dormers, a large exterior chimney serving corner fireplaces, and one-story shed-roofed wings with a front parapet. It has also been known as Aspen Cottage. *Privately owned. (Map B)*

Wall-Lackey-Rowe House (22)

Crossing Route 360 to the south side, continue west along this highway to the intersection with Route 201, then north along the west side of Route 360

Sunnyside (23) Royston Betts built this two-story brick house, with a gable roof and interior end chimneys, between 1834-1841. The original part of the house has a five-bay front with a center door flanked by single rooms. The two-story two-bay gable-roofed wing on the west side is thought to have been added very soon after. The front of Sunnyside, on both the original section and the west wing, is laid in Flemish bond, while the

Sunnyside (23)

other sides are of five-course American bond. The property contains a number of carefully preserved outbuildings. *VLR and NRHP. Privately owned. (Map B)*

Heathsville United Methodist Church (24) This is a Gothic style frame church, built in 1894, with a front bell tower with an octagonal spire, and decorative pointed-head windows with tracery. Outside stands an obelisk memorializing Juliana Gordon

Heathsville United Methodist Church (24)

Hayes (1813-1895), born at Font Hill in Northumberland County and the first president of the Woman's Missionary Society of the Methodist Episcopal South Church. The adjoining parsonage dates from 1929. *(Map B)*

Tingle-Doby & Jones/Haislip/Daniel Houses (25) The Tingle-Doby house was built as a twin to the Jones/Haislip/Daniel house just to its north (see below), ca. 1830-45. Originally a simple frame house, it was enlarged in the 1890s and embellished with Victorian stylistic details, including a scroll-sawn apron in the front gable. *Privately owned. Endangered.*

The **Jones/Haislip/Daniel House**, built ca.1830-45 and pictured here, remains a $1^1/_2$ story three-bay frame house with a chimney at each end, a gable roof with two front dormers, and an English basement once used for cooking. The neo-colonial style front porch was added later. The property also contains a 19th century frame smokehouse. *Privately owned. Endangered. (Map B)*

Jones/Haislip/Daniel House (25)

Heathsville Methodist Protestant Church (26) The original church stood in courthouse square approximately where the Confederate monument now stands. After portions of the public square were sold off in 1852, the present church building in the Greek Revival style was built on the south side of the square beginning in 1860. Following the reunification of the Methodist Protestant and Methodist Episcopal churches after 1870, this church languished, and by 1903 the church property was sold.

With internal renovations, this building was later used as, among other things, a movie house, opera hall, and a town hall, and parts of it served at one time or another as a bank, a drugstore, the post office, a showroom for a funeral parlor, and various law offices. *Privately owned. Endangered. (Map B)*

Heathsville Methodist Protestant Church (26)

Old Courthouse & War Monuments (27) This was the site of several successive Northumberland County courthouses from 1681 to 1998. The present white brick building dates from 1851, but was substantially renovated at the turn of the 20th century, including the movement of the entrance from the north to the east side. The north and south wings were added in 1964 and 1974 respectively. This former courthouse now serves as a county office building, although the old courtroom upstairs contains marble tablets honoring various early local officials and the county's representatives to the Virginia constitutional conventions between 1774 and 1901-02. A new, larger Northumberland County Courts Building was completed in 1998, several hundred yards west of this building and Hughlett's Tavern. Refurbished portraits of a number of early county leaders and officials line the walls of this newer Courts Building.

The Confederate memorial, erected in 1873 in the center of the greensward in front of the old courthouse, is unusual in that the obelisk, containing the names of the many Northumberland soldiers who lost their lives in the Civil War, is topped by a classically robed young woman with an upwardly stretched arm.

In addition to plaques on the side of the old courthouse which honor local citizens fallen in World War II and the Korean and Vietnam conflicts, a granite World War I memorial in the form of a miniature Roman Doric temple, with a central inscribed podium, is located in a small plot just across Judicial Place in front of a local bank. *(Map B)*

Old Courthouse & War Monuments (27)

Rice's Hotel/Hughlett's Tavern (28) Built about 1795 in what later became known as Heathsville, likely on the site of earlier taverns, this two-story tavern and later hotel, graced by porches running the length of each floor, has been a key element at this county-seat since at least the late 18th century. Restored in

Rice's Hotel/Hughlett's Tavern (28)

the 1990s, it is now the home of a popular restaurant and is a center—together with several auxiliary buildings added in the first decade of the 21st century—for a number of community activities. One of these outbuildings is also home to a cross-section cut of the ancient Chicacoan Oak, which was long a local natural landmark. *VLR and NRHP. Historical Marker O-60. (Map B)*

Old Jail (29) The successor to a number of short-lived jails built on the courthouse square since 1681, this is a two-story brick structure, with end chimneys and a corbelled brick cornice. Situated on what is now called Back Street, the Old Jail was erected in 1839, partially destroyed by fire in 1843, and rebuilt in 1844. The original plan was a center hall on each floor flanked by large rooms for confinement. The Old Jail was modernized in 1918 with the installation of a metal cell block. On the eve of its closure as a jail in 1958, it was the third oldest county jail in Virginia still in use for purposes of incarceration. *Owned by the county, but placed in the care of the Northumberland County Historical Society, which has been renovating it and now has the building open to the public. (Map B)*

Old Jail (29)

Moss Cottage (30) This one-story frame house, built about 1845, originally had a side-hall plan, one room on the first floor, an attic room up a steep flight of stairs, an English basement, and an exterior chimney laid in American bond at the south side of the gable roof. Based on old drawings, plats and photos, this would appear to have been a typical Heathsville house in the early-to-mid 19th century. Additions were made later, as was the expansion of the front window area. *Privately owned. (Map B)*

Moss Cottage (30)

Rowe House (31) A 2¹/₂ story three-bay frame house with raised brick basement, a gable roof and interior end brick chimney, this side-hall house is thought to date from about 1851. The rear addition and the front porch were added in the early 20th century. *Privately owned. (Map B)*

Rowe House (31)

Oakley (32) Still situated on 28 acres in the heart of Heathsville, on Back Street, Oakley was built prior to 1841 and may date from the early 19th century. It is a

Oakley (32)

2¹/₂ story five-bay frame house with a high brick basement, interior end chimneys and a one-story Greek-style front porch. The small size of the original fireplaces in the basement suggest the kitchen was located in a separate building. The property still has several outbuildings, including a frame two-story barn built in the late 19th or early 20th century. The wing off the left of the house is a 20th-century addition. The home was once occupied by C. Harding Walker, a state senator and delegate to the 1901-02 Virginia Constitutional Convention, and Oakley is the site of a Constitution Oak planted that year to celebrate the new constitution. *VLR and NRHP. Privately owned. (Map B)*

Route 360 corridor
east of Heathsville

Short detour south on Rt. 201

Howland Chapel School (33) This largely board-and-batten one-room schoolhouse was built in 1867 by Emily Howland (1827-1929), one of several northern spinsters who, after actively promoting the cause of abolition (as well as women's rights) before and during the Civil War, decided to purchase land in the South for the purpose of educating and otherwise assisting emancipated slaves.

The original schoolhouse was built on a lot of a little over one-half acre, which was conveyed to a group of trustees for the purpose of building a school from which "no person is to be excluded on account of race, color or sex." The rest of the 350 acres which she had purchased in 1866 was sold over time to freedmen for the purpose of starting up their own farms. The 1½ story board-and-batten cottage nearby was built in 1870 for Emily Howland and later was used as a teacher's residence.

Unlike several of her like-minded abolitionist colleagues, in 1870 Howland returned to her home in upper New York State, where she maintained her permanent residence for her long life. The school was supported, however, by Miss Howland and the local African American community until 1921, when it was taken over by the Northumberland County Public School Board. The school continued to operate until 1958, and now serves as a community and adult education center. A similar school was established by a colleague of hers, Laura W. Stebbins, just on the other side of the Great Wicomico River, about 1870, but it is no longer standing. *VLR and NRHP. Visible from the road. Owned by the First Baptist Church. (Map A)*

Howland Chapel School (33)

First Baptist Church (34) Founded by former black members of Coan Baptist Church (10), the members of this congregation organized themselves into a church in 1866, and early on used the Howland Chapel School across the road as a meeting house. The first church building was constructed in 1892, and the present building dates from 1938. *Visible from the road.*

Other early Baptist churches organized in Northumberland County by the black community and which are still active today include Calvary Baptist Church, Macedonia Baptist Church, Mt. Olive Baptist Church, Shiloh Baptist Church, and Zion Baptist Church. *(Map A)*

First Baptist Church (34)

Back to Rt. 360 and east towards Burgess

Waterloo (35) This 1½ story frame house with three dormers and exterior end chimneys was built in 1848 by Joseph C. Downing. The dwelling has retained

Waterloo (35)

Northumberland County, Map C

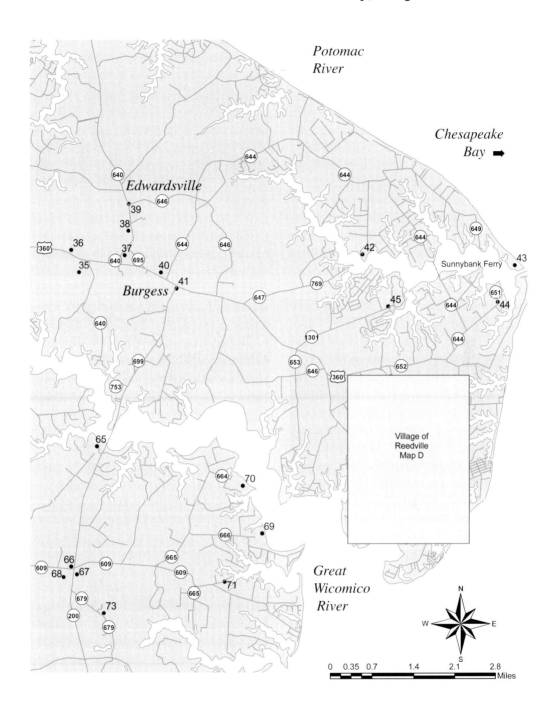

Potomac River

Chesapeake Bay ➡

644

644

640
Edwardsville
646
39
38
37
640
695
36
360
35
40
Burgess
41
644
646
647
769
42
Sunnybank Ferry
649
644
43
45
651
44
644
640
1301
644
699
653
646
360
652
753

65

Village of Reedville Map D

664
70

666
69

666
665
66
609
68
609
67
609
65

665
71
679
73
200
679

Great Wicomico River

N
W   E
S

0   0.35   0.7   1.4   2.1   2.8
Miles

interesting original interior woodwork, including the stairway, bannister, newel and mantelpieces. *Visible from the road; privately owned. (Map C)*

Brick House Plantation (36) It is considered that this two-story house was built by Col. Samuel Blackwell between 1827 and 1837. The building contractor may have been the same as for Springfield (16)—although this is a more modest structure, and may simply have been built to emulate the style of that manor house—as certain construction features are very similar, including inner walls of brick that reach to the top floor, and floor joists that are set directly into brick, instead of into wooden sills. The two-story portico is also similar to that at Springfield, which was built in 1828. *Visible from the road; privately owned. (Map C)*

Brick House Plantation (36)

Brief detour north on Rt. 640 towards Edwardsville

Arcadia (37) A small frame house had been built here ca. 1783 by John Doxey. Later owned by the Flynt family, it passed to the Blundon family in 1878. They expanded the house into a two-story three-bay structure with a double-story portico, and named it Arcadia. After standing vacant and deteriorating badly for three decades in the middle of the 20th century, the

house and its dependencies were carefully restored in the 1970s and 1980s. *Visible from the road; privately owned. (Map C)*

Arcadia (37)

Galilee Methodist Church (38) This church is directly descended from the first African American Methodist Episcopal congregation in Northumberland County, whose congregation obtained letters of dismissal from the Fairfields Methodist Protestant Church (39) to form the Fairfields Colored Church right after the Civil War. Later renamed Galilee Methodist Church, the old building burned and was replaced by the present one. (Another very early black Methodist Episcopal church in Northumberland County was located at Surprise Hill, but it no longer exists.) *Visible from the road. (Map C)*

Galilee Methodist Church (38)

Fairfields Methodist Church site (39) A Methodist meeting house or church was built here in 1789-90, only two years after Bishop Francis Asbury had preached nearby at a barn that the

Fairfields Methodist congregation had been using for meetings. After the 1830 Methodist schism, the Fairfields church became Methodist Protestant. A brick church stood here from about 1850 to the 1930s when it was torn down, having been replaced in 1926 by a new church building in the town of Burgess. An old cemetery remains on both sides of the road. *Visible from the road; church property. (Map C)*

Back to Rt. 360 and Burgess

Versailles (40) This two-story, five-bay frame house, with a double front portico and two interior brick chimneys at the gable ends, was completed in 1857 for Samuel Benedict Burgess, a farmer, gristmill operator, local justice, and pillar of the local Methodist church. The house sits atop an English basement, which housed the original kitchen. Both the interior and exterior of the house exhibit Greek Revival influences. Various additions were made to the rear of the house in the late 20th century. *VLR and NRHP. Visible from the road; privately owned. (Map C)*

Versailles (40)

Burgess Store complex (41) Three buildings make up this unusual complex of mid-19th century to early 20th-century structures that once were the commercial center of a crossroads community. (1) The Brent Store, a $2^1/_2$ story frame structure,

was built about 1850 on a foundation of brick piers. It has a one-story three-bay front porch, with square wooden posts resting on brick pedestals. One interior brick chimney rises above a standing seam metal gable roof. (2) The Brent House, also dating from about 1850, sometimes also functioned as a boarding house for travelling merchants and others. It is a $2^1/_2$ story frame structure with a more recent addition. (3) The Downing House was built ca. 1920 by S. J. Downing, then owner and operator of both the Brent Store and the Brent House. It is a $2^1/_2$ story frame house with single, gable dormers on all four sides, and is a good example of a an early 20th-century dwelling representing the American movement in architecture. *Visible from the road; private property. (Map C)*

The Brent Store (41)

North on Rt. 644 and on to Rt. 649

Flood Point (42) This is an early 19th century two-story five-bay frame house

Flood Point (42)

on a raised basement, with interior brick chimneys at each end, situated on Flood Point on the Little Wicomico River. An old burial ground is on the property. *Not visible from the road; privately owned. (Map C)*

Smith Point Lighthouse (43) There were earlier lighthouses in this area, beginning in 1802. In 1895, the then lighthouse was actually carried away and ultimately mostly destroyed by ice. A new lighthouse was built in 1897, but in 1971 the light was automated, and the need for resident lighthouse keepers ended. (The Great Wicomico River lighthouse, not shown here, was a hexagonal white wooden building on piles,

Smith Point Lighthouse (43)

and was put into operation in 1889. It was torn down in 1967 when it was replaced by a simple automated light.) *VLR and NRHP. Visible from the last part of Lighthouse Road (Rt. 649); privately owned but under the stewardship of the U.S. Coast Guard. (Map C)*

Back to Rt. 644 and south over Sunnybank Ferry

Rock Hall (44) Robert Coles is said to have built this two-story, five-bay frame house about 1850. The dwelling has interior brick chimneys at both ends, and sits atop an English basement. Tradition ascribes the home's name to its construction cost being met through an unusually large "haul" of rockfish.

The house is situated on Rock Hole Creek, a tributary of the Little Wicomico River. Union gunboats are said to have entered this creek during the Civil War, and the *Knickerbocker*, a Union steamer, was burned here by the Northumberland Home Guard. In one incident, the Union soldiers were turned away by the women of Rock Hall, and the soldiers' kidnapping of two young Coles boys was reputedly stopped through the pleas of one of the family's slaves. *Not visible from the road; privately owned. (Map C)*

Rock Hall (44)

Back on Rt. 651 to Rt. 652 west to Rt. 360 and north on Rt. 653

Locksley Hall (45) This house was built about 1865-70 by Dr. Hiram Edward Coles on the foundations of an earlier house that had been razed. The home is a wide two-story three-bay house with interior brick chimneys at either gable end.

On the first floor are unusual bay windows on either side of the front entrance. Inside, the front hall includes a prominent winding stairway. The earlier home appears to have been built by Coles's father, Col. Edward Presley Coles, in the second quarter of the 19th century. *Visible from the road; privately owned. (Map C)*

Locksley Hall (45)

Back to Rt. 360 and on towards Reedville

Rosenwald School (46) Established in 1917 in Beverleyville as the Northumberland County Training School, the school was erected with funds from the local African American community, which raised $7,000 for this purpose. Additional funding was received from the Rosenwald Fund, established by Julius Rosenwald, the wealthy philanthropist and benefactor of some 5,000 black

Rosenwald School (46)

schools throughout the rural south. The school's name was changed to the Julius Rosenwald High School in 1932, the year of the benefactor's death. The school's founder and first principal was the Rev. John M. Ellison, pastor of Shiloh Baptist Church. It was closed in 1958, when Central High School, near Claraville, was opened. *Historical Marker O-61. Visible from the road; privately owned. Endangered. (Map D)*

Roseland Cemetery (47) The first municipal planned cemetery in the Northern Neck, Roseland Cemetery was established in 1903 by a company of that name, headed by Albert Morris and other leaders of Reedville. With several purchases of land over the years, the cemetery now includes more than twenty acres. Its two imposing sets of iron gates were respectively given by Morris's widow and his brother-in-law, James C. Fisher, who along with Morris had come down from New Jersey to set up the large Morris-Fisher menhaden operation in Reedville (see Morris-Fisher smokestack (64)). Although Morris is buried in New Jersey, this cemetery contains a life-size statue of the benefactor, dedicated in 1909. *(Map D)*

Reedville Historic District

(All sites visible from the street.)

Entering Reedville from the north on Route 360, continue down the west side of Main Street to the end

Covington House (48) This $2^{1}/_{2}$ story four-bay weatherboarded Queen Anne style house, with a slate hip roof and one hip dormer, turned balustrade,

Covington House (48)

Doric columns and corner towers clad in shingles, was built about 1900. It is typical of the large homes along "Millionaires Row," so called because Reedville was reputed to be the wealthiest town per capita on the East Coast during the heyday of the menhaden fishing industry in the late 19th and early 20th centuries. *Privately owned. (Map D)*

Bethany United Methodist Church (49) The cornerstone of the present church, in Reedville, was laid in 1899 and the building was dedicated in 1901. This one-story Gothic Revival church has a slate gable roof and is laid in irregular bond brick. Its original frame bell tower was later replaced by the present brick tower with a pyramidal steeple and open belfry. *(Map D)*

Bethany United Methodist Church (49)

Walker House/Fishermen's Museum (50) The Walker house is part of the Fishermen's Museum, which opened in 1988. The museum tells the story of the menhaden fishing industry and the watermen of the lower Chesapeake Bay. The former dwelling is the oldest surviving house in Reedville, built on land purchased by William Walker from Elijah Reed in 1875. The house, originally a two-story vernacular shingled frame dwelling, with a center brick chimney, is said to have been built in one day, and had a separate kitchen attached to the house by a "dog trot." *(Map D)*

Walker House/Fishermen's Museum (50)

Elva C. Deck Boat (51) This is a typical Chesapeake Bay deck boat, designed by Gilbert White and built in 1922. The boat is 55 feet in length, and was used for pound net fishing and also as a "buy" boat that purchased and transported seafood. *VLR and NRHP.* It is located at the Fishermen's Museum. *(Map D)*

Elva C. Deck Boat (51)

Claud W. Somers Skipjack (52) A restored Skipjack built in 1911, this is a single-mast sailing vessel, 42 feet in

Northumberland County, Map D
Village of Reedville

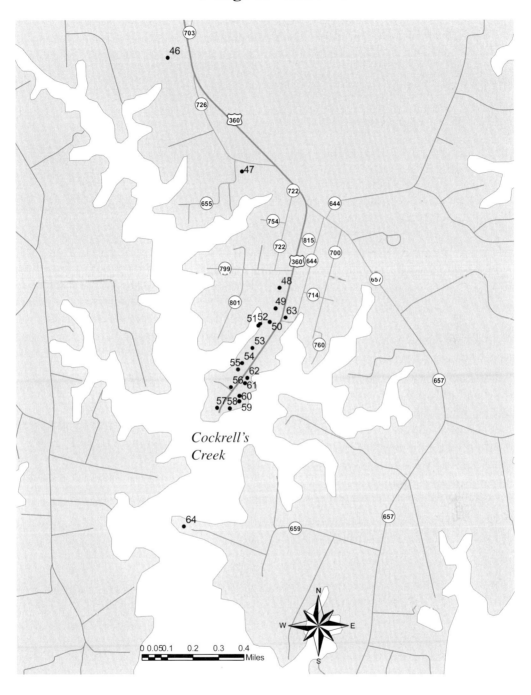

Cockrell's
Creek

Claud W. Somers Skipjack (52)

length, used for dredging oysters. *VLR and NRHP.* It is located at the Fishermen's Museum. *(Map D)*

Robinson-Haynie House (53) Built by Gamaliel T. Robinson on land purchased from Elijah Reed in 1875, this late 19th century two-story gable-roofed weatherboarded house with a large central brick chimney is the second oldest house still standing in Reedville. Its Doric columns and full pediment were added during the remodeling of the house by Miriam Haynie—author of *The Stronghold* (1959), an early history of the Northern Neck and its people—and her husband. *Privately owned. (Map D)*

Robinson-Haynie House (53)

Muir House (54) A Victorian vernacular 2¹/₂ story dwelling house built about 1906, the Muir House later was a favorite hotel for "drummers" (traveling salesmen), and also had a livery stable. The house has a standing seam metal gable roof, and a bracketed cornice, spindle frieze, and turned posts. *Privately owned. (Map D)*

Muir House (54)

Elijah Reed Monument (55) Elijah Reed, formerly of Maine and founder in 1874 of a viable menhaden processing plant here, died long before the establishment of Roseland Cemetery (47) and was buried here in 1888. His grave is marked by a marble obelisk surrounded by a wrought-iron fence, and shaded by magnolias and cedars. *Privately owned. (Map D)*

Elijah Reed Monument (55)

Albert Morris House (56) Albert Morris, one of the leading menhaden industrialists in Reedville, built his house on this site in 1874. That house was demolished in 1895, and was replaced by the current dwelling, constructed in Queen Anne style, about 1900. This two-story house is a weatherboarded and shingled structure with a slate hip roof, spindle frieze, paired tripled Tuscan columns, an octagonal turret with bell-cast roof, and decorative shingle patterns. *Privately owned. (Map D)*

Albert Morris House (56)

Peoples Bank of Reedville (57) This bank, a one-story Colonial Revival brick structure built in 1910, is said to have only closed for a very brief time during the nationwide "bank holiday" declared by President Franklin D. Roosevelt in 1933. Capt. James C. Fisher, the former partner of Albert Morris and by then quite elderly, is said to have driven to Washington, D. C. with a large amount of cash

Peoples Bank of Reedville (57)

which he persuaded officials he would deposit immediately in the Reedville bank so as to allow it to reopen. The building has a three-bay porch with brick Tuscan columns, full pediment and segmented-arched windows. *(Map D)*

Head back up the east side of Main Street, towards Route 360

The Gables (58) Built in 1909 for Capt. James C. Fisher, brother-in-law and partner with Albert Morris in their large menhaden fishing operation, this Queen Anne style house has 3 $\frac{1}{2}$ stories, a slate gable roof, and a six bay screened porch, and features a brick arcade and a turned balustrade. Also notable are the projecting front entrance portico with oval window in the gable, and the steeply-pitched cross gables with flanking smaller gables at the corners of the building. A frame building to the right of the house was used as a stable and carriage house. *Privately owned bed and breakfast. (Map D)*

The Gables (58)

George Reed House (59) George Reed, son of the town's "father" Elijah Reed, had this 2$\frac{1}{2}$ story Queen Anne style gable roof weatherboarded house built in 1897-99. Notably, the house includes shingled gables with a bracket cornice and returns, and a corner turret capped by a bell-shaped roof. *Privately owned. (Map D)*

George Reed House (59)

Bailey-Cockrell-Rice House & Dr. Cockrell's Office (60) The dwelling house is a 2½ story Queen Anne style weatherboarded structure with a standing seam gabled roof, built about 1890. It has a bay window, and a three-bay porch, spindle frieze, turned balustrade and sawn brackets. The old physician's office, next door, dates from about 1900, and is a weatherboarded one-story vernacular structure with a standing seam hip roof and Doric columns and broken pediment. *Privately owned. (Map D)*

Bailey-Cockrell-Rice House (60)

Blundon & Hinton Store (61) This structure was built as a department store,

Blundon & Hinton Store (61)

in the vernacular style, about 1890. Its decorative features include a bracketed cornice with returns. The storefront was altered in the 1940s, and it came to be known as the Reedville Market, and later as Elijah's Restaurant. It now houses Tommy's Restaurant. *(Map D)*

Bailey-Butler Railway & Rail Boat Shed (62) A vernacular early 20th century one-story gable-roofed wooden shed used for boat building, this structure is once again in use for its original purpose. The business has been in the same family for several generations. *Privately owned. (Map D)*

Bailey-Butler Railway and Rail Boat Shed (62)

Masonic Hall (63) Dating from about 1930, this 2½ story colonial revival brick structure is laid in Flemish bond, with four giant order pilasters laid in common bond, jack arches with keystones over the windows, a brick water table, and a pedimented gable end. Masonic lodges were prevalent in the Northern Neck region

Masonic Hall (63)

during this period, and this one was actually predated by some 35 years by the two-story frame Masonic lodge on the main street in Heathsville, still standing and surrounded by a late 19th-century cast-iron fence. *(Map D)*

Morris-Fisher Smokestack (64) This is a ca. 1902 fish factory brick chimney, belonging to the Morris-Fisher menhaden complex. While not part of the historic district per se, it is visible from Reedville. *Privately owned. (Map D)*

Morris-Fisher Smokestack (64)

Rt. 200 Corridor south from Burgess to Wicomico Church

Edge Hill (65) This 2½ story five-bay frame Federal style house was built by Dr. Hiram William Harding, probably in the 1830s. A good example of a mid-19th century I-house, similar to Shalango (69), this home, which sits atop a bluff, has a commanding view over the Great Wicomico River. In the mid-20th century it was the summer residence of Elsie (Ball) Bowley, a sister of Jesse Ball duPont, and the major benefactor of the Northumberland

County Historical Society. More recently the house was moved nearby from its original foundations. *Visible from the road; privately owned. (Map C)*

Edge Hill (65)

At Wicomico Church

Wicomico Methodist Church (66) Cyrus Harding, of nearby Snowden Park, is said to have erected the original frame church nearby in 1837. As the congregation grew and the little frame chapel became too small, Harding and his wife deeded one acre here for the construction of a larger, brick church in the Greek Revival style, which was dedicated in 1859. Although in 1862 Confederate soldiers used the sanctuary as a barracks, worship services continued at the church. *Visible from the road. (Map C and Map E)*

Wicomico Methodist Church (66)

Wicomico Parish Church & Memorial (67) The first church, probably a rudimentary frame structure, is believed to have been

Northumberland County, Map E

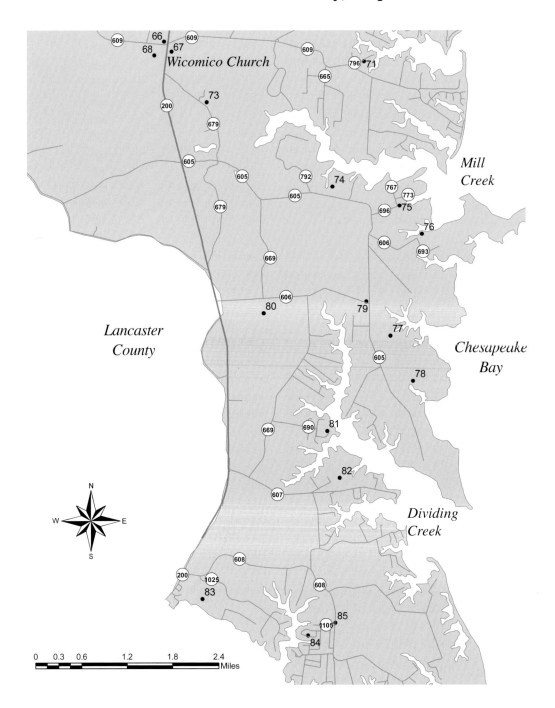

Wicomico Church

Mill
Creek

Lancaster
County

Chesapeake
Bay

Dividing
Creek

0   0.3   0.6   1.2   1.8   2.4
Miles

built here in the late 1640s or early 1650s. This church, along with the one at Cherry Point in upper Northumberland County, was one of the earliest Anglican churches to be built in the Northern Neck. A new church was built here by 1686, possibly of brick. In 1664, at the time of the death of Col. Richard Lee (see Cobbs Hall (81)), local leaders had chosen to rename the parish Lee Parish, but this name came to be disputed and ultimately was dropped. Nevertheless, his son, Hancock Lee of Dividing Creek, in his will of 1709, ordered that a silver chalice and matching paten be given to the "Parish of Lee."

A third brick church, of cruciform design, modeled on and built to exceed Christ Church (6) in Lancaster County in size, was completed here in 1772, but by the second decade of the 19th century, following disestablishment, it was in serious disrepair and the parish effectively had dissolved. The last ruins of that very large church were taken or sold off by 1840. After more than a half-century doing without a formal church building, the parish built the present church—since enlarged and added

Wicomico Parish Church & Memorial (67)

onto—in 1902, and a memorial monument to the early prominent families in the parish was erected in 1961. *Visible from the road. (Map C and Map E)*

Ingleside (68) This house began as a Federal style frame structure, the original part of which—a two-story five-bay single-pile gable roofed frame dwelling with exterior end chimneys and a central passage, hall and parlor plan—was built in 1840 by Hiram Ingram. It is believed that bricks and flagstones from the ruined Wicomico Parish Church (67) across the way were used in the construction of this house. Additions made in the 1850s, 1920s and 1990s have not materially affected the integrity of the frontal view of the house, or its core interior. The house has a number of original outbuildings. *Visible from the road; privately owned. (Map C and Map E)*

Ingleside (68)

Off of Rt. 609 east from Wicomico Church

Shalango (69) With a broad view of the Great Wicomico River, this $2^1/_2$ story single-pile five-bay frame house with interior brick chimneys at either gable end was built ca. 1855-56 for planter John Hopkins Coles. The house sits atop a high basement, which may have served an earlier dwelling on this spot. The present structure once had a two-story portico on its front side. The three-story, open-well stair is an impressive interior feature, along with both Greek Revival and Italianate style detailing. Shalango is one of the largest extant antebellum plantation houses in Northumberland County, and the home is still owned by descendants of its original owner. *VLR and NRHP. Visible from the road; privately owned. (Map C)*

Shalango (69)

Wicomico View (70) This 2¹/₂ story five-bay gable-roofed brick house, with wide interior end chimneys serving nine fireplaces, sits atop an English basement. While it looks older, the present house was evidently built in 1838. A noteworthy interior feature is a circular stairway—without a newel—that reaches to the attic level. The property, which stands close to the Great Wicomico River, was owned by the Hudnall family for generations. *Not visible from the road; privately owned. (Map C)*

Wicomico View (70)

Hopevale (71) Also known in the past as Little House Farm and Christmas Cove,

this frame house on Harvey's Neck near Ingram Bay may date from the late 18th century. Originally it was likely a one-over-one side-hall dwelling with one side chimney. Later, perhaps in the 1830s, the house was expanded to a center-hall plan, and dormers and a second side chimney were added. At least two later additions were made to what was originally the rear of the house, in the last quarter of the 20th century. The builder of the original dwelling is unknown. *Visible from the road; privately owned. (Map C and Map E)*

Hopevale (71)

Off of Rt. 609 west from Wicomico Church

Litchfield (72) The original part of this house may date to the 18th century, and may have been owned by the Taylor family. Later, it is thought to have belonged to the Broun family. Some further additions came with the establishment of a bed & breakfast here around the turn of the 21st century, but the core of the

Litchfield (72)

interior and the external appearance of the house has retained its integrity. An old office stands off to the right hand side of the house. *Visible from the road; privately owned. Endangered. (Map A)*

Route 200 corridor south from Wicomico Church to Kilmarnock

Towards the Bay on Rt. 679 and on to Rt. 605

West End (73) Also known as "Brick House," the 48-by-20 foot center section of this brick mansion is thought to have been built by William Blackerby by 1835, although parts of the house may date from the late 18th century. The 2½ story, five-bay center section has a gable roof with dormers, and is flanked by large 1½ story gambrel wings that were added about 1940 when the house underwent extensive restoration. *Visible from the road; privately owned. (Map C and Map E)*

West End (73)

The Anchorage (74) It is thought that the original part of this frame house, situated on Mill Creek, a tidal tributary of the Bay, was built in the second or third quarter of the 18th century, probably for Abraham Shears on ancestral property. This older 1½ story side-hall section of the house has a three-bay gambrel-roof structure seldom found in surviving houses in Northumberland County, but quite common across the Rappahannock River in Essex County. Of braced-frame construction, this older part has a massive double-shouldered brick chimney. Federal style elements were added when the house was remodeled about 1800.

The house was enlarged in 1856 when William C. Kent added a two-story wing with Greek Revival features, set atop an English basement. The third section, on the right hand side, was formerly a separate building on the property and was added to the house in 1948. *VLR and NRHP. Visible from the road; privately owned. (Map E)*

The Anchorage (74)

Gascony (75) The original home, with a 46-foot wide central block flanked by 20-foot wings, and with views of both Ingram Bay and the Chesapeake, was long the residence of the prominent Gaskins family, and is said to have been burned by British privateers during the Revolution. While some evidence suggests a later house may have stood here by the time of the War of 1812, the Gaskins family sold the property to John Hopkins Harding in 1845, and in 1848 his

Gascony (75)

son Lucius T. Harding is said to have built the present house on the original foundations. Tradition has it that during the Civil War, Gascony was visited by raiding Union soldiers, but that they spared the house after finding a Masonic apron in a trunk.

The present house is a two-story five-bay frame structure with interior brick chimneys at both gable ends, with an English basement. The two wings were added in the late 1960s. *Visible from the road; privately owned. (Map E)*

Guarding Point (76) This house stands on property that had remained in the Dameron family for almost 200 years after Lawrence Dameron purchased it in 1655 from the original patentee. The tract, also often referred to as Garden Point, was purchased from the Damerons by John H. Harding of nearby Clover Dale (now abandoned and in ruins) prior to the Civil War. He gave this property and nearby Dameron's Marsh to his son, John H. Harding Jr., and the two-story five-bay gable- roofed house with interior end chimneys possibly predates the War. The 1¹/₂ story section off the rear of the house is said to have been an earlier overseer's dwelling. The present double front portico was added sometime after 1970. *Visible from the road; privately owned.* The house faces east to the 316-acre Dameron Marsh Natural Area Preserve. *(Map E)*

Guarding Point (76)

Hurstville (77) Although the foundations of this dwelling are thought to date from the 17th century, the earliest section

of the present house was most likely erected soon after 1776, when this property, on a tidal creek with a view of the Bay, was purchased by Thomas Hurst. This section is a 1¹/₂ story frame house with a steeply pitched roof, with a large double-shouldered chimney on its south side, laid in Flemish bond with unusual tumbled courses. This part of the house also has a rare four-room plan. In 1940 the house was purchased by the philanthropist Jesse Ball duPont, who had it restored. *VLR and NRHP. Not visible from the road; privately owned. (Map E)*

Hurstville (77)

Salt Pond (78) Located on Ball's Neck, this property belonged to the Ingram family from the late 17th to the early 19th centuries, acquiring its name as allegedly the principal source of salt for the lower Northern Neck in the late 18th and early 19th centuries. The present two-story five-bay frame house with exterior brick chimneys at both ends was built by Robert W. Carter in 1856. The double front door opens under an attractive portico. Two large two-story wings off to the rear, each

Salt Pond (78)

with a tall exterior chimney at the gable end, were probably added later. *Visible from the road; privately owned.* A bit farther down the road is the entrance to the Hughlett Point Natural Area Preserve, a 204-acre beach where Dividing Creek flows into the Chesapeake Bay. *(Map E)*

Hard Bargain (80)

a bluff overlooking Dividing Creek and lower Ball's Neck. *Visible from the road; privately owned. (Map E)*

Back up Rt. 605 and then west on to Rt. 606

Shiloh School (79) Built in 1906 on Ball's Neck, this rare example of a basically unaltered one-room school building was actively used as a school until 1929. After that it was utilized mainly as a farm storage shed, until it was donated to Northumberland Preservation, Inc. in 1987 and gradual restoration of the schoolhouse began. Jesse Ball duPont, the philanthropist, was raised locally on Ball's Neck and taught at this school in 1906-07. *VLR and NRHP. Visible from the road; periodically open to the public. (Map E)*

Shiloh School (79)

Hard Bargain (80) This unpretentious rectangular 1½ story frame, two-end chimney house was probably built in either the late 18th or early 19th century. It is not known who built the house. Owned by the wealthy landowner William Harding of Springfield (16) at the time of his death in 1878, he devised it to his nephew John Emory Harding who was then living on the property. The home is situated on

South on Rt. 669 to Rt. 690 and then to Rt. 607

Cobbs Hall (81) Part of the Dividing Creek land patented in 1651 by Col. Richard Lee—a close associate of Royal Governor William Berkeley and progenitor of the Lee family of Virginia—this tract devolved to his son Charles Lee. The present house, a two-story five-bay brick Federal style dwelling with an English basement and four chimneys serving ten fireplaces, has center downstairs and upstairs halls each measuring 36 by 12 feet, and dates from the mid-1850s. The house, built by Lewis and Martha (Lee) Harvey, is situated on Dividing Creek, with a view directly to Hughlett's Point and beyond to the Chesapeake Bay. *VLR and NRHP. Historical Marker J-88. Visible from the road; privately owned.*

Cobbs Hall (81)

Nearby, off to the south of Cobbs Hall Lane, which leads up to Cobbs Hall, is the Lee burial ground in which are buried Col. Richard Lee the immigrant (1618-1664) and his wife Anne Constable, whom he married at Jamestown in 1640. *Historical Marker erected by The Society of the Lees of Virginia. Not visible from the road; privately owned. (Map E)*

Ditchley (82) Erected on a section of the land at Dividing Creek patented in 1651 by Richard Lee (see Cobb's Hall (81)), the present mansion, built ca. 1762 by Kendall Lee, a great-grandson of Richard Lee, is an example of classic colonial Georgian architecture. The main block is a two-story, five-bay brick structure laid in Flemish bond with scattered glazed headers. It has a hip roof and very tall brick interior chimneys at each end which serve eight fireplaces. The chimneys are laid in American bond above the roof level, suggesting they were probably restored at some later date. The basement is laid in Flemish bond below a beveled water table. Much of the interior woodwork is preserved, and the house features a noteworthy stairway, located off from the right hand side of the center hall, which proceeds to the second floor. The south wing was added in the 1850s.

In order to help pay off debts, Kendall Lee's son William sold the house in 1792 to his cousin James Ball, a kinsman of Mary Ball Washington, the mother of the president. In 1932, Ditchley was purchased by Jessie Ball duPont and her husband; and now belongs to the foundation created in her name. It was at this time that the north wing, which houses a kitchen and service area, was added to the house. Two old smokehouses still stand on the property.

Across the road, in an old Ball cemetery, lies the tombstone of Hancock Lee (1653-1709), one of Richard Lee's sons and to whom the Ditchley property had initially devolved. *VLR and NRHP. Historical Marker J-88. Visible from the road; privately owned. (Map E)*

West on Rt. 607 and south on Rt. 200 to Rt. 608

Clifton (83) This uniquely configured house was built ca. 1785 by Landon Carter Jr., son of Robert Wormeley Carter and a grandson of Landon Carter of Sabine Hall (41) in Richmond County. Thought to have been originally constructed as a hunting lodge, Clifton was an important plantation among the tens of thousands of acres owned by Landon Carter in the Northern Neck.

The house is a $2^{1}/_{2}$ story frame three-bay structure with a gable roof and a central interior chimney and English basement. The front door opens onto a hall running sidewise and then emptying into two large rooms to the rear, each with a fireplace served by the central chimney. Upstairs, four bedrooms, each with a fireplace built diagonally into this chimney, are entered from side halls, which in turn are reached by separate stairways at either end of the downstairs hall. The wings were added later. *VLR and NRHP, and BHR*

Ditchley (82)

Clifton (83)

easement. Not visible from the road; privately owned. (Map E)

Lynhams (84) Although having an 18th-century aspect, the present house is believed to date from about 1820. Lynhams is a $1^1/_2$ story three-bay frame dwelling with a high pitched roof and two very tall end chimneys, each laid in common American bond. It contains four rooms on the first floor, and much of the interior woodwork and hardware is original to the house. Restoration of the house began in the 1960s. Situated near a creek on Bluff Point Neck, Lynhams was a target of a raid by a Union gunboat during the Civil War. *Visible from the road; privately owned. (Map E)*

Lynhams (84)

South on Rt. 669

Bluff Point Graded School (85) Possibly built in 1913, this rural school originally had only one room. It remained open until 1932, when school buses made possible the transport of students over longer distances. It is now used as a community center. *VLR and NRHP. Visible from the road; open to the public. (Map E)*

Bluff Point Graded School (85)

Selected Bibliography

Adams, Carroll W. "The History of the Ownership of Salt Pond Farm," *The Bulletin of the Northumberland County Historical Society* 3 (1966): 21-27.

Arnold, Scott David. *A Guidebook to Virginia's Historical Markers*. Charlottesville: University of Virginia Press, 2007.

Bates, Delma Conway. "Juliana Gordon Hayes of 'Font Hill,'" *The Bulletin of the Northumberland County Historical Society* 10 (1973): 6-17.

Bates, Mrs. W. G. "Lynhams," *The Bulletin of the Northumberland County Historical Society* 8 (1971): 67-78.

Beale, G. W. "Early Tombs in Westmoreland, Richmond and Northumberland Counties," *William and Mary Quarterly* 11(1902): 123-30.

Booker, J. Motley. "Mt. Zion and Its People," *The Bulletin of the Northumberland County Historical Society* 9 (1972): 3-10.

Davison, Doris M. "Smith Point Lighthouse," *The Bulletin of the Northumberland County Historical Society* 24 (1987): 67-76.

Earle, Edward Chase Jr. "'Gascony' and the Gaskins (Gascoyne) Family," *Northern Neck of Virginia Historical Magazine* 4 (1954): 315-326.

Foster, Joanne R. "Lighthouses of the Northern Neck," *The Bulletin of the Northumberland County Historical Society* 45 (1998): 101-111.

Gough, Isabel. "The History of Wicomico Methodist Church at Wicomico Church," *The Bulletin of the Northumberland County Historical Society* 4 (1967): 79-89.

Gough, Isabel. "The Name is 'West End' or 'Brick House,'" *The Bulletin of the Northumberland County Historical Society* 5 (1968): 28-36.

Gough, Isabel. "Clover Dale," *The Bulletin of the Northumberland County Historical Society* 22 (1985): 19.

Haynie, Miriam. "History of Bethany Methodist Church," *The Bulletin of the Northumberland County Historical Society* 4 (1967) 38-48.

Haynie, Miriam. "Rock Hall," *The Bulletin of the Northumberland County Historical Society* 9 (1972): 23.

Haynie, Miriam. "Mantua," *The Bulletin of the Northumberland County Historical Society* 10 (1973): 25-27.

Haynie, Miriam. *Reedville 1874-1974*. Reedville, Va.: The Men's Club of Bethany United Methodist Church, 1974.

Hudnall, Ada Kelley. "Shalango and Its People," *The Bulletin of the Northumberland County Historical Society* 23 (1986): 7-15.

Jett, Carolyn H. "History of Fairfields United Methodist Church," *The Bulletin of the Northumberland County Historical Society* 15 (1978): 43-55.

Jett, Carolyn H. "Brick House," *The Bulletin of the Northumberland County Historical Society* 18 (1981): 34-37.

Jett, Carolyn H. "Versailles," *The Bulletin of the Northumberland County Historical Society* 23 (1986): 16-19.

Jett, Carolyn H. "The Anchorage," *The Bulletin of the Northumberland County Historical Society* 24 (1987): 77-89.

Jett, Carolyn H. *Heathsville: Yesterday & Today*. Heathsville, Va.: The Woman's Club of Northumberland County, 2nd Ed., 1989.

Jett, Carolyn H. *Lancaster County, Virginia: Where the River Meets the Bay*. Lancaster, Va.: The Lancaster County Book Committee, 2003.

Jett, Carolyn H. "Courthouses of Northumberland County," *The Bulletin of the Northumberland County Historical Society* 41 (2004): 40-46.

Jett, David. "A Shifting Symbol: Clover Dale and the Greek Revival Style in the Northern Neck of Virginia," *The Bulletin of the Northumberland County Historical Society* 22 (1985): 12-18.

Lee, Edmund Jennings. *Lee of Virginia*. Baltimore: Genealogical Publishing Co., 1974; orig. published in 1895.

Loth, Calder. *The Virginia Landmarks Register*. Charlottesville: University Press of Virginia, Fourth Edition, 1999.

Lounsbury, Carl R. *An Illustrated Glossary of Early Southern Architecture and Landscape*. Charlottesville: University Press of Virginia, 1994.

McClure, Phyllis. "Rosenwald Schools in the Northern Neck," *Virginia Magazine of History and Biography* 113 (2), 2005: 114-145.

McKenney, Robert N. "Cherry Point, Northumberland County, Virginia—The Formative Years," *Northern Neck of Virginia Historical Magazine* 48 (1998): 5622-5629.

McKenney, Robert N. "The Legacy Lives On: A Study of the Morris Contribution to Reedville, Northumberland County, and the Northern Neck of Virginia," *The Bulletin of the Northumberland County Historical Society* 38 (2001): 3-16.

Nagel, Paul C. *The Lees of Virginia: Seven Generations of an American Family*. New York: Oxford University Press, 1990.

Nee, Linda E. and Sarah H. Young. "Virginia's Statue of Liberty: A Sallie Jane Wildy Blundon Contribution," *The Bulletin of the Northumberland County Historical Society* 34 (1997): 95-100.

Overholt, John L. and Arthur C. Johnson. *The History of Wicomico Parish, Including 1703-1795 Vestry Minutes*. Wicomico Church, Va.: Wicomico Parish Church, 1999, 2nd Revised Edition.

Potter, Stephen R. *Commoners, Tribute, and Chiefs: The Development of Algonquian Culture in the Potomac Valley*. Charlottesville: University Press of Virginia, 1993.

Rountree, Helen C., Wayne E. Clark and Kent Mountford. *John Smith's Chesapeake Voyages, 1607-1609*. Charlottesville: University of Virginia Press, 2007.

Trudell, Elizabeth B. "Cobb's Hall," *The Bulletin of the Northumberland County Historical Society* 30 (1993): 38-45

Waring, Lucy Lemoine. *Hardings of Northumberland County, Virginia and Their Related Families*. Wicomico Church, Va.: self-published, 1971.

Warren, Barbara. "History of St. Stephen's Church, Heathsville," *The Bulletin of the Northumberland County Historical Society* 46 (1999): 37-48.

Wells, Camille. "New Light on Sunnyside: Architectural and Documentary Testaments of an Early Virginia House," *The Bulletin of the Northumberland County Historical Society* 32 (1995): 3-26.

Wolf, Thomas A. "Another Place in Time: The Cherry Point 'Community' in the Late Colonial and Early Federal Periods, 1760-1810," *The Bulletin of the Northumberland County Historical Society* 48 (2006): 12-36.

Wolf, Thomas A. "Wrights: The Land, the House and Its People," *The Bulletin of the Northumberland County Historical Society* 44 (2007): 45-80.

Wolf, Thomas A. "A History of Northumberland County's Old Jail, 1839-1958," *The Bulletin of the Northumberland County Historical Society* 46 (2009): 23-58.

Chapter 6
Lancaster

Lancaster County was formally established in 1651, out of Northumberland and York counties. The county borders the Chesapeake Bay to its east, and the Rappahannock River to its south. Since 1743, its county seat has been located in the village of Lancaster Court House, now known simply as Lancaster.

The inland village of Lancaster, and the villages of Irvington on Carter's Creek and Morattico on the Rappahannock River, have been listed on the Virginia Landmark Register and the National Register of Historic Places as historic districts.

Lancaster County encompasses an area of 231.3 square miles, but only 133.1 square miles are composed of land. The population of the county in 1790 was 5,638, of which 43 percent was free. By 1940, the county's population had increased to 8,786, and by 2000 it totaled 11,567.

Historic Sites in Lancaster County

South on Route 200 towards Kilmarnock

Morattico Baptist Church (1) Built in 1856, this early Classical Revival style brick church has a three-bay front and a rectangular shape. Morattico is considered the "mother church" of the Baptist denomination in the lower Northern Neck. The original congregation was constituted in 1778 at Morattico Hall (2) in

Morattico Baptist Church (1)

Richmond County, the residence of Alexander Hunton. It was a direct outgrowth of the work of Lewis Lunsford, who came to the lower Northern Neck as a Baptist preacher from Stafford County in 1771. The cemetery adjacent to the church, in which Lunsford is buried, is well maintained. *Historical Marker JX-5. Visible from the road. (Map A)*

Bondfield (2) This Federal style house was erected in 1854 on the site of a Carter house built prior to 1810. It is a two-story five-bay frame structure, with end chimneys, sitting atop an English basement with walls laid in three-course American bond. The kitchen, once located in the English

Bondfield (2)

Lancaster County

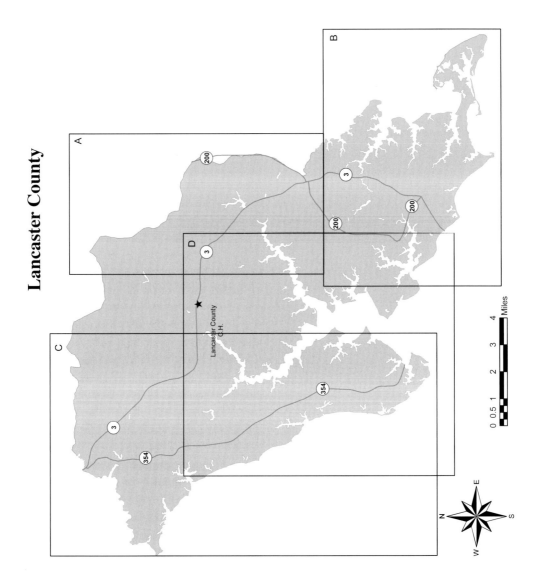

basement, was later moved to an addition to the main house. The property, still owned by descendants of the Bond-Carter family, has been recognized as a Century Farm for having been under cultivation by the same family for over a hundred years. *Visible from the road; privately owned. (Map A)*

Chilton House (3) A Queen Anne style 2¹/₂ story house located in the center of Kilmarnock, this residence was built around the turn of the 20th century. Located on a street with a number of handsome homes from that period, it has an attractive porch and a formal side entrance hall enhanced by fine woodwork. The house was built for Robert H. Chilton, the owner of a local automobile dealership in the 1920s and the mayor of Kilmarnock in the mid-1930s. Later, the house fell into neglect, but recently both the interior and exterior have been carefully restored. *Visible from the street; privately owned. (Map A)*

Chilton House (3)

James Brent House (4) This 2¹/₂ story two-bay frame house, sitting atop a raised basement, is a good example of a transitional mid-19th-century dwelling, although major alterations and additions have subsequently been made to this structure. It is situated in downtown Kilmarnock, some distance back from the street. *Visible from the street; privately owned. (Map A)*

James Brent House (4)

Following Rt. 200
south from Kilmarnock towards
Weems and Irvington

Corotoman site (5) Built in the early 1720s by Robert ("King") Carter (ca. 1663-1732), the wealthiest and most powerful planter in colonial Virginia, Corotoman was probably the most impressive house of that period in the thirteen colonies. It was a 40-by-90 foot two-story building with corner towers connected by a long verandah. The central passage was paved with marble, and the fireplaces, lined with a delft tiles, had a marble trim. Although the house burned in 1729, several years before Carter's death, an archaeological excavation carried out by the Virginia Department of Historic Resources in 1978 was able to recreate a picture of how this grand mansion must have looked.

Through his own business acumen and as a result of serving twice as the agent for the Northern Neck Proprietary in the early 18th century, "King" Carter amassed enormous land holdings, at one point exceeding 200,000 acres and located in fourteen Virginia counties at the time of his death. His estate inventory listed 47 different plantations or quarters, the land of which was cultivated by slave labor. *VLR and*

NRHP, and BHR easement. Historical Marker J-85. The site, behind the Campbell Memorial Presbyterian Church in Weems, is under the jurisdiction of Preservation Virginia. (Map B and Map D)

Historic Christ Church (6)

Corotoman site (5)

Historic Christ Church (6) John Carter, the immigrant and father of Robert "King" Carter of Corotoman (5), built a single-story frame earthfast structure, thought to have been named Christ Church, possibly very close to where the present church stands. By the early decades of the 18th century, this building had deteriorated badly, and Robert Carter proposed to the vestry of Christ Church Parish that a new church be built, at his expense. This offer was accepted by the vestry and Carter proceeded with his plan, having some 200,000 bricks made on the site, beginning about 1726-27. At the time of his death in 1732, the building was not yet complete, and he entrusted its completion to his three sons who were named his executors. They fulfilled their father's request and the church was completed by 1735.

Christ Church is one of the finest examples of extant Georgian architecture in the United States, and is without equal among colonial churches in Virginia in the degree to which its unrivaled architecture has been preserved. The church is of a cruciform plan, and its very fine exterior brickwork includes molded-brick doorways and heavily accented tall

arched windows. The paneled box pews, walnut altarpiece, and triple-decker pulpit are notable among the original interior woodwork. The tombs of Robert Carter and his two wives, near the east side of the church, have been recently restored.

Following disestablishment of the Church of England, the church remained in the Carter family. In 1835, a descendant, Mary Walker Carter Cabell of Nelson County, negotiated a 99-year lease with the Christ Church Episcopal vestry, turning over the stewardship of the building on the assumption that it would be well-maintained. By the 20th century, however, the church had been badly neglected and its membership had declined. The Foundation for Historic Christ Church was formed in 1958-59, and after assuming ownership of the property and initiating major renovations to the church, it was designated a National Historical Landmark in 1961. *VLR and NRHP, and BHR easement. Historical Marker J-86. Visible from the road. The church, museum and reception center are open to the public. (Map B and Map D)*

Chesapeake Academy (7) This private secondary school in Irvington was established in 1889. The original building was a simple framed weatherboard structure with a belltower. Co-educational and offering a very selective curriculum, it also was a boarding school and drew students from many parts of the Northern Neck region at a time before there was public secondary education in the area. With the advent of public secondary education in Virginia in 1907, the school was thought to be no longer needed and was closed. After the school's closure, the building was only modified slightly before becoming the King Carter Inn. Today it is the home of the three-story, double-porticoed Hope and Glory Inn. *Visible from the road. (Map B and Map D)*

Chesapeake Academy (7)

Wilder's Grant (8) Considered one of the oldest extant structures in the community of Irvington, Wilder's Grant probably dates to the late 18th century. The $1^{1}/_{2}$ story frame house appears to have been constructed initially on a side-hall plan. It takes its name from Michael Wilder, who in 1792 purchased this property from James Gordon, a prominent local figure and the likely builder of this house.

Wilder's Grant (8)

Wilder also bought an adjacent tract, and his property extended north to the Christ Church Glebe. A ten-acre portion of the property was acquired by the Baltimore and Rappahannock Steam Packet Company in the late 19th century and became the site of an active steamboat wharf. *Not visible from the road; privately owned. (Map B and Map D)*

Haydon Hall (9) The original part of this house, built in what is now the center of Irvington, about 1845, was a two-story five-bay single pile frame dwelling, with chimneys at either end. Later, a front-gabled two-story addition was made to the left-hand side of the house, and basic symmetry was achieved by altering the front of the right-hand two bays of the original building into a matching front-gabled structure. At some point, a $1^{1}/_{2}$ story gambrel-roofed wing was added to the right-hand side of the house. The house portrays many elements of the Classical Revival style, including its colonnaded front façade. It takes its name from one of its early owners, being a wedding gift to Tom and Sarah Haydon. *Visible from the street; privately owned. (Map B and Map D)*

Haydon Hall (9)

White Stone and Vicinity

A. T. Wright High School site (10) Originally called the Lancaster County Training School, a two-story wooden frame structure was erected here about 1917, drawing partly on funds raised by local black residents. Its philosophy incorporated ideas expressed in the curricula of the Hampton and Tuskegee institutes. The school was located some distance from the village of White Stone on James Wharf Road.

In 1921, Albert Terry Wright (1871-1944) became the school's principal, and the school—which had become a high school—was later named for him. The school was closed in 1959, when Brookvale High School was opened for all students of high school age. Before the black community was able to convert the building into a museum, it unexpectedly collapsed. *Historical Marker J-91. Site visible from the road; privately owned. (Map B)*

A.T. Wright High School site (10)

Pop Castle (11) While its date of construction is not known for certain, this house overlooking the Rappahannock River was partially damaged by a British naval bombardment during the War of 1812. The $2^1/_2$ story five-bay frame house has a standing seam gable roof with a front gable over a second floor front porch, and brick exterior chimneys are at either end.

Prior to the Civil War, the property was acquired by James W. Gresham, but soon thereafter it was considerably damaged by shelling from a Union gunboat, even while Gresham's mother remained in a wing of the house. The long screen porch on the principal façade was added sometime later. *VLR and NRHP. Not visible from the road; privately owned. (Map B and Map D)*

Pop Castle (11)

Crab Point (12) Also known as Francis Point, this site consists of fourteen acres on a point of land marking the entry from the Rappahannock River into Carter's Creek. In the 1890s, Isaac Francis acquired this tract and erected the Francis Point Hotel, a large three-story frame structure, with a cupola on the fourth floor. Built in the Queen Anne style, it is architecturally representative of many of the large waterfront summer resort hotels of that period. From the cupola, guests could easily follow the movement of steamboats on the Rappahannock River and its nearby tributaries. The

Crab Point (12)

old hotel is situated on the James Wharf road. *Not visible from the road; privately owned. (Map B and Map D)*

Locust Grove (13)   It is uncertain when or by whom this enormous house was built. It is a two-story seven-bay single pile frame structure, and over the years major alterations have evidently been made, including the erection of a two-story three-bay entry portico in the 1920s. The house is known to have been owned by several families, and a grave-yard off to the left of the long lane leading to the house includes interments of members of the Spriggs family. *Visible from the road; privately owned. (Map B)*

Locust Grove (13)

Pleasant Banks (14)   This two-story frame structure is thought to have been built in the early 19th century by a member of the Lawson family on a section of the original Lawson land patent. A three-bay structure with a gable roof and high brick exterior chimneys at both ends, the

Pleasant Banks (14)

wings were added later. The name of the house derives from the high banks of the nearby Rappahannock River. During the 20th century the property was sub-divid-ed into a number of smaller plots. *Not visible from the road; privately owned. (Map B)*

Dr. B. H. B. Hubbard Jr. Medical Office (15)   Dr. Hubbard, a native of the area, was a major medical figure in lower Lancaster County in the early decades of the 20th century. This office, a brick block structure consisting of three good-size rooms — waiting room, examining room and office — replaced an earlier very simple wood frame building. The most used entrance was from a porch facing Windmill Point Road, which opened di-rectly into the doctor's office rather than the waiting room. Although Dr. Hub-bard died in 1940, the office is scarcely changed and continues to be owned by his descendants. *Visible from the road; privately owned. (Map B)*

Dr. B.H.B. Hubbard Jr. Medical Office (15)

B. H. B. Hubbard Jr. House (16) Originally a simple two-story five-bay gable roof house, this Victorian-era home of Dr. B. H. B. Hubbard Jr. in the cen-ter of White Stone was probably built in the 1890s. Following the death of his first wife, Dr. Hubbard altered the house, most notably by adding a colonnaded front porch, the columns being made of cement blocks and discs actually manufactured locally by the firm of Humphries and McNamara. The formal entrance hall features highly crafted woodwork. This house has remained unoccupied for many years. *Visible from the street and privately owned. (Map B)*

B.H.B. Hubbard Jr. House (16)

East on Windmill Point Road (Rt. 695)

Lawson-Dunton-Kirk-Hall House (17) This two-story frame house with the long shed-like roof in the rear reflects the development of this site from a tavern to a dwelling house. Henry Chinn Lawson was granted a license to operate a tavern on this site by the county court in 1816. He called it the White Stone Tavern, taking its name from a very unusual object in the vicinity which is now thought to have been a survey marker for the original Lawson land patent. This object is the basis for the name of the present community of White Stone. In the early 1870s, Dr.

Lawson-Dunton-Kirk-Hall House (17)

William M. Kirk and his wife purchased this site from the Dunton family and added the two-story three-bay section now making up the front of the house, while retaining the old tavern structure with its large chimney. *Visible from the road; privately owned. (Map B)*

Off to the southeast on Rt. 641 towards Mosquito Point

Lawson Bay Farm (18) Thought to have been built by a descendant of the Lawson family in the 1830s, this property takes its name from a nearby tidal inlet off of the Rappahannock River. The house is a two-story five-bay frame Federal style structure with a standing seam gable roof and chimneys at either end, and with later one-story wings. Early in the 20th century this property was owned by an elderly couple who allowed the local citizenry to enjoy the sand beach adjoining the property. *Visible from the road; privately owned. (Map B)*

Lawson Bay Farm (18)

Muskettoe Point Farm (19) Situated on land patented in the mid-17th century by Roland Lawson, the original house is thought to have been built in the early 18th century, but with possible 17th century elements. It was a $1\frac{1}{2}$ story side-hall residence, to which another set of rooms was added at a later date. A similar structure was added next to the original house in the late 20th century.

It sits near Mosquito Creek. *Not visible from the road; privately owned. (Map B)*

Muskettoe Point Farm (19)

Cuttatawomen Indian site (20) Although Capt. John Smith did not mention visiting the downriver Cuttatawomen Indians during his exploratory voyage up the Rappahannock River in August 1608, he is thought to have encountered them. This group, whose name was later anglicized to Corrotoman, is estimated to have included about 135 people, and had towns strung along the north shore of the river from east of Mosquito Point to just west of what is now known as the Corrotoman River. The chief's house is thought to have been located here, just northeast of Mosquito Point. *(Map B)*

Back to Windmill Point Road (Rt. 695) to Windmill Point

Sanders-George-McCaig House (21) The main portion of this house, a two-story three-bay frame structure, probably dates from the early 19th century, and it is thought to have been there when James Sanders acquired part of Fleet's Island, originally owned by Capt. Henry Fleet, in 1825. Sanders is believed to have been a lighthouse keeper at Windmill Point. It would appear that the original house had a side-hall plan. The one-story addition to the left was added in 1857-58. In 1926,

the property was purchased by Benjamin Franklin George, who was the wharf master of the steamboat landing then located at the tip of Fleet's Island. The present owners have done much to restore the house to its original form. *Visible from the road; privately owned. (Map B)*

Sanders-George-McCaig House (21)

Fleets Bay area along
Route 3 between White Stone
and Kilmarnock

Enon Hall (22) An early property of the Hathaway family, whose descendants retained ownership until the early 20th century, Enon Hall was originally a simple $1^1/_2$ story three-bay frame house with a gable roof and an interior chimney, believed to have 17th century origins. On the inside, the center hall was flanked by a single room on each side, and a stairway led to the rooms above. Situated on Antipoison Creek. *Not visible from the road; privately owned. (Map B)*

Enon Hall (22)

Retirement (23) This antebellum Greek Revival style dwelling was built by Hugh Henry Hill ca. 1835-40. The house took four years to build, as most of the building materials were shipped from Baltimore. The house is a two story, five-bay gabled-roof structure, with interior chimneys at either end. Its entrance and central passage are embellished with both Greek and Classical Revival details. *Visible from the road; privately owned. (Map B)*

Retirement (23)

Somerset (24) Erected on what was once part of the Enon Hall (22) tract, Somerset is a two-story three-bay wood frame home with a single-pile central passage embellished with Greek Revival details. It was supposedly built for one of the Hathaway daughters of Enon Hall. Considerable restoration work has been carried out in recent years. *Visible from the road; privately owned. Endangered. (Map B)*

Somerset (24)

Bellows-Christopher House (25) Joseph Foster Bellows came to lower Lancaster County from Long Island, New York in the mid-1870s, and became the major entrepreneur associated with the menhaden industry in Lancaster County (also see the Reedville Historic District, in neighboring Northumberland County). He was the leading partner of the Bellows and Squires Menhaden Factory, and his wealth is manifest in his own residence and the several homes he had built for each of his children.

His own home, erected between 1880 and 1885, is known as the Bellows-Christopher house, a large 2$^1/_2$ story frame Queen Anne style dwelling with a steeply pitched roof enhanced by diamond shaped colored ties. (Other Bellows-related homes are those usually referred to by the names of his children: William Lorenzo Bellows, Fannie Bellows Hawthorne, Margaret Bellows Somervill, and Nina Bellows Lowe. Also there are the Bellows-Moore and Bellows-Humphreys houses.) *Visible from the road; privately owned. (Map B)*

Bellows-Christopher House (25)

Apple Grove at Chase's Cove (26) This house is thought to have belonged to

Apple Grove at Chase's Cove (26)

the Hubbard family at an early point in its history. The original structure, built in the early 19th century or possibly earlier, was a 1¹/₂ story three-bay double-pile frame structure with an imposing double-shoul-dered Flemish bond brick chimney on its south side. In 1840, a two-story three-bay addition, with a gable roof and its own exterior brick chimneys, was added to the north side of the original house. *Visible from the road; privately owned. (Map B)*

Dunton/Ring Farm (27) Once the home of Christopher S. Dunton, in order to reach it by land one had to follow the old road that led from Windmill Point to Christ Church, the remains of which are still in evidence. The farm passed into the Ring family in the 20th century, and although the original house no longer stands, the farmhouse of 19th-century vintage remains but has been incorpo-rated into a much more modern struc-ture. *Not visible from the road; privately owned. (Map B)*

Dunton/Ring Farm (27)

Public View (28) Believed to have been built in the mid-1830s, probably by William C. Currell, this early Classical Revival style house sits atop an English basement. A two-story five-bay home with a two-storied front portico, its gable roof is flanked by wide brick chimneys that are partially enclosed. Currell, a prominent lo-cal merchant, had his mercantile establish-

ment just across the road, which is now Route 3. The house has been in the Chase family for several generations. *Visible from the road; privately owned. (Map B)*

Public View (28)

Greenfield (29) Built ca. 1840, the original part of this house is a two-story, three-bay gabled-roof frame dwelling. Greenfield is one of the few extant ante-bellum dwellings in Lancaster County to have experienced a direct attack from Union forces during the Civil War. As a result of the capture of the Union ship the *Harriet De Ford* in early April 1865 by a Confederate force led by Capt. Thad-deus Fitzhugh, and its pillage and then de-struction in Dymer's Creek, seven Union gunboats sailed up the creek and shelled numerous homes, including Greenfield. Bits of shrapnel and other evidence of this shelling remain in the house to this day. *Not visible from the road; privately owned. (Map B)*

Greenfield (29)

Lancaster County, Map A

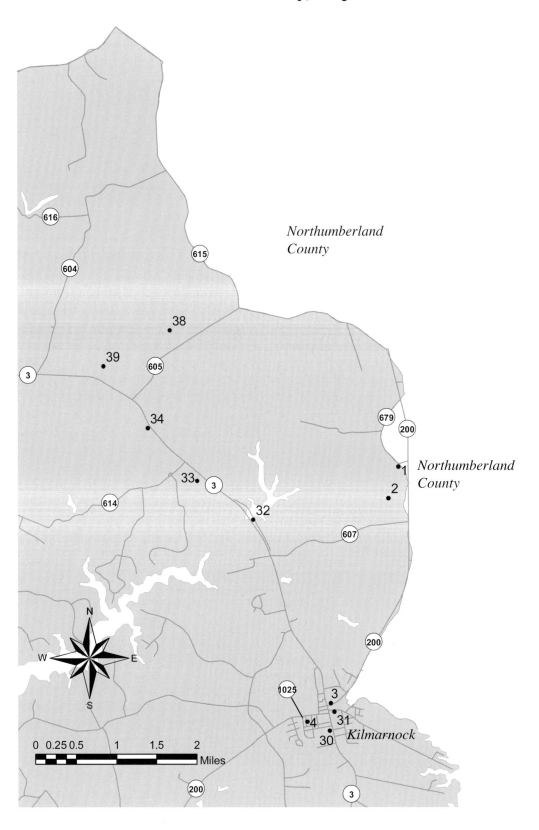

Northumberland County

Northumberland County

Kilmarnock

0 0.25 0.5   1   1.5   2
Miles

Grace Episcopal Church Chapel (30) By the mid-1850s, there had been a population shift away from the area around Christ Church (6) towards what is today Kilmarnock, and Christ Church had been virtually abandoned. In 1853, Col. Addison Hall, the father of Henrietta Hall Shuck, the first woman missionary to China, conveyed part of his tract of land called Waverly to the vestry of Christ Church parish. On this tract, the vestry built a small single story wooden frame sanctuary with a gable roof and a simple portico entry. Known as Grace Episcopal Church, this chapel served the Episcopalian community well into the 20th century. As Kilmarnock expanded in the mid-20th century, the need for a much larger sanctuary became apparent. A new brick church was built, and later two additions were made. In the process, it was decided that the original Grace Church be relocated immediately behind the newer structure, and it continues to be used. *Not visible from the street. (Map A)*

Grace Episcopal Church Chapel (30)

Chase Manor (31) A Classical Revival style structure built in 1849, this two-story five-bay frame dwelling with interior end chimneys sits on an English basement. Its most distinguishing feature is probably the two-story porch on the front with its Doric columns and pilasters. The home is named for its original owner, Lewson Chase, whom Col. Addison Hall recruited from Massachusetts to establish the Kilmarnock Seminary for females (although it later became co-educational before closing in 1892). This is considered the oldest extant structure in the community of Kilmarnock. *Not visible from the street; privately owned. (Map A)*

Chase Manor (31)

Northwest on Route 3 from Kilmarnock

Lancaster Rolling Mill (32) This is one of Lancaster County's most recognized landmarks. Believed to have been constructed by George Kamps and J. Carter in 1845, this water-powered mill ground wheat and corn into flour and meal. It is the last of the many mills that once dotted the horizon of Lancaster County. There is some thought that this mill might have been built on the site of Robert "King" Carter's "Great Mill." *Visible from the road; privately owned but open to the public. (Map A)*

Lancaster Rolling Mill (32)

Windsor Farm (33) Built for Hilkiah Ball, this two-story five-bay brick house is built over an English basement, and has flanking wings. It follows the traditional Georgian architectural plan, although it was erected in 1833. The standing seam gable roof is flanked by two wide brick chimneys. The bottom section of the brick walls is laid in American bond, while the upper part is Flemish bond. *Visible from the road; privately owned. (Map A)*

Windsor Farm (33)

White Marsh Church (34) This Greek Revival style rectangular church, built in the meeting house form, was erected in 1848. The congregation was founded in 1792, and was probably the second earliest Methodist church in the

Northern Neck, after Fairfields Methodist Church (39) in Northumberland County. The church has a seven-foot original medallion in its ceiling and a Gothic Revival cast iron railing encloses the wrap around the balcony. Out of this church came two bishops as regional leaders of Methodism. Due to a declining congregation, the church has been decommissioned. *Historical Marker J-83. Visible from the road. (Map A and Map D)*

White Marsh Church (34)

Side trip to the south of Route 3

Apple Grove (35) Located off of Devil's Bottom Road (Rt. 614), this house is a two-story gable-roofed frame structure over an English basement. It is thought to have had its origins in the colonial period, and underwent many additions in the 19th and 20th centuries. Most of these are considered to have had a negative impact on its architectural integrity. *Not visible from the road; privately owned. Endangered. (Map D)*

Apple Grove (35)

Lancaster County, Map B

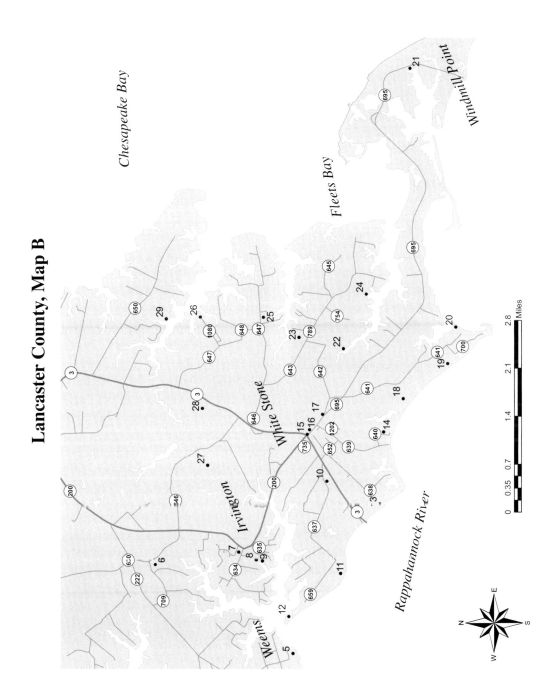

Chesapeake Bay

Fleets Bay

Windmill Point

Rappahannock River

Weems

Irvington

White Stone

Verville (36) The original part of this house is a 1¹/₂ story three-bay gambrel-roofed brick structure, laid in Flemish bond, one of just a few colonial buildings to have survived in Lancaster County. This portion was built in the 1740s by James Gordon, a Scotch-Irish immigrant who became prominent in the commercial and public affairs of the county. The wings were added in the early 19th century by Ellyson Currie, a justice of the General Court of Virginia. The interior contains some fine Federal woodwork. The house was later expanded with compatible additions. *Visible from the road; privately owned. (Map C and Map D)*

Merry Point Ferry Farm (37)

Verville (36)

Merry Point Ferry Farm (37) The original part of this house, a 1¹/₂ story three-bay frame structure, was built about 1767 for James Waddell, known as the "blind preacher." About 1840 it was enlarged by the addition of a 1¹/₂ story wing. The house has passed through many hands over the years. *Visible from the road; privately owned.*

Close by the farm is one of three ferries still operating on Virginia waters, known as Merry Point Ferry. It connects the Merry Point side of the western branch of the Corrotoman River to the Ottoman side, and operates on a regular schedule except in bad weather. *(Map C and Map D)*

Side trip to the north of Route 3 on Pinckardsville Road (Rt. 605)

Melrose (38) Melrose, believed to have been built in the 1840s and enlarged by Thomas H. Pinckard in 1857, is a fine example of Greek Revival architecture. The central part of the house is a two-story, five-bay structure with interior chimneys at each end, atop an English basement, and is flanked by two-story wings. The home is noted for its interior, and in particular the staircase in the center hall built by William Pierce, a highly skilled local craftsman. Pinckard's daughter married a Dunaway, the brother of the builder of nearby Levelfields (39), and Melrose remained in the Dunaway family until 1922. *Visible from the road; privately owned. (Map A)*

Melrose (38)

Levelfields (39) Thomas S. Dunaway, who along with several of his brothers was a distinguished Baptist minister, built this two-story, five-bay hip roof frame house in 1859. Once the manor house for an 800-acre plantation, Levelfields has a double portico and four interior chimneys. Accepting a call to the First Baptist Church in Fredericksburg, Dunaway moved there prior to the Civil War and sold Levelfields in 1866. *Visible from the road; privately owned and currently operated as a bed and breakfast. (Map A and Map D)*

Levelfields (39)

Lancaster Tavern (40) This ordinary (tavern) was built by Henry Hinton ca. 1790, and is sometimes confused with the early, but no longer extant, Job Carter's Tavern. Situated on the north side of the road, this structure may later have been enlarged, and for many years it served as the private home of the clerk of the county court. Over time it has undergone some major changes, some of which threaten

Lancaster Tavern (40)

the historical integrity of the structure. *Visible from the road; a public eating facility. (Map C and Map D)*

Old Clerk's Office (41) The west end of this building was completed in 1797, but its eastern addition was not built until 1833/34. It then became a rectangular brick structure with a gable roof and interior chimneys at each end. While today it stands very close to the south side of the road, it actually faces south, suggesting that the county road at the time of its construction passed south of the building. It was used as the county clerk's office until 1938, when the office was moved to the 1861 courthouse (44) after its wings were added. Near the old clerk's office is a Confederate memorial from 1872, thought to be one of the earliest in Virginia. *Visible from the road; owned by the county and open to the public. (Map C and Map D)*

Old Clerk's Office (41)

Lancaster House (42) The original part of this house, which stands back some distance from the south side of the road, was a two-story single-pile side-hall structure known to have been erected about 1827/28 by William Dandridge on what was then public land associated with the courthouse grounds. The house was later sold to Daniel P. Mitchell Jr. who added the two-story west wing and made other changes. In the middle of the 19th century it was the residence of Warner Eubank, a

Lancaster County, Map C

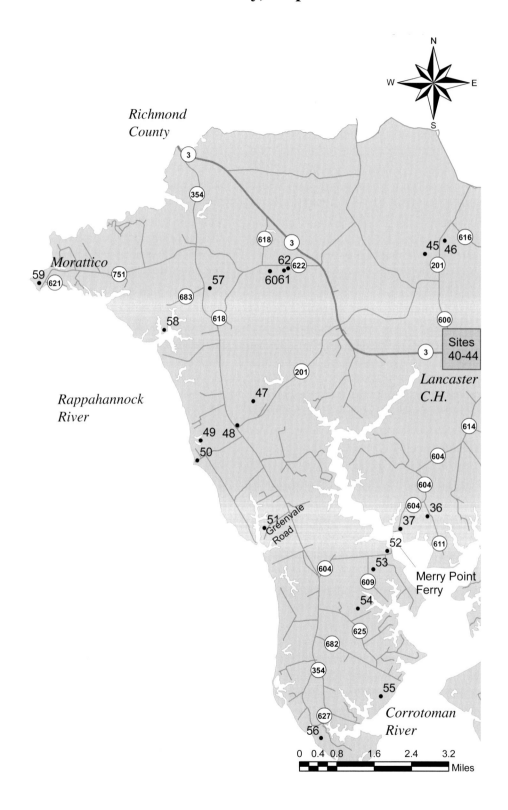

Richmond County

Morattico

Rappahannock River

Lancaster C.H.

Sites 40-44

Greenvale Road

Merry Point Ferry

Corrotoman River

59
621
751
354
3
618
3
57
683
618
58
201
47
49 48
50
51
604
609
54
625
682
354
627
56
62
622
6061
45 46
616
201
600
3
614
604
604
604 36
37
52
611
53
55

0 0.4 0.8   1.6   2.4   3.2
Miles

N
W   E
S

long-time clerk of the county court. The building currently serves as the headquarters for the Mary Ball Washington Library and Museum. *Visible from the road; open to the public. (Map C and Map D)*

Lancaster House (42)

Old Jail (43) Farther along on the south side of the road is the Old Jail, built about 1819. The right hand part of this building was laid in Flemish bond, while the left side—designed to house criminals and to separate them from imprisoned debtors or other detainees—was laid in American bond when it was added on several years later. The original jail in this area is thought to have been built about 1743, when the county seat was moved to this location from Queenstown (now a lost site) on the western bank of the Corrotoman River. This building burned in 1817, however, and the present Old Jail was built in the same proximity. The Old Jail was taken out of use in 1937, when a new jail was added as a wing to the existing Courthouse (44) across the road. *Visible from the road; open to the public. (Map C and Map D)*

Old Jail (43)

Courthouse (44) It is unknown where exactly the first courthouse in this village was located, following the move of the county seat from Queenstown in 1743. By 1860, the need was seen for a new courthouse, and a two-story rectangular brick structure was built on the north side of the road and opened on April 15, 1861, at the beginning of the Civil War. The building was not substantially changed until it was remodeled in the 1930s under the aegis of the federal Works Progress Administration (WPA). Wings were added to the original structure to include the clerk's office and a new jail, and the colonnaded front was also constructed at this time. The large entrance foyer with its graceful staircase leading to the second floor is a portrait gallery of officers of the court and the county, and several marble memorial plaques also list the names of notable Lancaster County citizens. *Visible from the road; open to the public.*

In 2010, a modern judicial center building, with new court rooms and judicial chambers, and extensive parking space, was opened behind the 1861 courthouse. *(Map C and Map D)*

Courthouse (44)

Side trip on Rt. 201 north of Route 3

Wake Forest (45) Likely built about 1840 for Thomas Dunaway Eubank and his wife Elizabeth Eudora Downing, this house may have been erected by his brother,

William O. Eubank, a local builder. Wake Forest was and remains a two-story frame structure with a gable roof, sitting atop an English basement, and its center hall contains a very skillfully crafted stairway to the floor above. After the tragic death of the Eubanks during the Civil War from typhoid fever brought home by one of their sons, the house was sold out of the family and an I-shaped wing was later added. Renovation of the house has been underway for a number of years. *Visible from the road; privately owned. (Map C)*

Wake Forest (45)

Edgely & Edgely Cemetery (46) Samuel Downing, later Judge of the Northumberland County Court, built Edgely about 1853. This two-story, five-bay frame house with a gable roof and interior chimneys at either end, and a front gable over the single-story front porch, was given this name because it stands literally on the edge of the boundary line between Lancaster and Northumberland counties. Downing's sister was the wife of Thomas Eubank of nearby Wake Forest (45). His son, Thomas J. Downing, was a locally renowned lawyer and served in the Virginia State Senate. During his tenure in the General Assembly, he sponsored the bill to build the first bridge connecting the Northern Neck with the outside world. When it was completed in 1927, it became known as the Downing Bridge (see site (49) in Richmond County), connecting the peninsula with Tappahannock in Essex County. *Visible from the road; privately owned. (Map C)*

In addition to the Downing family cemetery at Edgely, there is another cemetery by that name bordering on the Edgely estate. On that site there was once a small two-room public school, but after it closed for want of enough pupils, the Edgely Methodist Church was built there and served the area until well into the 20th century. *Visible from the road; open to the public. (Map C)*

Edgely (46)

Back down Rt. 201 and across Route 3 to the southwest

Fox Hill Plantation (47) An L-shaped Federal style two-story brick house, Fox Hill recalls the Georgian style of an earlier generation with its five-bay façade and hip roof, and tall brick interior end chimneys. Probably built in the first decade of the 19th century by Richard Selden II, Fox Hill was recently given this name by Marjorie Eastwick, a late 20th-century owner who chose to so honor the 17th-century owner of this property,

Fox Hill Plantation (47)

David Fox. A detached two-story hip roof kitchen laid in Flemish bond, and a brick smokehouse, are likely remnants of an early complex of outbuildings. *VLR and NRHP. Visible from the road; privately owned. (Map C and Map D)*

St. Mary's White Chapel Church (48) A church evidently existed on this site as early as 1669. A cruciform structure was built here in 1739-41 which may have included some parts of the older church. In 1752, St. Mary's White Chapel Parish was merged with Christ Church Parish. After disestablishment the church was abandoned, but it was reoccupied in 1832. The small congregation tore down the deteriorated chancel and nave and used the bricks to repair the transepts. Although the 18th -century plan has thus been significantly altered, two sets of altar tablets from the early 1700s are preserved inside, and the well-maintained cemetery contains many early tombstones, including that of John Stretchley, a late 17th-century clerk of the Lancaster County court. This parish church was that of the family of Mary Ball, the mother of George Washington. *VLR and NRHP. Historical Marker J-82. Visible from the road. (Map C and Map D)*

St. Mary's White Chapel Church (48)

Midway (49) Thought to have been built about 1842, the house is named for being "midway" between nearby Monaskan (50), which is closer to the Rappahannock River, and Maidley, which once stood up the hill a bit. While it is uncertain who built the house, an early owner was Addison L. Carter. The home sustained severe damage during the Civil War from an attack by the Union's Potomac Flotilla.

Midway is a two-story five-bay gabled-roof wooden structure with dual chimneys at either end, and sits atop an English basement. Its north and south porticos are both supported by Doric columns, while the porches on the east and west are smaller but also with Doric column support. *Not visible from the road; privately owned. (Map C and Map D)*

Midway (49)

Monaskan (50) Predating its neighbor Midway (49), Monaskan is an example of Early Classical Revival architecture. A two-story, five-bay structure with a gable roof, the front and back sides are frame but the side walls are brick, laid in Flemish bond, as are the double-shouldered end-chimneys. The two-story portico on the principal façade is supported by Tuscan columns. *Visible from the road; privately owned. (Map C and Map D)*

Monaskan (50)

Greenvale Manor Farm (51) Built about 1840 on the foundations of an earlier structure, this is an altered Greek Revival frame house overlooking the Rappahannock River and Greenvale Creek. It is a two-story five-bay single pile structure with a center-hall plan. Matching wings were added at a later date. *Visible from the road; privately owned. (Map C and Map D)*

Greenvale Manor Farm (51)

Spring Hill Farm (52) This house dates to the early 19th century or possibly even earlier. It is a 1½ story three-dormered frame house, with tall dual external chimneys at each end of the gabled roof. The entrance is slightly-off center. One-story wings were added later. The property was owned by Raleigh Dunaway in the early 19th century. *Visible from the road; private property. (Map C and Map D)*

Spring Hill Farm (52)

Level Green (53) This early 1½ story frame house with end chimneys has undergone many changes over time, including the addition of a front gable and a front porch, and probably added windows on the front. *Not visible from the road; privately owned. (Map C and Map D)*

Level Green (53)

Locustville (54) The persistence of Georgian influences is seen in this mid-19th century frame farmhouse, possibly built or enlarged for its owner, John A. Rogers. Its symmetrical two-story five-bay form, with gable roof and interior end chimneys, is enlivened with a Greek Revival dwarf portico over the front entrance. The name of its builder, F. A. Pierce, is inscribed on a back wing, along with the date of 1855. *VLR and NRHP. Visible from the road; open to the public. (Map C and Map D)*

Locustville (54)

Millenbeck Archaeological Sites (Ball's Point) (55) These archaeological sites, now covered over, are near the western shore of the lower part of the

Lancaster County, Map D

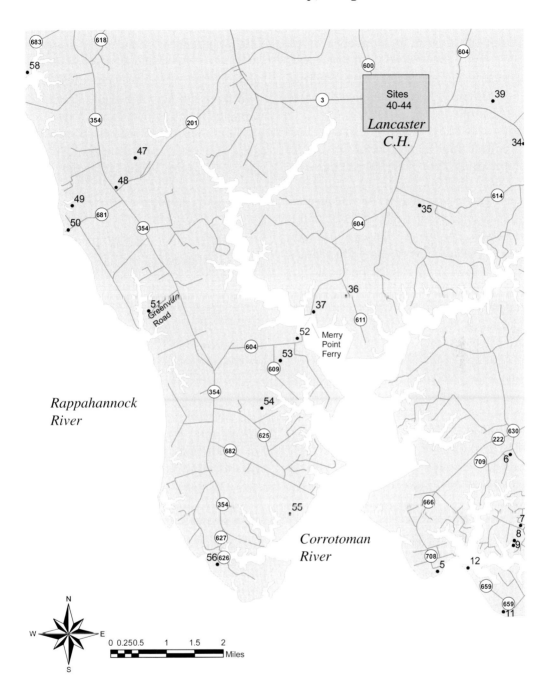

Sites
40-44

Lancaster
C.H.

Rappahannock
River

Merry
Point
Ferry

Corrotoman
River

Greenvale
Road

N
W   E
S

0 0.250.5   1   1.5   2
Miles

Corrotoman River. They include the excavated remains of a fort at Ball's Point, established about the time of Bacon's Rebellion of 1676, and evidence of the late 17th-century home of Hannah Ball, a great-grandmother of George Washington. *VLR. Not visible from the road; privately owned. (Map C and Map D)*

Chowning Ferry Farm & Towles Point sites (56) The frame house at Towles Point, overlooking the Rappahannock River, was already an endangered site when photographed by WPA architectural historians in the 1930s, and had thoroughly collapsed by the late 20th century.

The 18th century house once standing a bit upriver from Towles Point belonged to Capt. William Chowning, who served in the local militia during the Revolutionary War. His family had migrated to this part of Lancaster County from the south side of the Rappahannock, which was part of Lancaster until Middlesex County was established out of Lancaster in 1669. This was the site of Chowning's Ferry, which was the only ferry that connected upper Lancaster County and lower Richmond County with the port town of Urbanna on the south side of the river. Little remains of the original structure. *Both sites are visible from the road; privately owned. (Map C and Map D)*

Chowning Ferry Farm site (56)

Backtrack on Rt. 354 to north of Rt. 201

Edgehill (57) Given the steep pitch of its roof, the original portion of this house, which was a 1½ story structure with three dormers and a large chimney at one end, possibly dates from the 18th century. A large two-story addition has been attached where a matching chimney may have been. *Visible from the road; privately owned. (Map C)*

Edgehill (57)

Belle Isle (58) This two-story, three-bay hip roof Georgian manor house with very tall brick interior end chimneys was built in the mid-18th century, and one-story wings were added about 1790. Whether its original owner was a member of the Burwell or the Downman family is disputed. Much of the original woodwork was acquired by the Henry Francis duPont collection at Winterthur, Delaware in the 1920s. The plantation complex, including two brick outbuildings, was restored in

Belle Isle (58)

the 1940s under the direction of the architectural historian Thomas T. Waterman. In more recent years, most of the property surrounding the complex has been incorporated into Belle Island State Park, a late 20th century recreational development in Lancaster County. *VLR and NRHP. Visible from the road; privately owned. (Map C and Map D)*

Morattico Village (59) After the Civil War this area became known as Whealton, taking its name from the Whealtons who relocated here and sought to make it a center for seafood processing. Their efforts were unsuccessful, and smaller tracts were sold off to local residents who together were able to establish a viable seafood-based community. One of its leaders was Dr. Frank Lewis, a physician and educator. He built a large Victorian style house and a separate one-story frame office. In time, the community came to be known as Morattico, deriving its name from the early Joseph Ball homesite nearby (also see Moraughtacund Indian village site (4) in Richmond County). In more recent years, the Morattico Waterfront Museum has been established in this community, in one of the original country stores. *VLR and NRHP. Visible from the road. (Map C)*

Return from Morattico to Route 3 along Morattico Road (Rt. 622)

Oakley site (60) The original portion of the house that until recently stood on this site, thought to date from the 18th century, was a 1¹/₂ story structure with dormers and a shed-like roof. It stood on property owned by Joseph Chinn, who had acquired the land from his uncle, Joseph Ball I. In the 19th century the five-bay frame Greek and Gothic Revival

addition was built, with its high style portico and supporting columns dominating the front façade. This house was burned down in January 2010. *Visible from the road; privately owned. (Map C)*

Oakley site (60)

Holyoke (61) The main block of Holyoke, probably a modest house with a hall-parlor plan, is thought to date from before the Revolution. It was substantially enlarged about 1840, and major renovations were made again in the 1870s. The rear ell was added in the 1920s. At present the house is a two-story five-bay double-pile structure. The earliest owners of this property have not yet been identified. *Visible from the road; privately owned. (Map C)*

Holyoke (61)

Epping Forest (62) This two-story five-bay gabled-roof frame house with dual interior chimneys at either end, is a very interesting and controversial site.

In the late 17th and early 18th centuries, Joseph Ball I owned an inland tract known in his day as the Forest Quarter, while he resided at his home called Morattico near the Rappahannock River (see Morattico Village (59)). Sometime after the death of his wife, he negotiated with his children a series of deeds having to do with his personal and real estate. In one of the deeds he said he reserved a room "in the new home he was then building." This is thought to be the beginnings of Epping Forest, on Forest Quarter, the site of the birthplace of Mary Ball. After spending a good part of her childhood on Cherry Point in Northumberland County, she moved to Westmoreland County where she married Augustine Washington and gave birth to George Washington. Epping Forest as a name for this property, however, did not arise until the mid-19th century, and alterations and additions have brought many changes to the original house. *Historical Marker J-80. Visible from the road; privately owned. (Map C)*

Epping Forest (62)

Selected Bibliography

Arnold, Scott David. *A Guidebook to Virginia's Historical Markers*. Charlottesville: University of Virginia Press, 2007.

Brown, Katharine L. *Robert "King" Carter: Builder of Christ Church*. Irvington, Va.: The Foundation for Historic Christ Church, 2001.

E. H. T. Traceries. *Historic Architecture Survey Report of Lancaster County, Virginia; Final Report*. Richmond: Department of Historic Resources Archives, File LA-17, 1997.

E. H. T. Traceries. P*hase II of a Historic Architecture Survey in Lancaster County, Virginia: Final Report*. Richmond: Department of Historic Resources Archives, File LA-19, 1999.

Farrar, Emmie Ferguson and Emilee Hines. *Old Virginia Houses: The Northern Peninsulas*. New York: Hastings House, 1972.

Foster, Joanne R. "Lighthouses of the Northern Neck," *The Bulletin of the Northumberland County Historical Society* 45 (1998): 101-111.

Jett, Carolyn H. *Lancaster County, Virginia: Where the River Meets the Bay*. Lancaster, Va.: The Lancaster County Book Committee, 2003.

Loth, Calder. *The Virginia Landmarks Register*. Charlottesville: University Press of Virginia, Fourth Edition, 1999.

Lounsbury, Carl R. *An Illustrated Glossary of Early Southern Architecture and Landscape*. Charlottesville: University Press of Virginia, 1994.

McClure, Phyllis. "Rosenwald Schools in the Northern Neck," *Virginia Magazine of History and Biography* 113 (2), 2005: 114-145.

McKenney, Elizabeth B. *History of the Town of White Stone*. White Stone, Va.: privately published, 1976.

Rountree, Helen C., Wayne E. Clark and Kent Mountford. *John Smith's Chesapeake Voyages, 1607-1609*. Charlottesville: University of Virginia Press, 2007.

Simmons, Carroll Jackson. *Irvington: An Album of Its First Generation*. Virginia Beach, Va.: Donning Co., 1992.

Wilson, John C. *Virginia's Northern Neck: A Pictorial History*. Virginia Beach, Va.: Donning Co., 1984.

Chapter 7
Richmond

Richmond County was formally established in 1692, out of that part of (Old) Rappahannock County which was north of the Rappahannock River. (Old Rappahannock County had been formed in 1656 out of the upriver sections of Lancaster County, which in turn had been formed from Northumberland and York counties in 1651.) Richmond County borders the Rappahannock River to its southwest. Its county seat has been located at what today is known as the town of Warsaw since very early in the county's history.

Richmond County consists of 216.4 square miles, of which 191.5 are land. The population of the county in 1790 was 6,985, of which 43 percent was free. By 1940, the county's population had fallen slightly to 6,634, but by 2000 it had risen to 8,809.

Historic Sites in Richmond County

Heading north on Route 3

Side trip west on to Rt. 608 and Rt. 606

Farnham Baptist Church (1) This gable-roofed brick rectangular church was dedicated in 1856. The earlier wooden church building, erected about 1790, was used as a hospital during the small pox epidemic of 1855-56. Afterwards it was burned, and the present church was built across the road. In 1866, black members of the church were granted letters of dismissal and they established Mount Zion Baptist Church (6), one mile away in Downings. *Visible from the road. (Map A)*

Farnham Baptist Church (1)

Morattico Hall site (2) This 1½ story side-hall house with a small wing was torn down in the late 1920s, after erosion of the bank of the Rappahannock River had undermined its chimney end. Despite this loss, the interior of its one room has been preserved at the Winterthur Museum in Delaware. Given the fine finish of that room, it is unlikely that this had always been simply a one-room house with a loft. Rather, the room originally was most likely either a wing of a larger house from the 18th or early 19th century, or the remaining part of a central hall house of that period with a large room on either side of the hall, one of these rooms having been removed before the 1920s. *Site not visible from the road; privately owned. (Map A)*

Richmond County

Town of Warsaw

B

C

D

A

3

360

3

0 0.5 1   2   3   4
Miles

Edge Hill site (3) Edge Hill was built in 1770 for John Chinn. It possibly was designed by the renowned architect and master-builder William Buckland (1734-1774) (see Mount Airy (42)), who lived in Richmond County around this time. This large brick two-story five-bay house had a hip roof and interior end chimneys. It was torn down by the Chinn family in the 1930s and the bricks were used in buildings in the city of Richmond as well as in a descendant's house in Tappahannock across the river in Essex County. *Site is not visible from the road; privately owned. (Map A)*

Moraughtacund Indian village site (4) The name of this Indian group was anglicized to Morattico, hence Morattico Creek and the present village of Morattico (59) in Lancaster County, on the south side of Lancaster Creek. The Indian village here was visited by Capt. John Smith in mid-August 1608, on his way up the Rappahannock River on his second exploratory voyage, and again in late August during his return downstream. This was evidently one of several Moraughtacund towns—within what is today upper Lancaster and Richmond County—which may have included as many as 340 people, including 80 fighting men, at the time of Smith's visit. *Site is visible from the road; privately owned. (Map A)*

Indian Banks (5) Although a brick near the front door is incised with the date 1699, the house was probably built in the 1720s for Capt. William Glasscock, whose wife Esther Ball was a first cousin of George Washington's mother. The name of this property is derived from the Moraughtacund Indian village (4) that once existed in this immediate area.

Laid in Flemish bond with glazed headers, and with tall interior end chimneys with flared caps, the house is of particular interest as it is transitional between Jacobean and Georgian architecture. From the land

Indian Banks (5)

side the steep L-shaped hip roof appears medieval, but from the water approach the house looks distinctly Georgian with its symmetrical two-story five-bay façade. The scrolled soffit of the jack arch over the front entrance—a common feature in England—is said to be one of only two known in Virginia. Some of the original interior woodwork has survived. A 1976 one-story addition was designed to blend in with the earlier architecture. The property includes an 18th century frame outbuilding and an old cemetery. *VLR and NRHP. Visible from the road; privately owned. (Map A)*

Mount Zion Baptist Church (6)

Mount Zion Baptist Church (6) Established as a congregation in 1866 by black members of Farnham Baptist Church (1) who had requested letters of dismissal, the first church was built that very year. The present frame church with its simple steeple and tall Gothic Revival arched windows sits on a brick foundation, and was completed in 1890 after re-laying the cornerstone of the old church in the new building. Additions were added in the 20th century. An extensive cemetery lies behind the church and continues across the road. *Visible from the road. (Map A)*

Wilna (Chinn) (7) Joseph William Chinn of Oakley built Wilna in 1820. It is typical of Federal houses of the period, having a five-bay principal façade, a gable roof with interior brick chimneys at either end, and a center hall with double doors in both the front and the rear. The house is of brick construction with a separate 1½ story brick kitchen. The home commands a sweeping view of the Rappahannock River. The family cemetery is 100 yards west of the house. Family lore says that the house was named Wilna for the Lithuanian capital of Vilnius, out of sympathy for the Polish-Lithuanian struggle for freedom in the 1830s. *Not visible from the road; privately owned. (Map A)*

Wilna (Chinn) (7)

Northern Neck Industrial Academy site (8) This school was founded in 1898 by the Northern Neck Baptist Association, composed of African American Baptist churches in the Northern Neck area. The academy, housed in a large 2½ story frame structure with a high roof and cupola and with very tall windows to let in plenty of light, was built on a 100-acre tract near present-day Ivondale and opened its doors in 1901. It was the first high school for blacks in Richmond County, but also had students from Essex, King George, Lancaster, Northumberland and Westmoreland counties. Students from Richmond County came for the day, while those from the other counties often lived in on-site dormitories. With the opening of the public Richmond County High School for blacks in 1939, the academy was closed. The last building on this site burned in 1974. *Historical Marker J-99. Site is visible from road; privately owned. (Map A)*

Side trip west onto Rt. 642

Woodford (9) Woodford is a 1½ story three-bay brick house with a clipped gable roof, dating from the mid-18th century. It is an example of Virginia's transitional vernacular architecture, combining elements of a simple colonial cottage with the more formal Georgian style. The center hall is somewhat off-center because of the uneven sizes of the flanking rooms, which is a transitional feature. The presumed builder of the house was Billington McCarty, Jr. and it is thought that an old burial ground is on the property

Woodford (9)

Richmond County, Map A

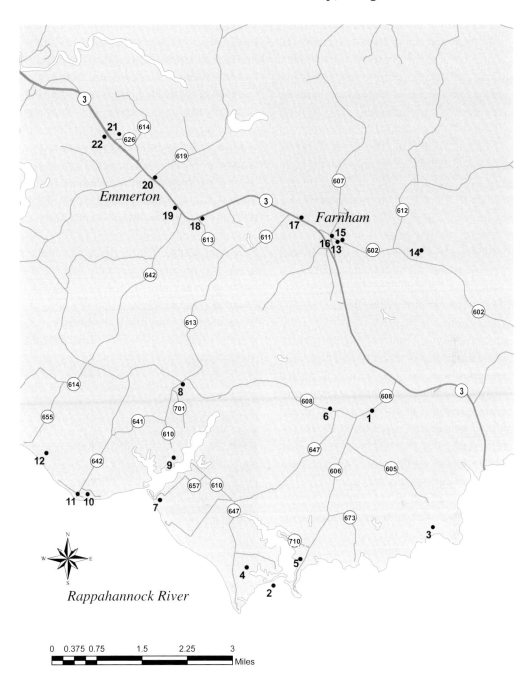

which contains the graves of the builder's heir, Col. William McCarty, and his wife Martha Hall Corbin. No archaeological survey has been done, but at least one and possibly two earlier houses existed here prior to construction of the present structure. *VLR and NRHP. Not visible from the road; privately owned. (Map A)*

Milden Hall (10) The present house was built in 1803, replacing the original home erected in the 18th century. In dry weather the outline of the original house may be seen. The two-story five-bay house is constructed of brick laid in Flemish bond, and has a raised English basement with exposed hand hewn chestnut beams. It is set back from the Rappahannock River behind an allée of pecan trees.

The home is named after the English birthplace of Samuel Peachey, who owned the property as early as 1664. His great-grandson, William Peachey, served as a captain under George Washington in the French and Indian War, was a colonel in the Continental Army during the Revolution, and after the War was elected to both the House of Delegates and the Senate in the Virginia General Assembly. The house was sold out of the Peachey family in 1824. *Not visible from the road; privately owned. (Map A)*

Milden Hall (10)

Sharps (11) Sharps is a Victorian waterfront village that grew up around Milden Hall plantation after the Civil War.

It is named for Dewitt Clinton Sharp, who developed shipping facilities here. In its prime it had hotels, stores, saloons, a crabhouse, an oyster house, schools, a bank and a post office. The village was called Milden until about 1890, and both names were used interchangeably until the early 20th century. Sharps Wharf was an important steamboat stop until the Downing Bridge (49) was built in 1927, linking the Northern Neck with Essex County and the rest of Virginia to the south.

Much of old Sharps still exists on Rt. 642, including on Front Street the L.E. Mumford Bank building (1910), the Downing Hotel, Milden Lodge, another hotel, the one-room schoolhouse (now a cottage) at the end of the street, Milden Presbyterian Church (1888), and the former school for black students (1930) which is on the way into Sharps. *(Map A)*

Sharps (11)

Riverdale (12) Riverdale farm on the Rappahannock River has been in the Barber family for over 250 years except for two decades in the mid-19th century. The oldest portion of the house dates to 1801 according to a dendrochronological study. It was added onto in 1832 and again in 1895, and the last addition was made in 1962. The main part of the present house is a two-story gable-roofed structure with interior end chimneys, to which a large screen porch has been added. Upon the repurchase of the property by the Barber family in 1874, the farm was divided, with the river frontage named Riverdale and the land side given the name of Tanglewood. Riverdale farm is the site of a family cemetery and was also the site of the old steamboat landing, Union Wharf. *Not visible from the road; private property. (Map A)*

Riverdale (12)

Continuing on Route 3 north towards Warsaw

Side trip east on to Cedar Grove Road (Rt. 602)

Farnham schools (13) From the mid- to late 19th to the early 20th century there were several schools in Farnham, all within a quarter mile of each other. Farnham Academy, a private school for boys, was begun in 1850. It closed for the duration of the Civil War, reopening in 1866. In this later period, the school was known locally as Williamson's School, after the name of its headmaster. Offering a full curriculum—including English literature, natural science, mathematics, Latin, Greek and German—it closed in 1890. A co-educational school, known as the Farnham Institute, was also open during much of this period. Somewhat later, a private school for girls, known as "Miss Addie's School" for Addie Veazy Payne, who taught there for many years, was opened. The schoolhouse later became part of a larger, private home. The Farnham Public

Addie Veazy Payne's School (13)

School was also erected here in the late 1800s. *All are visible from the road; private property. (Map A)*

Cedar Grove (14) Dr. Erasmus Derwin Booker purchased Cedar Grove in 1851 from Thomas Oldhams. It is a white two-story gable-roofed clapboard house built in the late 18th or early 19th century with an 1856 addition. The oldest part of the house is an L-plan with a spacious hall and a room on each floor. There are double doors on either end of the first floor hall. Dr. Booker was active as a local official and served as a medical officer during the Civil War. In 1863 his wife died as a consequence of a Union raid in the area.

The name Cedar Grove also appears in connection with the family of Dr. Nicholas Flood. While this house does not appear to fit the description of Dr. Flood's home, the property may have been at one time a part of Dr. Flood's estate. *Visible from the road; privately owned. (Map A)*

Cedar Grove (14)

The Cottage (15) The original part of the Cottage was built about 1830 on part of the Cedar Grove property, although its first owner is unknown. It was simply a 1½ story side-hall structure, which accounts for its name. The house was added on to over the years until by the 1870s it looked about as it does today: a two-story, three-bay frame house with a graceful front porch with filigreed columns. *Visible from the road; privately owned. (Map A)*

The Cottage (15)

Farnham Church, North Farnham Parish (16) The present church was built in 1737 in the shape of a Latin cross, with the brick above the water table laid in Flemish bond with glazed headers, and laid in English bond below. These exterior brick features are the only ones remaining from the recurring damage to which the 1737 structure was subject over the next 150 years. This building had replaced a church built in 1660 three miles west, closer to Farnham Creek.

After the Revolution and disestablishment of the Church of England, services continued to be held at the church, even after 1802 when the church furnishings and glebe lands had been sold at auction. The silver, a gift from Queen Anne, had been purchased by John Tayloe and given to St. John's Church in Washington, D.C., but it was later returned to Farnham Church in 1876.

During the War of 1812, a skirmish with the British was fought in 1814 on the church grounds and bullet holes are still visible in the transept. By 1838, the church had been restored and reconsecrated, but it was used as a stable by Union soldiers during 1863-65 and partially destroyed. Having once again been restored in 1871, a fire on Easter Monday in 1887 in the village of Farnham destroyed the roof and the interior of the church, although the furnishings were saved. Restoration began again, and by 1922 it was completed.

Although it has been conjectured that the original roof line of this church was similar to that of Christ Church (6) in Lancaster County, sketches in an 1841 letter written by a tutor of the Tayloe children of Mount Airy (42) reveal the roof line to have been as it is today. During its most recent period of restoration (ca. 1888 to 1922), the congregation worshipped at Emmanuel Church in Emmerton, a board-and-batten church in the Gothic Carpenter style, built in 1888. After Farnham Church was restored, Emmanuel Church was deconsecrated and torn down in the 1940s. North Farnham Parish still owns the property and cares for the cemetery at that site where at least one Confederate soldier is buried, and also a parrot, whose tombstone reads "Our Polly." *VLR and NRHP. Historical Marker J-77. Visible from the road. (Map A)*

Farnham Church, North Farnham Parish (16)

Linden Farm (17) Possibly the oldest extant house in Richmond County, Linden Farm is a rare example of a colonial vernacular farmhouse. This 1 ¹/₂ story frame dwelling was probably built for the Dew family about 1700, and originally was a side-hall one-room structure with a loft. It was enlarged to its present size in the second quarter of the 18th century, and it has remained virtually unchanged since that time. The house is flanked by two massive asymmetrically-placed chimneys, and much of the original beaded weatherboarding on the front portion of the house is nailed with hand-forged, rose-headed nails. Most of the original 18th century interior woodwork and a fireplace has survived. The staircase is an example of closed string Jacobean stairs, and the steps show the indentations of more than 250 years of footsteps. *VLR and NRHP. Visible from the road; privately owned. (Map A)*

Linden Farm (17)

Calvary Methodist Church (18) This is a frame church built in 1856. The steeple and vestibule were added in 1953 and a rear addition made in 1954. The front gable eave has a highly decorative cornice. The founding pastor, William Crocker, (1825-1901) is buried in the church cemetery. *Visible from the road. (Map A)*

Calvary Methodist Church (18)

Middleton House (19) The center block of this house probably dates from the early 19th century, with the wings believed to have been added by Dr. Benjamin Smith Middleton after the Civil War. The house is unusual in that the gable ends of the wings face forward. The porch columns appear to be Egyptian Revival style and are said to be made of concrete, not wood. Dr. Middleton was born in 1816 in Westmoreland County and after his marriage to Caroline Virginia Coffin in 1855 they lived in Emmerton where he practiced medicine. *Visible from the road; privately owned. Endangered. (Map A)*

Middleton House (19)

Lemoine-Griffith House (20) This two-story five-bay simple frame Victorian house was built by the Griffith family about 1880. Located in Emmerton, it stands out as not only the largest house in the village, but it is architecturally very unusual for its

Lemoine-Griffith House (20)

third story central tower. The house in the past has served as a hotel. The family graves once on the property have been moved to Farnham Church, North Farnham Parish. It was the home of the grandparents of W. Tayloe Murphy, a member of the House of Delegates from 1982 to 2000 and Virginia's Secretary of Natural Resources from 2002 to 2006. *Visible from the road; privately owned. (Map A)*

Pleasant View Farm (21) The original part of this house, a hall-and-parlor dwelling with mortised and tenoned hand-hewn timbers, probably dates to the mid-18th century. The original owner is unknown. A frame addition was built onto the west side of this house in the 19th century, and another addition was made in the 20th century. The present house has large exterior chimneys at either end. *Visible from the road; privately owned. (Map A)*

Elmore House site (22) The Elmore House, still standing at least as late as about 1940, was probably the best surviving example in Richmond County of a very early tobacco farmer's house, with two rooms on the first floor and a steep loft above. Today all that remains is a native sandstone chimney. The building is thought to have served as a small tavern until the late 1860s. It is the site of the Elmore family cemetery. *Site is not visible from the road; privately owned. (Map A)*

Walnut Lawn (23) The Garland family built this house between 1853 and 1856. Walnut Lawn is a large two-story three-bay frame house set on an English basement. Two large semi-interior chimneys at each gable end serve fireplaces in each of the four rooms on each floor. The bottom parts of the chimneys were built with their outer faces exposed in order to reduce the risk of fire. The center hall runs through to the rear of the house. The property contains two cemeteries, one a family graveyard. In the late 19th century a second Garland house, Greenwood, was built not far from Walnut Lawn with a similar floor plan, but with fully interior chimneys. *Visible from the road; privately owned. Endangered. (Map B and Map D)*

Walnut Lawn (23)

Pleasant View Farm (21)

Richmond County, Map B

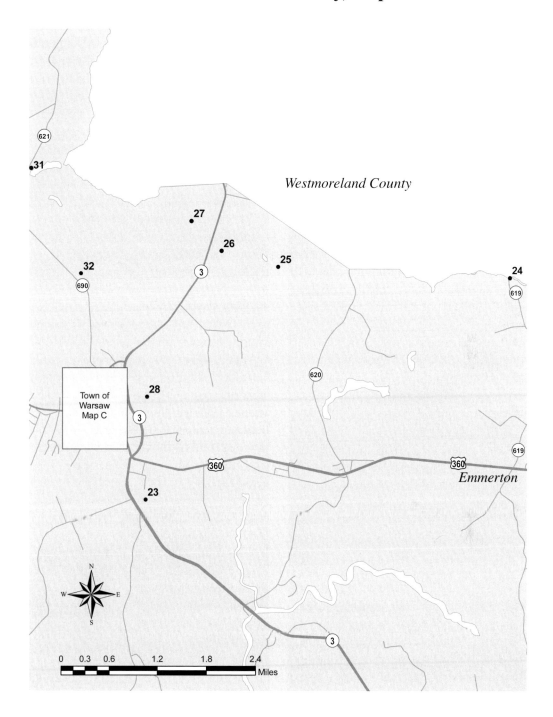

Continuing on Route 3 north and east around Warsaw

Purcell's Mill (24) This 19th century structure still stands, although not as a working mill, on the Richmond-Westmoreland County line. *Visible from Rt. 619; private property. (Map B)*

Purcell's Mill (24)

Bladensfield site (25) The original part of Bladensfield was built in the third quarter of the 18th century by Robert ("Councillor") Carter, of Nomini Hall (57) in Westmoreland County, for one of his sons-in-law. It evolved into a 2 ½ story gabled-roof frame house with dormers, which included an addition made in 1854 by the Rev. William N. Ward for the purposes of a seminary for girls. The house combined a Georgian plan with both Federal and Greek Revival features. Unfortunately the house burned in 1996. *Prior to its destruction, it had been on the VLR and NRHP since 1980. Site not visible from the road; privately owned. (Map B)*

Bladensfield site (25)

Hickory Thicket (26) This two-story frame gable-roof house was built in the mid-19th century, perhaps on the foundations of an earlier structure. A wing was added in 1895. It is a well-preserved example of a 19th-century tenant house. *Visible from the road; privately owned. (Map B and Map D)*

Hickory Thicket (26)

Plain View (27) Plain View is a striking early 19th-century Federal style house with an elegantly simple design not atypical of the early republic. *Visible from the road; privately owned. (Map B and Map D)*

Plain View (27)

Belle Ville (28) Major Moore Fauntleroy Brockenbrough built Belle Ville sometime between 1826 and 1830. This two-story five-bay Federal house atop a high English basement is laid in Flemish bond bricks made on the property, and the depression where the bricks were made is now a pond. The house stands at the end of an allée of locust trees. The original 18th-century frame house, which stood behind and to the left of the present home, was being used as servants' quarters when it burned in 1873. Prior to the Civil War and as late as 1870, Belle Ville was known for its gardens, which were terraced with an allée that led back to the barn. The property also contains several outbuildings, including an old law office off to the left of the main house as well as a schoolhouse built about the same time as the present house. Intended mainly for educating the children of the family and some neighboring children, the school was called the Warsaw Female Institute. Boys were educated there as well, including locally born Henry St. George Tucker (1874-1959), who became the presiding Bishop of the Episcopal Church of the United States. *Visible from the road; privately owned. (Map B and Map D)*

Belle Ville (28)

Rt. 690 to the northwest of Rt. 3

Menokin Baptist Church (29) Letters of dismissal were granted in 1837 by the Nomony Meeting House to create this church, which was completed in 1841. Three different styles of masonry were used in its construction. In 1868, letters of dismissal were granted to the former slaves who had attended the church, and they formed Clarksville Baptist Church several miles away. One Thomas Thomas, who belonged to William Tayloe, joined Menokin Baptist Church in 1864.

He later became known as Reverend Tom and was instrumental in founding the Clarksville Baptist Church. *Visible from the road. (Map D)*

Menokin Baptist Church (29)

Menokin (30) Commissioned by John Tayloe II of Mount Airy in 1769, Menokin and the 1,000 acres on which it stood was given as a wedding present by Tayloe to Francis Lightfoot Lee (of Stratford Hall (26) in Westmoreland County) and his daughter Rebecca Tayloe, upon its completion about 1775. Lee was a colonial statesman and one of two brothers to sign the Declaration of Independence the next year. The Lees lived at Menokin until their deaths in 1797.

The house, a two-story three-bay square structure, had stuccoed local sandstone walls that contrasted with the dark stone trim, giving it an unusual degree of formality for its size. The two brick chimneys stood high over a hip roof. The front entrance contained heavy pilasters topped by a delicate fanlight and an unusual keystone with floral carvings. Both the dining room and the master bed chamber featured Georgian woodwork and chimney pieces. The manor house was flanked by an office and kitchen dependencies. Terraced gardens provided a view to Cat Point Creek.

Over the years the house went into decline, and it was abandoned in the 1940s. Much of the interior woodwork was removed in the 1960s, however, for

Menokin (30)

safekeeping. After further deterioration, T. E. Omohundro gave the house, woodwork, and 500 acres of the original plantation to the Menokin Foundation in 1995, for the purpose of architectural conservation and archaeological study. Currently, the site serves to inform the public about building practices in the 18th century. A restored chimney piece and other samples of the original woodwork, architectural drawings, and photographs are displayed at Menokin in the Martin Kirwan King Conservation and Visitors Center. *Menokin has been designated a National Historic Landmark and is open to the public. VLR and NRHP, and BHR easement. Located off of Rt. 690 four miles northwest of Rt. 3. (Map D)*

Connellee's Mill (31) This is one of only a very few water-powered grist mills still standing in the Northern Neck region. It was operated by the Settle family from 1765 until 1915, when it was sold to John Connellee. It remained in operation until about 1942. *Not visible from the road; privately owned. (Map B and Map D)*

Cloverdale Farm (32) The original part of Cloverdale Farm is a two-story three-bay side-hall Federal style frame house with a gable roof and one exterior end chimney. The house was built ca. 1800-1825 but its original owner is unknown. The foundation is local sandstone and the original part of the house consists of four rooms. Additions to the back and

one side were added in 1992 and in 2000-2001. The summer kitchen and smokehouse are believed to have been built at the same time as the main house. *Visible from the road; privately owned. (Map B and Map D)*

Cloverdale Farm (32)

Back to Route 360 and through Warsaw

(All sites visible from the street unless otherwise indicated.)

St. John's Church, Lunenburg Parish (33) Saint John's Church was built in 1835 to replace the earlier Lunenburg Lower Parish church erected in 1732 and abandoned after the Revolution. St. John's exemplifies the resuscitation of the Episcopal Church in Virginia under the leadership of the Rt. Rev. Richard Channing Moore, elected Bishop in 1814. He inspired such men as the Rev. George Washington Nelson who, as their rector, led the rebuilding of North Farnham and Lunenburg parishes in Richmond County and Cople Parish in Westmoreland County.

The church is of brick construction, laid in Flemish bond. It has an unusual arcade with its three arches supported by two unplastered brick columns. The doors are Gothic Revival. Inside, the old pews and communion rail have been replaced, and a stained glass window has been

St. John's Church (33)

placed in the wall over the altar.

St. John's of Lunenburg Parish and Farnham Church, North Farnham Parish have shared a rector for over one hundred years, and today the two churches also share the silver communion service given to Farnham Church in the 18th century. *(Map C)*

Jones Monument (34) The people of the Philippines commissioned this bronze and marble monument over the grave of U.S. Congressman William Atkinson Jones (1849-1918) in St. John's churchyard. The monument honors his role in passing legislation that ultimately led to national independence for the Philippines. Jones, who served in Congress from 1891 to 1918, was a native of Richmond County. The monument, erected in 1924, was created by Mariano Benilliure, the most famous Spanish sculptor at that time. *(Map C)*

Jones Monument (34)

The Old Jail (35) Although built in 1872, the old Richmond County Jail was characteristic of many buildings constructed before the Civil War, with its hip roof and interior chimneys. Its walls are laid in five-course American bond, and there are four courses of corbelling at the eaves. The jail has a small "hanging chamber" on the second floor, which apparently was used only once. The building served as the county jail well into the 20th century. *It is presently the home of the Richmond County Museum and is open to the public. (Map C)*

The Old Jail (35)

Richmond County Courthouse (36) This building in the center of Warsaw is said to be the oldest courthouse in continuous use in Virginia, its construction in 1748 having been supervised by Landon Carter of Sabine Hall (41). It is a one-story brick Palladian structure which once had open porticoes on either side to allow

Richmond County Courthouse (36)

Richmond County, Map C
Town of Warsaw

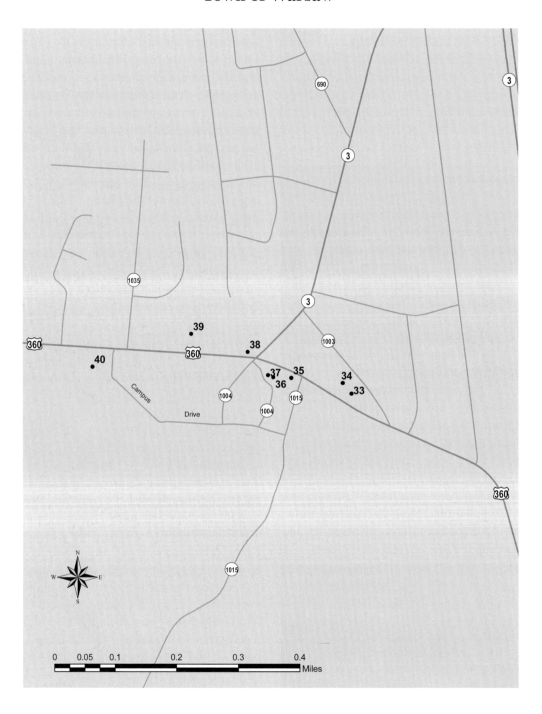

for the stabling of horses and respite from inclement weather. These porticoes have been enclosed with windows since 1877, when Baltimore architect T. Buckler Ghequiere directed an extensive remodeling of the building. *VLR and NRHP.*

The town of Warsaw was originally called Richmond Court House. In 1831, the town was renamed Warsaw out of support for the 1830-31 Polish uprising for freedom which was put down by Imperial Russia. *(Map C)*

Clerk's Office (37) Although the Richmond County Clerk's Office would appear to date from the same period as the courthouse, it was not built until 1816. The building's foundation is of roughly cut local brown sandstone laid in oyster shell mortar. Above the stone, the construction is of brick covered with whitewashed plaster. The Clerk's Office has a high loft with two narrow four-over-four windows in the west end and a door in the east gable. The external doors are double batten with two panels each, and the windows are six-over-six. This structure, which is presently used as an attorney's office, is part of the Richmond County Courthouse complex in the center of Warsaw. *(Map C)*

Clerk's Office (37)

The Saddlery (38) This building carries this name because it is known to have been used as a saddlery in the 19th century. More recently, the building housed at different times a dentist's office, an attorney's

office and a real estate office. Built in the mid-19th century, the Saddlery is unusual for its very high basement, rising six feet above ground level, and its different styles of brick work. The gable end towards the street and the side towards the courthouse are laid in Flemish bond, while the bricks on the other two sides are laid in irregular American bond. *Privately owned. (Map C)*

The Saddlery (38)

Jones House (39) The Jones House is a three-story Victorian-era house built by U. S. Congressman William Atkinson Jones and his wife, Claude Douglas Motley, in 1887. This is the second home to be built on the property, the first having been burned during the Civil War. Congressman Jones served as Chairman of the Insular Affairs Committee in the early 1900s and is best known for authoring the Jones Act of 1916, which provided for the independence of the Philippines (see Jones Monument (34)).

The house sits on four acres in the heart of Warsaw, with the yard bordered by

Jones House (39)

original wrought iron fencing. A columned entranceway leads to the front door. A second floor French door with unusual sidelights, and third floor fanlights, add to the distinctive look of the house. A gazebo in the side yard covers a thirty-foot deep icehouse. *Privately owned. (Map C)*

Chinn House (40) This Colonial Revival house was built in 1908 for Justice Joseph W. Chinn and his wife Sarah Fairfax Douglas, on property belonging to her parents. Justice Chinn—also serving as Commonwealth's Attorney for Richmond County and later as a Virginia Supreme Court Justice—and Mrs. Chinn were active in the political, economic and educational life of the Northern Neck.

The house features classical porticoes, located on the north, east and south facades. Leaded sidelights flank the front hall door. The first floor contains five fireplaces with oak mantels and overmantel treatment. The parlor has a cylindrical bow window with curved glass, and the carved oak staircase contains all original newels, handrails, balusters, and a paneled stair seat. In 1969, the house and its immediate grounds were donated to the Commonwealth of Virginia in the memory of Justice Chinn and Mrs. Chinn by their family. From these roots came the Warsaw Campus of the Rappahannock Community College, and the Chinn House now houses some administrative offices. *(Map C)*

Chinn House (40)

Sabine Hall (41) Considered one of the finest extant Georgian mansions in the United States, Sabine Hall was built about 1738 by Landon Carter (1710-1778), the fourth son of Robert "King " Carter of Corotoman (5) and the builder of Christ Church (6) in Lancaster County. Originally a classic Georgian brick structure, the mansion reflects alterations by both the builder and later generations. In 1764, the south wing was built as a covered passage to the kitchen. The Roman Style portico or "piazza" on the river side of the house was added by Landon Carter and documented in a 1797 insurance policy. The enormous paneled entrance hall, which runs through the house, is one of the country's finest colonial rooms.

In the 1820s, influenced by the new Classical Revival architecture, Landon Carter's great-grandson Robert Wormeley Carter II lowered the roof, added a large portico on the land side and a classical pediment on the river side, and added

Sabine Hall (41)

several classical architectural elements to the interior. He also painted the exterior of the house white. The north wing was added in 1929 by Armistead Wellford when the home became a two family dwelling. Sabine Hall is situated on a ridge of the Rappahannock River with six terraces sloping toward the water. The garden retains its original 18th century design. The property continues to be owned by descendants of Landon Carter. *Sabine Hall has been designated a National Historic*

Landmark. VLR and NRHP, and BHR easements. Not visible from the road; privately owned. (Map D)

Mount Airy (42) Acclaimed as one of the most beautiful Palladian style houses in the United States, Mount Airy was begun by John Tayloe II in 1753 on land the Tayloe family had acquired in 1682. The entire architectural plan, completed in ten years, included a main two-story house connected to symmetrical dependencies on either side by curved passageways, a formal forecourt facing a deer park, and terraced gardens. Although cautioned about using soft local sandstone, Tayloe chose to build Mount Airy of local brown sandstone, three feet thick and quarried on the farm. The house is trimmed with contrasting buff sandstone quarried from Aquia Creek north of Fredericksburg.

A recessed loggia with four Doric columns leads to the front door which is flanked by floor-to-ceiling windows. The architect and master builder William Buckland, who had moved to Richmond County, was hired to complete the house's interior in 1762. His work, however, was destroyed when the house burned in 1844. The interior was then rebuilt in a plain Greek Revival style. Several outbuildings and one wall of the orangery remain, as does the 18th century stable which housed many thoroughbreds in colonial days. The Tayloes were a founding family of American horse racing.

Francis Lightfoot Lee, a signer of the Declaration of Independence and his wife Rebecca Tayloe Lee, for whom Menokin (30) was built by her father, are buried in the Tayloe family cemetery here at Mount Airy. The property remains in the Tayloe family. *Mount Airy has been designated a National Historic Landmark. VLR and NRHP, and BHR easement. Visible from the road; privately owned. (Map D)*

Mount Airy (42)

Rt. 360 Corridor west of Warsaw

Side trip on Newland Road (Rt. 624) and other roads to the north

Chestnut Hill (43) This property was patented in 1673 by Thomas Beale and remained in the Beale family until about 1846. The original part of this house, sitting atop an English basement, dates to 1820 with some doors and woodwork thought to derive from an earlier dwelling. The house was enlarged ca. 1850 and about 1900 it was raised to two stories. Col. Thomas Beale's flat and weathered tombstone, from 1679, was moved from Chestnut Hill to Menokin Baptist Church and portrays the earliest extant example of a coat of arms used in Richmond County. *Visible from the road; privately owned. Endangered. (Map D)*

Chestnut Hill (43)

Richmond County, Map D

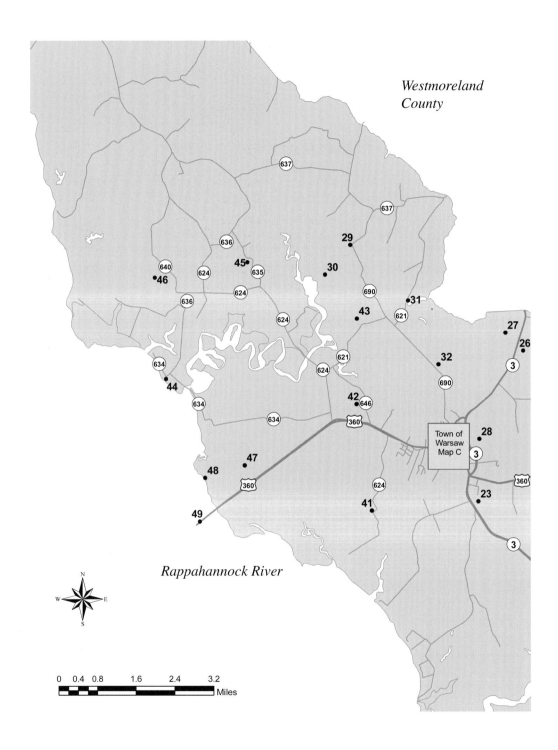

Westmoreland County

637

637

29

636

30

45
635
640
624
46
624

690
31
43
621

27
26
3

621
624
634
32
690
44
634
42
646
634
360
28
3
Town of Warsaw Map C
47
624
360
48
23
360
41
49
3

Rappahannock River

N
W   E
S

0   0.4   0.8   1.6   2.4   3.2

Miles

Naylor's Hole site (44)   William Fauntleroy (1713-1793), a Richmond County justice and militia officer, and member of the Virginia House of Burgesses (1740-1749), built this house in 1737 shortly after his marriage to Margaret Murdock. The early Georgian home dated from about the same time as Sabine Hall and they shared many features. It had twelve rooms and three halls. The abundance of halls was due to Margaret (Peggy) Fauntleroy's fondness for dancing, according to a letter written by her great-granddaughter. The house was torn down in the 1890s, but a drawing survives.

In 1927, Col. Powell C. Fauntleroy, a descendant, had a pyramid-shaped monument erected using bricks from the ruins of the house. It held a bronze tablet honoring Moore Fauntleroy (d. 1663/64), the immigrant and progenitor of the Fauntleroy family in Virginia and one of the first settlers, about 1650, in what is now Richmond County. The monument was torn down in 1943 and the bronze tablet was given to the war effort; all that remains is its concrete base. *Site is visible at Naylor's Beach. (Map D)*

Grove Mount (45)   Grove Mount is a fine example of a Georgian plantation home built between 1780 and 1800 by Robert "Councillor" Carter, of Nomini Hall (57) in Westmoreland County, for his daughter Priscilla Carter and her husband Robert Mitchell IV. A two-story five-bay house constructed of frame and brick nogging with a hip roof and tall interior chimneys, atop a full cellar and foundations laid in English bond, it remains basically unchanged since it was built. The original dairy stands to the west of the house.

With a few exceptions, the interior woodwork is original. The staircase is similar to that at nearby Menokin (30). The formal parlor has twin alcoves and cupboards, while the dining room contains twin closets flanking a fully-paneled chimney breast. In the 1950s, a kitchen was added, and the orangery was built in 1988. Sited on a high ridge, Grove Mount offers broad views of the Rappahannock River valley. *VLR and NRHP, and BHR easement. Visible from the road; privately owned. (Map D)*

Grove Mount (45)

Wilna (Mitchell) (46) This is a $2\frac{1}{2}$ story three-bay frame house with a gable roof and exterior end chimneys with a raised basement. The front entrance is covered by a two-story portico. The main house is thought to have been built by Carter Mitchell between 1800 and 1820. The unusual side entrance with its columned porch belies a carefully proportioned and detailed interior. All the mantels incorporate Federal details, and the flooring throughout is walnut. An outbuilding on the property is believed to have been the old kitchen. *Not visible from the road; owned by the Rappahannock River National Wildlife Refuge. (Map D)*

Wilna (Mitchell) (46)

Back to Route 360 and west
to Essex County

Island Farm (47) The last farmhouse seen upon leaving Richmond County by way of Rt. 360 and the Downing Bridge is Island Farm, an early 19th-century $2^{1}/_{2}$ story frame side-hall entrance dwelling. This property was once part of the extensive Fauntleroy holdings and in the 18th century was known simply as "The Island," as it is surrounded by marsh. *Visible from the road; privately owned. Endangered. (Map D)*

Island Farm (47)

Zack Johnson's House (48) This two-story house, standing at the edge of the Rappahannock River close to where the old ferry from Tappahannock used to land in Richmond County, was built from material salvaged from the *Caponka*, a decommissioned World War I cargo ship. Plumard J. Derieux had purchased this ship and had it brought up to Tappahan-

nock where it ran aground on a sandbar and later burned. The present wooden structure, which includes the ship's pilot house, is locally known as Zack Johnson's house, after the former ferryman who is said to have continued to live on this spot, hunting and trapping, long after construction of the Downing Bridge (49)—from which, incidentally, the house can be seen upriver. *Visible from the road; privately owned. Endangered. (Map D)*

Downing Bridge (49) The earliest known regular ferry to connect the Northern Neck peninsula with the west side of the Rappahannock River at Tappahannock operated from 1659 to 1769. When the Downing Bridge, with a drawbridge in the middle, was erected in 1927, it ended more than $2^{1}/_{2}$ centuries of ferry service. Moreover, until 1927, the Northern Neck had been largely tied in with the economy of Baltimore through the numerous steamboats that plied the waters of the Chesapeake Bay and its tributaries. With the opening of this first bridge to the Northern Neck—named for state senator Thomas J. Downing (see Edgely (46) in Lancaster County) who had introduced legislation for its construction—and the paving of Route 360, travel to the southern part of Virginia became much quicker and easier. Now cars and trucks largely replaced water traffic and Richmond replaced Baltimore as the main commercial connection. The present bridge replaced the original drawbridge in 1963. *(Map D)*

Zack Johnson's House (48)

Selected Bibliography

Arnest, H. Lee III. "Andrea Palladio, the Venetian High Renaissance and the Northern Neck of Virginia," *Northern Neck of Virginia Magazine*, 34 (1974): 2898-2911.

Arnold, Scott David. *A Guidebook to Virginia's Historical Markers.* Charlottesville: University of Virginia Press, 2007.

Booker, Lucille. *North Farnham Parish: 1683-1991.* Lottsburg, Va.: Lottsburg Printing, 1991.

Delano, Frank. *Richmond County Historic Sites Survey Papers.* Warsaw, Va.: Richmond County Museum archives, 1992.

Delano, Robert Barnes. "Northern Neck Farming in Historical Perspective," *Northern Neck of Virginia Magazine* 50 (2000): 5941-5946.

Harper, Robert R. *Richmond County Virginia, 1692-1992: A Tricentennial Portrait.* Alexandria, Va.: O'Donnell Publications, 1992.

Kinsley, Ardyce and Don Kinsley. *Passage to Sharps: From Plantation to Village.* Sharps, Va.: Gazebo Books, 1996.

Kohr, Andrew D. "Case Study: The Menokin Terraces," Section III of *A Terrace Typology: A Systematic Approach to the Study of Historic Terraces during the Eighteenth Century in the Mid-Atlantic Region of the United States.* Muncie, Ind.: Masters Thesis, College of Architecture and Planning, Ball State University, 2005.

Lorenz, Otto. "William McKay, Rector of North Farnham Parish in Richmond County, 1744-1775," *Northern Neck of Virginia Magazine* 46 (1996): 5398-5409.

Loth, Calder. *The Virginia Landmarks Register.* Charlottesville: University Press of Virginia, Fourth Edition, 1999.

Lounsbury, Carl R. *An Illustrated Glossary of Early Southern Architecture and Landscape.* Charlottesville: University Press of Virginia, 1994.

McClure, Phyllis. "Rosenwald Schools in the Northern Neck," *Virginia Magazine of History and Biography* 113 (2), 2005: 114-145.

Pearson, Virginia Drewry McG. and Joseph Belfield, M. D. "Doctors of Yesteryear," *Northern Neck of Virginia Magazine* 24 (1974): 2619-2622.

"People, Places and Stories of Farnham as Recorded by the Seventh Grade Students of Miss Essie Harrison's 1935-1936 Classes," *Northern Neck of Virginia Magazine* 52 (2002): 6214-6226.

Pitts, Buren, Louis Courtney III and Virginia Clapp. "The Princely Tomato: Down Memory Lane," *Northern Neck of Virginia Magazine* 50 (2000): 5947-5952.

Rountree, Helen C., Wayne E. Clark and Kent Mountford. *John Smith's Chesapeake Voyages, 1607-1609.* Charlottesville: University of Virginia Press, 2007.

Ryland, Elizabeth Lowell, ed. *Richmond County: A Review Commemorating the Bicentennial.* Richmond: Whittet and Shepperson, 1976.

Semsch, Suzanne Hadfield. "Francis Lightfoot Lee: A Brief Political Sketch," *Northern Neck of Virginia Magazine* 26 (1976): 2574-2881.

Waterman, Thomas T. "Architectural Notes on the Room from Morattico Hall, Lancaster County, Virginia." Winterthur, Del.: Winterthur Museum Archives, October, 1940.

Wells, Camille. "Field Methods in Architectural History: Documenting Old Buildings." Fredericksburg: Mary Washington College, Department of Historic Preservation, 1991.

Chapter 8
Essex

Essex County was formally established in 1692, out of that part of (Old) Rappahannock County which was south of the Rappahannock River. (Old Rappahannock County had been formed in 1656 out of the upriver sections of Lancaster County, which in turn had been formed from Northumberland and York counties in 1651.) Essex County borders the Rappahannock River to its northeast. Its county seat has been in Tappahannock since 1728.

The county seat and old port town of Tappahannock, earlier known as Hobb's Hole, has been listed on the Virginia Landmarks Register and the National Register of Historic Places as an historic district.

Essex County encompasses 285.9 square miles, of which 257.8 square miles are land. It is the largest county in this six-county region, in terms of both land and total area. The population of the county in 1790 was 9,122, with 40 percent of the population being free. By 1940, the county's population had fallen to 7,006, but it had increased to 9,989 by the year 2000. It is the least densely populated of the six counties.

Historic Sites in Essex County

Route 17 south from Caroline County

Port Micou (1) An antebellum granary and a former overseer's house still survive from what was once a bustling tobacco and later grain wharf and complex located right on the Rappahannock River. The first known house here was built by Paul Micou, a French Huguenot immigrant who had established a thriving tobacco business and public warehouse here by the early 18th century. His daughter Mary married Joshua Fry, the commander of the

Port Micou (1a)

Port Micou Granary (1b)

Essex County

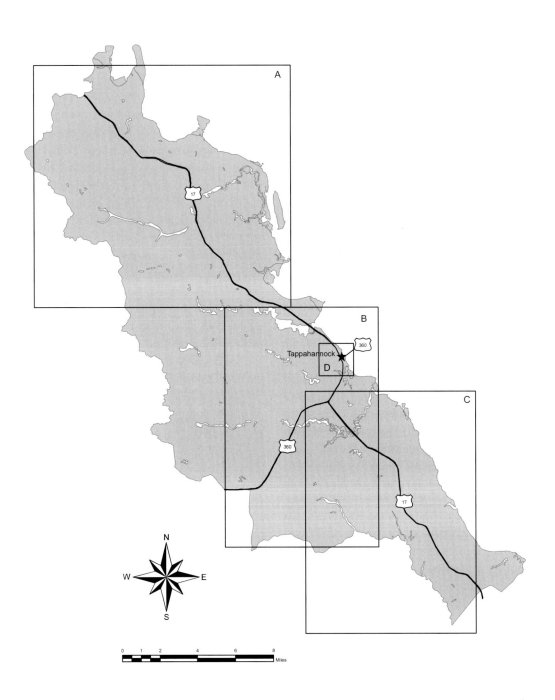

Virginia forces at the outset of the French and Indian War and a prominent surveyor, who along with Peter Jefferson, father of the president, composed the famous Fry-Jefferson map of Virginia in 1751.

By the first half of the 19th century, the wharf and land had passed into the hands of the Waring family, and then to the Baylors (see Kinloch (5)), and it was at this time that the extant granary and overseer's house were built. The large two-story granary-barn is noteworthy for such features as doors composed of three-layer batten boards. The one-story frame overseer's house has a high English basement and a single chimney. *VLR and NRHP. Not visible from the road; privately owned.* (Map A)

Vauter's Episcopal Church (2) This church is now thought to have been erected about 1719, with the addition making it a cruciform completed in 1731. It was the principal church of St. Anne's Parish. As with many colonial churches, it is of simple cruciform configuration. The exterior walls are of Flemish bond with glazed headers, rubbed-brick corners, gauged-brick arches and molded-and-gauged pedimented doorways. The original communion silver service, which is still in use, was donated by the Crown.

Following the Revolutionary War and disestablishment of the Church of England, Vauter's lacked an active congregation for some time. It was later saved from outright destruction, however, by parishioner Muscoe Garnett of nearby

Vauter's Episcopal Church (2)

Elmwood, who claimed as his own the land on which the church stands. The church was remodeled in 1827 upon the resumption of regular services. It escaped damage during the Civil War. *VLR and NRHP. Historical Marker N-23. Visible from the road. (Map A)*

Mt. Pleasant Barns (3) These are all that remain of a plantation complex developed in the course of the 18th century by James Garnett Sr. and which became the ancestral home of the Essex County family by this name (also see Elmwood (7)). The manor house and most of the outbuildings were destroyed during the Civil War, but two wooden barns and three log-sided corncribs remain intact and date from the early 19th century or possibly earlier. One of the barns is 18-by-33 feet, the other is 18-by-38 feet. *Not visible from the road; privately owned. (Map A)*

Mt. Pleasant Barns (3)

Rose Mount (4) This $2^1/_2$ story single-pile home, constructed atop a high English basement, was built in the second half of the 18th century by William Gray. It is situated on the top of a hill, and looms above the surrounding countryside. Sometime after coming into the Sale family in 1848, the brick walls were covered with cement. Its two end chimneys serve six fireplaces. A one-story addition, with its own chimney, continues the style of the original house. Also still standing on this property is a two-level barn, measuring 18-by-45 feet, which dates to the first half of the 19th century or possibly even earlier. It may be the oldest surviving barn in Essex County. The door and windows suggest it may have been used at one time as a dwelling, perhaps a tenant house. *Visible from the road; privately owned. (Map A)*

Rose Mount (4a)

Rose Mount Barn (4b)

Kinloch site (5) This manor house, which burned in 1947, was the seat of the Baylor family, whose name is closely associated with many old sites in upper Essex County. Richard Baylor Sr., who is said to have owned the greatest number of slaves in Virginia on the eve of the Civil War, built this imposing Greek Revival house near Supply in the 1840s. Three stories over an English basement, the house also had an observation deck on top from which one could see into Caroline, King George and Westmoreland counties, as well as surrounding Essex County.

The mansion had twenty rooms, 18 of which had fireplaces served by four chimneys, one at each corner of the house. The mantels and hearths were marble, four having been imported from Italy. The façade of the house had a porch with a balcony on the second floor, supported by four Ionic columns. The grounds around the house were said to be beautifully landscaped. After the 1947 fire, the Baylor family graves were moved to Vauter's Church (2). *Site not visible from the road; privately owned. (Map A)*

Kinloch site (5)

Wheatland & Saunders' Wharf (6) Built on the site of earlier homes right on the Rappahannock River, Wheatland was constructed during 1849-51 by John Saunders, a merchant and planter. Combining both Federal and Greek Revival styles, this large two-story frame house sits on an English basement, and has two-story porticos on both its front and the river facades. The house has a center-hall plan on all three floors, with each hall entering on to two rooms on each side. A one-story kitchen wing is thought to have survived from an earlier house on this site. Wheatland has remained in the extended family for over 150 years.

During the Civil War, a Union gunboat commander is said to have ordered everyone out of the house before shelling it, but the family refused to leave and the gunboat shelled the granary instead, although it survived until burning to the ground in the 1950s.

The property includes Saunders' Wharf, which is said to be the best preserved steamboat wharf on either the Rappahannock or lower Potomac rivers. The wharf, which at 70-by-40 feet was quite large, helped the Saunders family through the difficult Reconstruction years and was visited by steamboat packets as late as 1937. *VLR and NRHP, and BHR easement. Not visible from the road; privately owned. (Map A)*

Wheatland (6a)

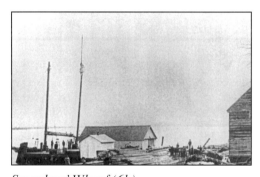

Saunders' Wharf (6b)

Elmwood (7) Built by Muscoe Garnett Sr. in 1774, this 100-foot long single-pile brick manor house has remained in the Garnett family to this day. Built in the mid-Georgian style, the austere formality of the façade contrasts with the highly ornamented interior woodwork, much of which is original. Most of the house is laid in Flemish bond, with a molded water table and a rubbed brick belt course. The two interior chimneys serve ten fireplaces. Many of the Italianate changes introduced by a remodeling of the house in

1852 were reversed by renovations in the late 20th century.

Included on the Elmwood property are the Garnett family graveyard, and an overseer's house built in 1849 and now used as a tenant house. Mary Picton Stevens Garnett, the New Jersey-born widow of the Confederate legislator Muscoe Russell Hunter Garnett Sr., reluctantly left Elmwood in 1864 after her influential father arranged for a Union gunboat to escort her to safety. *VLR and NRHP, and BHR easement. Barely visible from the road; privately owned. (Map A)*

Elmwood (7)

Brooke's Bank (8) Completed by the widow Sarah Taliaferro Brooke about 1751, this classic Georgian style house is laid in fine brickwork. The unusual diamond patterning formed by the glazed headers on the towering chimneys is thought to reflect the Brooke family's beliefs as to how to protect themselves from evil spirits.

The house sits only a hundred yards back from the Rappahannock River, and

Brooke's Bank (8)

in the 18th century was the center of bustling activity connected with the tobacco trade. Sarah Brooke is said to have maintained an informal ordinary here, and it was a favorite stop for the Rev. Robert Rose of St. Anne's Parish, who lived a bit down river at the Glebe (9).

After falling into considerable disrepair in the late 19th and early 20th centuries, Brooke's Bank has undergone a series of restorations since the 1930s. *VLR and NRHP, and BHR easement. Not visible from the road; privately owned. (Map A)*

St. Anne's Parish Glebe (9) Known as Cloverfield after it became a private residence following disestablishment of the Church of England following the Revolutionary War, this glebe house is one of the finest and oldest glebe houses in Virginia. The two-story, single-pile Georgian style house, laid in Flemish bond brickwork, may have been built about 1731, not long after nearby Vauter's Church (2) which has similar brickwork. The Rev. Robert Rose was the first occupant of this house.

Although the Glebe has periodically been open to the elements in recent decades, some of the fine interior woodwork survives. *VLR and NRHP. Visible from the road; privately owned. Endangered. (Map A)*

St. Anne's Parish Glebe (9)

Edenetta (10) Built by Robert Payne Waring Jr. about 1828, this 2$\frac{1}{2}$ story mansion was built over a high English

Edenetta (10)

basement. Waring was one of the largest landowners in Essex County in his time, and both he and his wife, Lucy Latané Waring, came from among the oldest and most prominent Essex families. Their daughter married a Baylor, (see Kinloch (5)) and the house remained in the Baylor family for well over a century.

The principal façade of the house contains a very large two-story portico with massive Tuscan columns. The brick 30-inch walls are laid in Flemish bond, but the house was painted white years ago. The chimneys on either side of the house each serve three fireplaces. The house underwent major restoration beginning in the 1980s. Two very old outbuildings survive: a brick smokehouse and a two-story brick structure that once served as an exterior kitchen and servants' quarters. *Not visible from the road; privately owned. (Map A)*

Bloomsbury (11) The original house on this site was built before 1793 by John Spindle. After a fire partially destroyed the home about 1850, it was rebuilt by his descendants into a 2$\frac{1}{2}$ story house

Bloomsbury (11)

Essex County, Map A

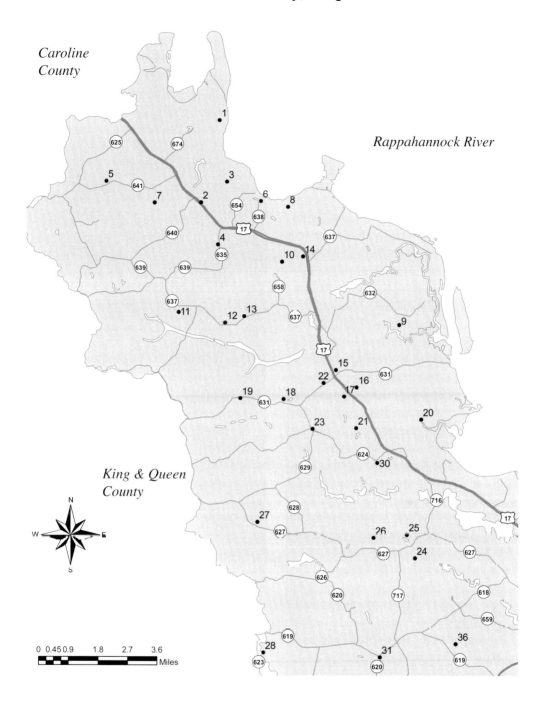

Caroline
County

Rappahannock River

King & Queen
County

with a large hall and eight fireplaces. The house remained in the Spindle family until the 1990s.

The property contained a gristmill, known as Spindle's Mill, which supplied meal and grain-feed to both the Revolutionary and Confederate armies. It also included a store and a blacksmith operation. The mill was abandoned in the 1930s, and it collapsed during a hurricane in the 1950s. *Not visible from the road; privately owned. (Map A)*

Oakalona (12) This two-story center-hall brick home atop an English basement was built by John G. Bentley over a ten-year period in the 1830s and 1840s. The house has four chimneys, two at each end of the house, and large porches adorn both the front and back facades. The home has belonged to the Taliaferro family for more than a century. *Visible from the road; privately owned. (Map A)*

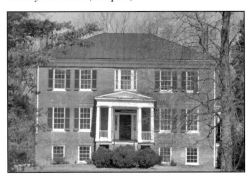

Oakalona (12)

Epping Forest (13) The two-story frame house with an English basement was built in 1849 by Benjamin Rice Baird, and is the third home to be built on this ancestral property. Notable are the ten-light windows on the front and the rear of the house, which extend practically from the floor to the ceiling. The downstairs doors are of commensurate height, inside as well as out. The property includes a cemetery with the graves of several generations of Rouzies and Bairds.

Captain E. R. Baird served in the Confederate army on the staff of General George Pickett, best known for the ill-fated Pickett's charge on the last day of Gettysburg. Just after the end of the Civil War, former Confederate Secretary of State R. M. T. Hunter of Fonthill (18) was captured at Epping Forest while having supper, when the house was surrounded by Union troops. *Visible from the road; privately owned. (Map A)*

Epping Forest (13)

Glencairn (14) The original section of this 1½ story frame house is believed to date from about 1730, when a one-room house was built by Col. Thomas Waring. The longer east side of the house was added in the fourth quarter of the 18th century, and the long rear porch was added at that time. The shed dormers are believed to date from the mid-19th century.

The house has an English basement and the roof is made of wood shingles.

Glencairn (14)

The chimneys at each end of the house are laid in Flemish bond and each serves three fireplaces. The interior contains some interesting woodwork. A two-story brick kitchen stood on the property before its bricks were used for renovation of the main house. *VLR and NRHP. Visible from the road; privately owned. (Map A)*

St. Matthew's Episcopal Church (15) This church, built between 1860 and 1865, belonged to St. Anne's Parish (see the Glebe (9)). It replaced a nearby colonial Church of England structure known as "Sale's." St. Matthew's was decommissioned in 1970, and the building thereafter was known as "The Old Church Store." *VLR and NRHP. Not visible from the road; privately owned as a store. (Map A)*

St. Matthew's Episcopal Church (15)

Poverty Ridge (16) Once known as the Rennolds Place, this 1½ story single-pile house was probably erected prior to 1827 by James Cox or a member of the Garnett family. Most of its English basement is above ground, so the house has the appearance of a 2½ story structure. Its façade is laid in Flemish bond brickwork, while the other three sides are in American bond. The large chimneys at either end each serve three fireplaces, and ten dormer windows help light the top floor. *Not visible from the road; privately owned. (Map A)*

Linden (17) This three-bay side-hall plan Federal style brick house was

Poverty Ridge (16)

completed ca. 1825 for Lewis Brown, who had inherited the property and probably an earlier house on that site. The house is three stories on an English basement, most of the brickwork being Flemish bond. The two porches, on the east and north sides, are believed to be original to the house. The house underwent considerable renovation and additions in the 1990s, in a style broadly consistent with that of the original house. The frame barn on the property, with wooden peg construction and a sandstone foundation, is thought to have been built in the mid-19th century. *VLR and NRHP. Visible from the road; privately owned. (Map A)*

Linden (17)

Fonthill (18) Built in 1832 by Robert Mercer Taliaferro Hunter Sr. (1809-1887), this two-story house is sided with brick nogging covered with clapboards. The house has a basement and two wings, and its chimneys at either end of

Fonthill (18)

the main five-bay house serve six fire-places. An early surviving outbuilding on the grounds has been used as an office, school house and bachelor's quarters.

Hunter was Speaker of the U. S. House of Representatives from 1841-43, and a U.S. Senator from 1847 until the outbreak of the Civil War. He served as the Secretary of State of the Confederacy during 1861-62, and was a member of the peace commission that met with Union representatives near Fort Monroe in February 1865. After the war, Hunter served as Treasurer of Virginia from 1874 to 1880.

During the Civil War, Union troops raided Fonthill in 1863 and again in 1865, causing much destruction. The house continues to be owned by descendants of R. M. T. Hunter. *Historical Marker N-20. Not visible from the road; privately owned. (Map A)*

Smithfield (19) The original house on this site was built by John Lee, born in Maryland but a great-grandson of Richard Lee the immigrant (1618-1664) (see Cobbs Hall (81) in Northumberland County). John Lee succeeded his cousin as the Essex County Clerk of Court in 1761, and was one of five members of the Lee family who served as clerk or deputy clerk of the Essex court between 1744 and 1814. The house was probably named for John Lee's wife, Susanna Smith. The original house burned before 1932, at which time a modern home was built on its foundation. *Not visible from the road; privately owned. (Map A)*

Blandfield (20) Built by Robert Beverley by 1774, on land patented by his ancestor of the same name about 1660, Blandfield was inspired by English Palladian architecture and is one of the grandest of the American colonial homes. Robert Beverley married a daughter of Landon Carter (see Sabine Hall (41) in Richmond County), and was a successful planter and respected member of the county gentry. He was a political conservative at the time of the Revolution, but despite his lack of enthusiasm for this cause he later managed to be elected to various county posts.

Situated on 3,500 acres overlooking the Rappahannock River, Blandfield remained in the Beverley family until 1983. At that time, after the plans of a developer had been defeated by local opposition, the house was purchased by James C. and Wiley H. Wheat of Richmond, who decided to restore Blandfield to its original 18th century appearance. The new owners meticulously restored the house, both inside and out, drawing on Robert Beverley's own writings and their consultations with leading architectural historians and craftsmen, and utilizing the fragments of many original materials.

The architectural plan for Blandfield had been inspired by illustrations in James Gibbs's *Book of Architecture*, published in 1728. The mansion consists of a large two-story central structure flanked by two-story dependencies connected to the main house by one-story hyphens, all built with exceptionally fine brickwork.

Blandfield (20)

The two central halls of the main house measure 25-by-30- feet, with 13-foot ceilings. The original interior woodwork had been replaced with plain Greek Revival trim in 1844, but this was reversed in the restoration that took place following 1983. *VLR and NRHP. Not visible from the road; privately owned. (Map A)*

Lily Mount (21) The original part of this house, a two-story, side-hall brick structure over an English basement, was built ca. 1740 by Thomas Fogg. Later, a crude two-story frame addition was made to the side of the house, but this addition was brought more into line with the original house in the mid-20th century. The interior of the addition was enhanced with paneling from Mahockney (25), and a fireplace mantel from the Munday House. *Not visible from the road; privately owned.* (Map A and Map B)

Lily Mount (21)

Antioch Baptist Church (22) This church, located in upper Essex County in Champlain, was organized in 1867, drawing its African American members from Upper Essex Baptist Church, Elon Baptist Church and Logan Methodist Church. The congregation first met in an old house above Occupacia, but as the membership grew it was decided to build a frame church. Later, it was decided to erect a new, larger church, and in 1895 the cornerstone of the present brick structure was laid. In 1952, as small rural

schools were being abandoned in favor of a larger consolidated school for blacks, the church acquired the Champlain Colored School (built about 1897) across the street to serve as a church annex. *Visible from the road. (Map A)*

Antioch Baptist Church (22)

Upper Essex Baptist Church (23) Founded in 1772, the first assembly place for this congregation is believed to have been the Diamond Meeting House on Springfield farm. The present Greek and Gothic revival church was erected about 1825. Local lore has it that a member was "turned out" of this church because she had bought a piano for her daughter, and another was "unchurched" for wearing a red dress to a service, both acts deemed too frivolous for the Church of God. After the Civil War, its black members left to help form Antioch Baptist Church (22). *Visible from the road. (Map A and Map B)*

Upper Essex Baptist Church (23)

Essex County, Map B

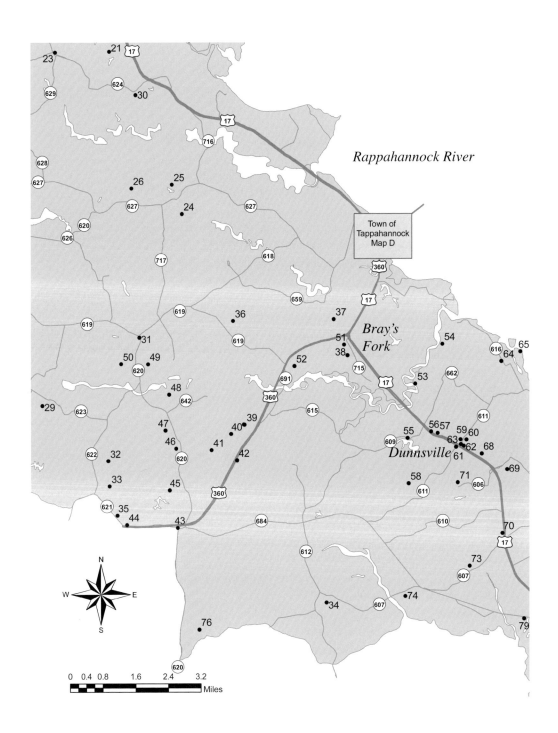

Rappahannock River

Town of Tappahannock Map D

Bray's Fork

Dunnsville

N
W E
S

0 0.4 0.8   1.6   2.4   3.2
Miles

Mount Landing Road (Rt. 627) west of Tappahannock

Paynefield (24) The original home on this site was a 1½ story, two-bay clapboard house with a gable roof, over an English basement. Likely built by Robert Payne Jr., and dating from the late 17th or early 18th century, Paynefield probably had one room on each level, with the top floor being a simple loft.

A much larger two-story, five-bay center-hall frame addition, placed on the east eave of the original house and having its own English basement, was built in the 1820s. Its second floor has smaller windows and lower ceilings than the 12-foot high ceilings found on the first floor Standing on the property is a brick barn or storehouse thought to date from the early 19th century. Recently badly damaged by fire, the house is undergoing careful restoration. *Visible from the road; privately owned. (Map A and Map B)*

Paynefield (24)

Mahockney (25) The original part of this house, possibly built in the second quarter of the 18th century, was probably a 1½ story frame structure, with an unusual chimney that begins as a single eight foot wide structure and then divides into two separate chimneys about half way up. Sometime later, a Mr. Crutchfield raised this house to two stories. In 1820, William Latané built a two-floor brick addition, laid in Flemish bond on its east and west sides, and three-course American bond on its north side. The chimney for this part of the house extends fully to one corner, and forms closets for the basements. A large frame addition to the rear dates from the 20th century.

Mahockney was the home of William Roane, an Essex County justice and militia major who participated in the Stamp Act demonstrations aimed at the Tappahannock merchant Archibald Ritchie (see the Ritchie House (90). *Visible from the road; privately owned. (Map A and Map B)*

Mahockney (25)

Rockland (Rennolds) (26) The original part of this frame house is thought to have been built ca. 1690 by Thomas Sthreshley, making it one of the oldest extant structures in Essex County. This was a 1½ story two-bay single-room house, with a gable roof and two dormers on each side. A large exterior chimney stood at the northern eave end.

In 1755, a larger section was built onto the original house at a right angle, forming an L-plan. With this addition, the house now

Rockland (Rennolds) (26)

is a 1 ¹/₂ story, five-bay dwelling with a center hall, a gambrel roof with three dormers on the front side, a chimney at each end, and an extended English basement. Sthreshley's daughter married John Rennolds, and the house has remained in this family up to the present time. *Not visible from the road; privately owned. (Map A and Map B)*

Greenway (27) The original portion of this house may date to the mid-17th century, and is one of the oldest extant structures in Essex County. Its earliest recorded owner, from 1690, was James Rennolds. This part of the frame house is a 1¹/₂ story three-bay structure, with a steeply pitched gable roof, and it sits atop an English basement. The large brick chimney on its west gable end is laid in English bond.

A two-story three-bay addition was made to the east gable end in 1827, probably by Edward Wright. The addition has an attic and a chimney on its east end. The entire house contains original floorboards and period hinges and locks. Careful restorations were carried out in the late 20th century. *Visible from the road; privately owned. (Map A)*

Greenway (27)

Liberty Hall (28) This house is made up of two discrete frame houses of different vintages and styles. The earlier house was built in 1769 by Abram Montague, and resembles the "saltbox" style found throughout New England. The 1¹/₂ story

house sits on a low foundation, and on its west side the roof changes pitch to become a sweeping Cape Cod-like catslide, dropping to within just a few feet of the ground. Its central chimney is surrounded by four rooms on the first floor and two on the second.

The second house was built in 1820 by Reuben Garnett—who had purchased the original home from the heirs of Abram Montague—as a home for his daughter and her husband. The combined home served as a boarding school in the mid-19th century, and after a series of owners, it was carefully restored in the late 20th century. *Not visible from the road; privately owned. (Map A)*

Liberty Hall (28)

The Meadow site (29) This 2 ¹/₂ story five-bay frame house, built on a high English basement by Henry Waring Latané Sr. in 1824, had tall porches on both the front and rear sides, and attractive chimneys. Paneled double doors with transoms opened into a central hall and an enclosed winding stairway rose from the back of

The Meadow site (29)

the hall. Capt. William Latané of the Essex Light Dragoons, 9th Virginia Cavalry lived here, and his burial, after being killed during Stuart's daring ride around Gen. McClellan's army in October 1862, inspired a poem and painting called "The Burial of Latané" which later became one of the symbols of The Lost Cause. Unfortunately, the house was torn down in the 1950s. *Site not visible from the road; privately owned. (Map B)*

Locust Grove (30)   The enormous stone exterior chimney of this house is thought to date from the 17th century, when it would have abutted a $1^1/_2$ story log dwelling with no basement. The house was substantially altered in the late 18th or early 19th century, when a typical hall and parlor plan, with a loft and an English basement, were added onto the log structure, which in turn was replaced by a frame section. The names of the owners just before the Civil War are known, but those of its earlier residents are not. The house has undergone other alterations, but careful restoration work was begun in the late 20th century. *Visible from the road; privately owned. (Map A and Map B)*

Locust Grove (30)

Mt. Zion Baptist Church (31)   This congregation was first organized in 1774 as Piscataway Baptist Church on the site of what is now Beulah Baptist Church. In 1818, Capt. Robert G. Haile gave land near Piscataway Post Office—now Dunbrooke—for a new meeting house. The present structure, a traditional rectangular form with Gothic embellishments, was built in 1854, and in 1856 the congregation changed its name to Mt. Zion Baptist Church. *Historical Marker O-41. Visible from the road. (Map A and Map B)*

Mt. Zion Baptist Church (31)

Elton/Burnetts (32)   It is thought that the original part of this frame house, to the far left, was built by a Mr. Burnett and dates from the mid-18th century. It likely consisted of one or two rooms on the first floor, with a loft above, all built atop an English basement. This house had two large exterior chimneys on the left hand side. Sometime later, a wide hallway was added to the right side, and the loft and English basement extended. This made the house, now almost a square, a three-bay gambrel roof house with three dormers. A smaller wing was added more recently onto the right of the older house, which it echoes. *Visible from the road; privately owned. (Map B)*

Elton/Burnetts (32)

Retreat (33) Probably built by John Jones sometime between 1789 and 1803, this frame dwelling originally was a small 1¹/₂ story house with a hall and parlor plan and a shed which ran across the back, standing atop an English basement. This dwelling had a gambrel roof and a double chimney on the northern eave. A few years later, the house was extended to the south and two more chimneys were added, giving the house a five-bay, center hall plan. The foundations and chimneys are a mixture of English and Flemish bond brickwork. The bedrooms on the second floor have very deep window seats, reflecting the very steep pitch of the lower part of the gambrel roof. The house was renovated in the 1960s. *Visible from the road; privately owned. (Map B)*

Retreat (33)

Rockland (Cauthorn) (34) This two-story, five-bay brick house, built in a center hall plan over an English basement, dates from at least the mid-19th century, and was likely built by a member of the Cauthorn family. The chimneys on the gable ends are interior, and the only windows on these gable ends are on the third, or attic, floor. The brickwork is five-course American bond. *Not visible from the road; privately owned. (Map B and Map C)*

Midway site (35) Thought to have been built by Benjamin Jones in the mid-to-late 18th century, Midway was a 1¹/₂ story frame house with an English basement and a double porch in front. The house was named for its location midway between the Rappahannock and Mattaponi rivers. Sometime before 1840, Dr. Jefferson Minor established the Midway Female Academy here, in a separate building. The main house burned in 1893, and the only outbuilding that has survived to the present time is the post office, which was served by a large four-horse stage coach.

Given its location on the main road to Richmond, it is not surprising that the grounds of Midway were occupied as a campground, at different times, by both Confederate and Union soldiers. *Site not visible from the road; privately owned. (Map B)*

Young House (36) Originally a 1¹/₂ story hall and parlor plan frame house, with one room on the second floor and a chimney laid in unhewn local ferrous sandstone, this dwelling was built by

Rockland (Cauthorn) (34)

Young House (36)

Ambrose Young, an emancipated slave, in the late 1860s. The gable roof had two dormers on the front. A two-story addition with its own chimney was appended to the north side of the original house in the late 19th century, and a one-story wing was added to the rear, and a screen porch on the front, in the early 20th century. The house remains in the Young family to this day. *Not visible from the road; privately owned. (Map A)*

Route 360 west from Bray's Fork to Dunbrooke Road

Mt. Clement site (37) Measuring 62-by-24 feet, this two-story, five-bay gable-roofed house was built by Dr. John Clement in 1752. From its hilltop setting, it provided magnificent views of the Rappahannock River and the town of Tappahannock. From the mid-19th century, the house passed through a succession of hands and was later leased to a long list of tenants. The long-neglected house was unfortunately demolished in the 1960s to make way for a new hospital. It is a cautionary tale of what can happen to a noted historic structure that is not carefully preserved, and which is then subjected to the whims of developers.

The house was laid in Flemish bond, with interior chimneys. Palladian arches covered both the front and back doors. The center hall had large rooms on either side, and the six-foot high windows were finished with low window seats with side

Mt. Clement site (37)

paneling. The house was one of the most elegant in the county, and the property included a race track in the flats below the house. *Site not visible from the road; privately owned. (Map B and Map C)*

Poplar Spring (38) Located on high ground west of Bray's Fork, the original house, built ca. 1780 by Dr. Mace Clements, had a simple hall and parlor plan, with a basement and an attic. In 1833, this house was expanded to a $1^1/_2$ story five-bay gambrel-roofed frame dwelling. The parlor contains early wainscoting, mantels, window frames and door facings. *Not visible from the road; privately owned. Endangered. (Map B and Map C)*

Poplar Spring (38)

Woodfarm (39) Built prior to 1815, this dwelling is thought to have been built by the Wood family, of nearby Woodville (41). Constructed of massive hand-hewn oak timbers and broad floorboards, this $1^1/_2$ story five-bay frame house with a center-hall plan has a dormered gambrel roof and a chimney at each end, and is set atop

Woodfarm (39)

an English basement. All of the interior woodwork is original. The property passed into the Croxton family (see Cherry Walk (47)) by 1815, and it remained in the extended family until the early 21st century. In 2007, the house unfortunately had to be moved off the property to avoid being torn down by a developer. *Not visible from the road; privately owned. (Map B)*

Mt. Pisgah (40)   Built prior to the Civil War, probably by the Cauthorn family, this house was originally a $1^1/_2$ story small hall and parlor plan residence, with an exterior chimney laid in American bond. Somewhat later, the roof was raised, and an addition was constructed on the right side, giving the house a roughly symmetrical appearance. Much of the interior woodwork has been replaced over time. Wings were added to the home during a 1989 remodeling. *Not visible from the road; privately owned. (Map B)*

Mt. Pisgah (40)

Woodville (41) The original section of this brick structure was the 17-foot square hall and parlor section to the right side, built by a member of the Wood family over an English basement and likely dating to the late 17th century, is one of the oldest extant dwellings in Essex County. The second floor of this original house was probably a loft, with the dormers added later. The double set of small windows in the south end of the second floor and the quoin-like placement of the corner bricks are clues to its very early construction. Its square-stacked interior chimney, which serves fireplaces on the first and second floors, is laid in Flemish bond and stands

on a foundation of ferrous sandstone.

Early in the 18th century this house was extended on its north side. In 1989 a long two-story perpendicular wing was added to this extension, broadly matching the original square house in style. *Visible from the road; privately owned. (Map B)*

Woodville (41)

Woodlawn (Trible) (42) While taking its subsidiary name from Samuel W. Trible, who came into ownership of the house in 1860, and his descendants, this $1^1/_2$ story, two-bay frame house was built in the late 18th century by the owners of Woodville (41) as a gift to one of their daughters. Still a hall and parlor home in its original configuration, it has an English basement and a side hall and stairs to the second floor. The roof is gambrel with two dormers in the front, but catslide, or saltbox, in the rear. Two large brick chimneys on the south side flank an entry to the basement, and serve five fireplaces on three floors including the basement. The siding is said to be original.

Two very old outbuildings, a meathouse and a playhouse, have survived. In the 1970s, the Virginia Historic Landmarks

Woodlawn (Trible) (42)

Commission survey observed that Wood-lawn (Trible) had been long abandoned, subject to vandalism, and in a general state of neglect. At this point it was bought by a person devoted to its stabilization and preservation, much of which she carried out herself, in many instances with pe-riod-type tools. *VLR and NRHP. Visible from the road; privately owned. (Map B)*

Millers Tavern site (43) The earliest known owner of this important local social center was a Mr. Miller. The building is believed to have been erected in the early 18th century, and was a stopping place for stage coaches making semi-weekly trips between Richmond and Tappahannock on the then quite primitive main road.

In early February 1861, prior to the calling of a statewide secession conven-tion, delegates from Essex and King and Queen counties met here and adopted the "Millers Resolutions." These affirmed the right of states to withdraw from the Union, argued that Virginia was commit-ted to the defense of the South, and called for Virginia to leave the Union.

The original building is thought to have had 1½ stories and three bays, probably laid out in a center-hall plan, with dormer windows, and built over an English base-ment. A later two story addition, made to the east end, had two tall chimneys that were partially exterior but whose interior sections were the basis for closets. In an advanced state of deterioration, this im-portant historic structure was destroyed by

Millers Tavern site (43)

a controlled burn in 2005. *Site not visible from the road; privately owned. (Map B)*

St. Paul's Episcopal Church (44) This church was erected in 1838 on a por-tion of Midway plantation donated by Dr. Jefferson Minor, right on the line separat-ing Essex from King and Queen counties. Like St. John's Church (96) in Tappahan-nock, with which it shared a rector until 1972, St. Paul's is descended from the two colonial churches of South Farnham Parish which were destroyed during post-Revolution disestablishment and neglect. This Gothic revival church is one of but two Virginia churches with a center pul-pit, characteristic of the 19th-century An-glican movement. *Visible from the road. (Map B)*

St. Paul's Episcopal Church (44)

Dunbrooke Road (Rt. 620) north

Shelba (45) This was originally a small 1½ story frame house, dating from the mid-18th century, with a hall and parlor plan and a large kitchen fireplace served by one chimney. In the late 18th century an addition was constructed which trans-formed this dwelling into a symmetrical center-hall five-bay gambrel-roofed home with chimneys at either end, serving a total of eight fireplaces. A closed turned stair-way rises from the back of the central hall. During the colonial era the home belonged to Col. Bohannon. A perpendicular wing was added to the rear of the house in the early 19th century, thereby forming an L-shaped structure. *Not visible from the road; privately owned. (Map B)*

Shelba (45)

Woodlawn (Sandy) (46) This mid-18th-century house, like Woodlawn (Trible) (42), was probably built by members of the Wood family of Woodville (41). The home was bought by Capt. P. A. Sandy in 1859, thereby acquiring its current name.

Woodlawn (Sandy) may originally have been a simple hall and parlor style house, to which later was appended a smaller addition. Today the house has a center-hall, two-room plan, with double doors that open into a front hall that leads to a closed, turned stairway at the back. A kitchen dependency still remains on the property. In the early- to mid-20th century, the property was known as the "Circus House," it being the headquarters for a traveling circus, the Johnny J. Jones Exposition, Inc. *Visible from the road; privately owned. (Map B)*

Woodlawn (Sandy) (46)

Cherry Walk (47) Built by Carter Croxton in the last quarter of the 18th century, Cherry Walk is a four-bay brick house with a steep dormered gambrel roof, a tall chimney at either end, and an English basement. It is a characteristic example of a Tidewater plantation complex of the middling class, with an unusually complete set of outbuildings consisting of two dairies, a smokehouse, a privy and a kitchen, and farm buildings that include an early frame barn, a plank corncrib, and a late 19th century blacksmith shop. These buildings, erected over the course of about a century, provide a revealing look at the various construction techniques in use during this period.

The house and its vast array of subsidiary buildings remained in the same family and was well cared for until the early 1980s, when it was purchased by the current owners who have carefully preserved the property. *VLR and NRHP, and BHR easement. Visible from the road; privately owned. (Map B)*

Cherry Walk (47)

Beaver's Hill (48) Capt. Richard Gaines Haile Sr. built this Federal style home during 1818-22 on land patented by an ancestor in 1694. The house is a $2^1/_2$ story brick house with a full basement, and high chimneys at each end. The walls are laid in Flemish bond. Double doors on the front and back porches lead to a wide center hall, and from the back porch is a view of extensive meadow lands. Most of the interior woodwork is original. The house has remained in the extended Haile family for all but a few years in the 1920s and 1930s. *Not visible from the road; privately owned. (Map B)*

Beaver's Hill (48)

Adam's Spring (49) This two-story three-bay frame house has a gambrel roof with an exterior chimney, laid in American bond, at both ends. The English basement is of ferrous sandstone, said to have been quarried on the property. Both floors have a wide center hall entering into two rooms, and all interior doors are of batten construction. Built ca. 1800, the house has retained its original unbeaded clapboarding. The attached kitchen was once a separate dependency. The original owner of this house has not yet been identified. *Visible from the road; privately owned. (Map B)*

Adam's Spring (49)

Fountain Run (50) A hall and parlor home believed to date from the 18th century, Fountain Run is a $1^{1}/_{2}$ story three-bay frame structure with a gambrel roof, dormers, and a chimney at both ends. Both chimneys are laid in Flemish bond, whereas the foundations of the English basement are English bond. An enclosed winder stair connects the first and second floors. An early kitchen, once a separate dependency, has been connected to the house.

While the builder of this house has not yet been identified, from about 1812 it was occupied by the Montague family for the rest of the 19th century. Two of the Montagues served successively as pastors of Mt. Zion Baptist Church (31) for a total of 64 years during the middle decades of the 19th century. Significant restoration of the house began towards the end of the 20th century. *Visible from the road; privately owned. (Map B)*

Fountain Run (50)

Route 17 south from Bray's Fork

Berry Hill (51) This side-hall brick dwelling, with more the look of a town house than a farmhouse, is thought to have been built by James Roy Micou in the early to mid-19th century. The exterior brickwork is five-course American bond, and given the very high set English basement and the garret, the house is essentially a four-story structure. Although the front entrance and portico are on the west side, the north-side gable end effectively, and unusually, serves as the façade

Essex County, Map C

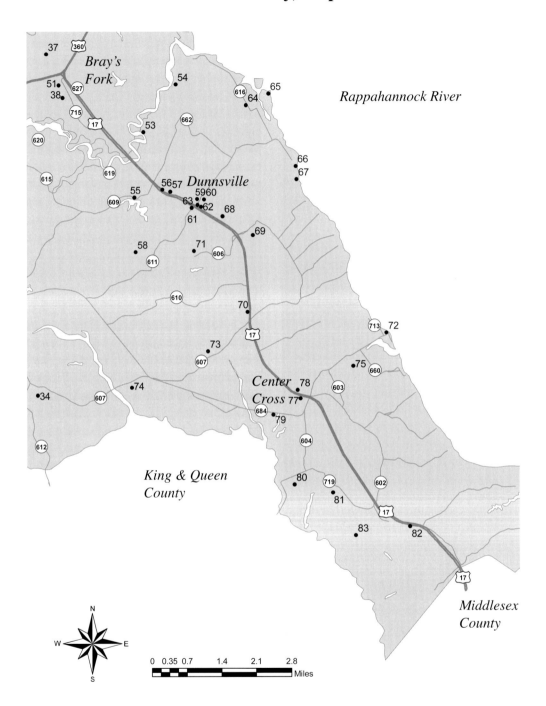

Bray's Fork

37 360

Rappahannock River

54

51 627
38
715
17
620

53 662

615

619

66
67

55
609

5657 *Dunnsville*
5960
63 62 68
61

58
611

71
606

610

70

17

713 72

73
607

75 660

34
607

74

Center Cross 78
77
684 79
603

604

80 719
81
602

17

83 82

17

King & Queen County

Middlesex County

N
W E
S

0   0.35 0.7   1.4   2.1   2.8
                                        Miles

of the house. The dwelling contains many examples of early fine woodwork, and the basement fireplace is unique in that it consists of bricks covered by painted mortar. The house was near ruin by the 1960s, when it underwent a careful restoration. *Not visible from the road; privately owned. (Map B and Map C)*

Berry Hill (51)

Cedar Level site (52) Destroyed by a controlled burn in 2002, this image of this house stands as an object lesson of what may easily happen if an historic structure is long abandoned and neglected.

The $1^1/_2$ story part of this dwelling probably dated from the 18th century, and was notable for its two chimneys on the north eave, laid in Flemish bond, one having disappeared by the time this photo was taken in 2001. The larger section to the right, dating from the early 19th century, was a full two-story addition with a low English basement and an attic. Its tall chimney had been laid in irregular American bond. Much of its interior woodwork was still extant at the

Cedar Level site (52)

time of this photo. *Site not visible from the road; privately owned. (Map B)*

Clydeside (53) The property on which Clydeside stands contains a plethora of artifacts suggesting that houses preceded it on this site possibly as early as the late 17th century and the second quarter of the 18th century. It is unknown exactly when the original part of the present house was built, but it was presumably before the Revolutionary War.

The Scottish loyalist, Archibald McCall, was managing the property at that time, but he fled with his family to Scotland during the War, and only returned to Clydeside about 1786 (see the McCall-Brockenbrough House (101))

The oldest part of this house is the $1^1/_2$ story structure on the right hand side, with an exterior chimney and a saltbox roof at the rear. In the mid-19th century, the two-story hall and room section was added to the left side of the original house. Since then, rooms have been added to the rear sides of both sections. The house underwent careful restoration in the mid-20th century. *Not visible from the road; privately owned. (Map B and Map C)*

Clydeside (53)

Dunnsville Area

Bathurst site (54) Another lost site is Bathurst, torn down about 1940 due to its advanced state of decay. This house was built in 1692, partly with materials shipped from Britain, by Francis Merriweather, the first clerk of Essex County, which was formed from old Rappahannock County in that year. It is believed that George W. Smith, the only Virginia governor from Essex County (and who died in the terrible Richmond theater fire of 1811, after only nine months in office), was born in this home.

This now departed house, the subject of many tales of lovers and ghosts, exemplified the early Tidewater architectural genre. Flanked by large double-shouldered chimneys laid in Flemish bond, this 1 1/2 story structure had a wide center hall and paneling that extended from floor to ceiling. At some point, a perpendicular wing was added to the rear of the house. *Site not visible from the road; privately owned. (Map B and Map C)*

Bathurst site (54)

Essex Mill (55) Erected in 1808, this mill replaced Covington's Mill, which was either torn down or burned. The mill included a "bake house," at which bread was made to sell to the ships then docking at Tappahannock (the name being changed from Hobb's Hole that very year). The water to power this mill came from Mill Stream, a tributary of Piscataway Creek, which later flows into the Rappahannock.

Old-timers used to recall seeing farmers drive their horse-drawn wagons of grain to the mill to be ground, where they could often expect the miller to charge a "toll" equal to 25 percent of their cargo, which was either corn to be ground into meal, or wheat to be ground into flour, with the by-products to be used as feed for livestock.

By the early 1900s, water power proved insufficient to drive both the corn and wheat mills, and the old machinery was supplanted by a turbine and gasoline engine auxiliary. Despite ever-mounting difficulties facing the old mills in the region, Essex Mill actually continued in limited operation until 1976. *Visible from the road; privately owned. (Map B and Map C)*

Essex Mill (55)

Woodland (56) This two-story five-bay brick home sits atop an English basement, and is flanked by interior chimneys. While often attributed to the mid-19th century, in many respects this house resembles some of the finer homes built in Essex County a century earlier, and may actually date from the mid-18th century. It is unknown at this

Woodland (56)

time who built this home, but it is known that Peter Trible owned this property in the late 1840s and conducted a girls' school here. From the entrance one enters a wide hallway, with one room to each side, and two more rooms are on the second story. Each room has a fireplace, with its original mantelpiece. *Visible from the road; privately owned. (Map B and Map C)*

Hill and Dale (57) The original part of this house—the left hand wing and the now center hallway—probably dates from the early 19th century. It was a small 1½ story house sitting atop an English basement, with an exterior chimney, both laid in five-course American bond. The later, right hand wing is set on brick piles, and has an interior chimney. The downstairs windows in this wing are quite a bit larger than those in the original section, reflecting the building styles of the mid-19th century.

This dwelling was the home of several generations of Garnetts beginning in the 1850s, including William C. Garnett, a noted southern educator and the author of the popular *Tidewater Tales. Visible from the road; privately owned. (Map B and Map C)*

Hill and Dale (57)

Johnville (58) This home remains in the Trible family, which may have owned it for 2½ centuries. The original part was a small 1½ story house, but in the 1860s a small rear wing was added and the home was expanded to two full floors and three bays, flanked by exterior chimneys. The English basement contains the dining room,

kitchen and a pantry. Prior to the Civil War, a school was conducted at this house. The name of the house probably is attributable to the large number of John Tribles known to have lived in Essex County since the 1730s. *Not visible from the road; privately owned. (Map B and Map C)*

Johnville (58)

Riverview (59) As the name suggests, this two-story five-bay hip roof frame home, which blends Federal and Greek Revival styles, overlooks the Rappahannock River—as well as about two miles of lowland in between—from its hilltop perch. The original house, built in 1838, was severely damaged by a fire in the 1870s, but much architectural detail has survived from the earlier period. On each floor, four rooms are divided by a center hall. Prior to construction of the house in 1838, the Riverview property belonged to Bathurst (54) plantation, and an old family cemetery contains an obelisk in memory of Governor George W. Smith. An old cannery, which put up fruit

Riverview (59)

and vegetables under the "Old Dominion Brand" label in the early 20th century, still stands on the property. *Not visible from the road; privately owned. (Map C)*

Rose Hill (Dunn) (60) This frame house was built about 1781 by James Dunn, and remained in the possession of his descendants for a little over two centuries. The original part of the dwelling was the two-story house on the right, with two rooms off of a side hall. After a 1 ½ story addition was built in 1847, the entrance hall became a center hall. Many of the original hand-blown window panes in the older part have survived. Curiously, one of the chimneys on the right side of the earlier dwelling has been laid in English bond, while the other is of Flemish bond. *Not visible from the road; privately owned. (Map B and Map C)*

Rose Hill (Dunn) (60)

Rappahannock Christian Church (61) Located in Dunnsville, this is one of the oldest churches of the Disciples of Christ, whose basic precepts are that the church should be one, and that its teachings should be based on those of Christ and the Apostles, as set forth in the New Testament, and not based upon creeds or theology. This congregation, dating from 1832, met at first in members' homes. In 1834, the Rappahannock Meeting House was erected on donated land, and construction of the present building was commissioned in 1858, with completion in 1860. The exterior is of classical design, while its spacious sanctuary exhibits a strong colonial influence. Important restorative work was carried out in 2005-06. *Visible from the road. (Map C)*

Rappahannock Christian Church (61)

Hundley Hall (62) The original part of this brick three-bay four-square house was built between 1820 and 1840. The property was bought by Dr. William Lowery Waring in 1841 who may have rebuilt the house or torn it down and erected another. The home has a hip roof, four exterior chimneys, and a vernacular Greek Revival porch with an unusual set of four square columns. John T. Hundley, a distinguished educator then living at Clydeside (53), bought the property in 1869 as his new residence. A one-story wing was added to the rear in the early 20th century. *Not visible from the road; privately owned. (Map B and Map C)*

Hundley Hall (62)

The Grove (63) This 1½ story three-bay frame house originally had one room and a hall on the first floor, a loft above, and no basement. It is thought to be the oldest surviving structure in Dunnsville. The house was expanded several times during the 19th century. Once known as Byron Park, the building was used as a cantonment and training area for both the 9th Virginia Cavalry and the 55th Virginia Infantry during the Civil War. Later in the 19th century it became a two-room schoolhouse. After a period of gradual deterioration in the late 20th century, it was carefully restored in the 1990s. *Visible from the road; privately owned. (Map B and Map C)*

The Grove (63)

Fairview (64) Erected about 1762 by John Lowry as an overseer's house on his plantation known as Tuscarora, Fairview originally had a side-hall plan, with two stories and a loft standing atop an English basement which was the kitchen. Each room had its own fireplace. The house was built with bricks made on the property, joined with oyster shell mortar. The façade is laid in Flemish bond, while the rear side is American bond. Thomas Lawson Waring added a

Fairview (64)

two-bay section to the north end about 1840, and this transformed the house into a five-bay plan.

During the Civil War, this house served as a picket station of nearby Fort Lowry (65). After a period of great neglect, restoration of the house began in 1942. The house remains in the hands of the builder's descendants. *Visible from the road; privately owned. (Map B and Map C)*

Fort Lowry site (65) General Robert E. Lee ordered the construction of this eight-gun water battery on the Rappahannock River in 1861, to protect Fredericksburg from Union naval forces. The installation was built by both free blacks and slaves, and its ramparts were made of layer upon layer of marsh sod covered with sand. Fort Lowry was garrisoned by elements of the 55th Virginia Infantry, who lived nearby in tents and wooden barracks. Its ordnance included three 8-inch Colombiads, two long 32-pounders, two short 32-pounders, and a heavy rifled gun known as "Long Tom."

Fort Lowry never fired a round against Union forces, and it was abandoned in 1862, with most of its weaponry dispatched to the Army of Northern Virginia. As late as 1945, before being bulldozed for development, the fort's five-foot high line of fortifications could still be seen, and cannon balls could still be found here. *Historical Marker N-24. Privately owned. (Map B and Map C)*

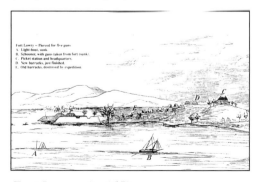

Fort Lowry site (65)

Waterview (66) This frame structure was originally an overseer's house, built by Captain Henry Young before 1750. The initial house likely consisted of just one large room with a loft above. It later was the home of Robert Lowry Ware Sr., who operated nearby Ware's Wharf in the 19th century. Additions and reconstruction following a 1977 fire have substantially altered the appearance of the house. Still visible, however, is the large Flemish bond chimney and the early part of the basement. *Visible from the road; privately owned. (Map C)*

Waterview (66)

Bellevue site (67) This house was built in the mid-18th century, probably by Henry Young. It was a two-story frame structure, with a dormered gambrel roof, two tall chimneys on the north end and one on the south. Its paneled parlor was 25-feet square, with six windows providing views of the Rappahannock River. Situated on a hill, Bellevue was one of the most noticed houses from the water.

In February 1863, Union gunboats moving upriver towards Fredericksburg fired on the house, where a number of

Bellevue site (67)

friends and family had gathered to pay their last respects to the then master of the house, Edward Macon Ware I. It is said that a family slave, Randall Segar, got the boats to stop firing by running back and forth in front of the house waving a white flag. Later, the dwelling became a tenant house, fell into disrepair, and was torn down in 1962. The paneling and some other materials, however, were salvaged. *Site not visible from the road; privately owned. (Map C)*

Ephesus Baptist Church (68) Erected in 1858, this brick church with frame entablature was built in the style of a Roman basilica and replaced an earlier structure that had been built on the same site in 1844. Following the Civil War, its black members left the church to establish Angel Visit Baptist Church (70) just a few miles away. *Visible from the road. (Map B and Map C)*

Ephesus Baptist Church (68)

Ben Lomond (69) This Georgian foursquare house was actually constructed in two very different periods. The original part, a brick dwelling erected ca. 1735 over an English basement, had a wide hall on both floors, each opening onto two rooms on the west side. There were two chimneys, which served six fireplaces. There is also evidence that a chimney with three flues had at some point been built into the east exterior wall, which with remnants of a foundation on that side suggest a frame three-story addition had at some point been erected.

About 1840, Muscoe Garnett bought this property from his father-in-law and replaced the frame addition with the east-end brick enclosed rooms that are seen today, and which gives the house its Georgian symmetry. Prior to the Civil War, the manor house had a brick outbuilding opposite each corner. Garnett, who lost both of his sons serving in the Confederate military within a very short period in 1862, went on to become the first Essex County judge after the long-standing plural county courts were eliminated by the Virginia Constitution of 1869. *Not visible from the road; privately owned. (Map B and Map C)*

Ben Lomond (69)

Angel Visit Baptist Church (70) This congregation was formed by blacks who left Ephesus Baptist Church (68) after the Civil War, under the leadership of Brother Anderson Lindsey. In its early days, the congregation met in private homes during the winter, and under oak trees or brush arbors in the summer. Later,

Angel Visit Baptist Church (70)

land was purchased, and a church building erected. It was destroyed by fire in 1917, however, and the present structure was built in 1919. *Visible from the road. (Map B and Map C)*

Center Cross Area

Aspen Grove (71) Built by James Cauthorn in 1721, this frame house originally had one room and a hall on the first floor, and an enclosed stairway to the bedroom upstairs. The present parlor and a second upstairs room were added ca. 1810, and the house took on a more asymmetrical aspect. Although sadly neglected for years, and for a long time used as a barn, the house—first undergoing serious restoration in the late 1970s—still retains a good deal of interior woodwork from the 18th century. *Visible from the road; privately owned. (Map B and Map C)*

Aspen Grove (71)

Bowlers (72) This house was erected about 1669 by Thomas Bowler, the founder of Bowler's Wharf on the Rappahannock River and which remained a bustling port up through the end of the steamboat era in the 1930s. The house, one of the oldest surviving in Essex County, is a $1\frac{1}{2}$ story structure with dormers, and has chimneys at each end with $10\frac{1}{2}$ foot wide bases.

Bowler's Wharf was the scene in 1776 of the recapture by Essex County patriots of a grain boat that had earlier been taken by the British from Bathurst (54) upriver. Another violent encounter with the British fleet, during the War of 1812, did not end so happily, as gunboats managed to blow off the north porch of Bowlers. Through all of this, the home still is owned by the descendants of Thomas Bowler. *Visible from the road; privately owned. (Map C)*

Bowlers (72)

Marigold (73) This is another house with likely late 17th century origins, believed to have been built by Thomas Bowler (see Bowlers (72)) in the late 1670s on inland property that he called Mary Gold. The original house was a small 1½ story frame house with a hall and stairs connecting single rooms up and down. Later, the house was widened to a five-bay structure with halls on both floors and it was raised to two full stories. The two-story brick addition on the right was built somewhat later, using bricks from the ruins of old Lower Piscataway, a colonial church that had stood nearby. *Visible from the road; privately owned. (Map B and Map C)*

Marigold (73)

Plainview (Smith) (74) This large Federal style frame home is believed to have been built about 1840, by William F. Smith. As with many other old houses, it was constructed in two stages. The original part of the house had a side-hall plan, and was two stories over an English basement. Later, an addition was made to the left side of the house which resulted in a five-bay symmetrical dwelling with a center hall. The chimney and English basement are laid in American bond. What appears to have been the original kitchen on the property has survived as an outbuilding not far from the main house. It consists of a brick first story with a large cooking fireplace, with second floor living quarters, and an attic above. This may predate the manor house, and might have been the original dwelling on the property. *Visible from the road in the winter; privately owned. (Map B and Map C)*

Plainview (Smith) (74)

Monte Verde (75) Built in 1816 by Joseph Janey, a French immigrant who opened an import-export business at Bowler's Wharf, this two-story, four-bay frame house has a central passage flanked on each side by one room on all four of its floors (including an attic and English basement). The interior is notable for its high style Adam mantels in the public rooms on the first floor. The additions date from the late 19th and mid-20th centuries. *VLR and NRHP. Not visible from the road; privately owned. (Map C)*

Monte Verde (75)

Harewood (76) Believed to have been built by lawyer James Webb in the last quarter of the 18th century, Harewood is located on the north side of Dragon Run swamp. The house was originally a 1½ story frame structure with one room on each floor and a high English basement. Later this gable roof house was expanded and made into a three-bay center-hall plan. Surviving outbuildings include a kitchen, smokehouse and laundry. *Not visible from the road; privately owned. (Map B)*

Harewood (76)

Level Green (77) Although the builder of this ca. 1835 house is not known for certain, an early owner was George W. Dillard. The two-story, five-bay clapboard home has a gable roof and an interior chimney at each gable end, and sits atop a high English basement. The original house is single-pile, and central hallways on each floor are flanked by single rooms. A kitchen dependency, which may

predate the house, stands on the property. Additions to the house were made in the 1930s and 1970s. *Visible from the road; privately owned. (Map C)*

Level Green (77)

Holly Springs (78) The exterior of the original brick portion of this house measures only 18-by-18 feet, and with 18-inch thick walls, the interior is fifteen-by-fifteen. This structure stands on an English basement, and the south main façade is laid in Flemish bond. On the north side of the house, a five-foot deep brick portico leads out of the English basement. The other exposed sides of the original dwelling are in five-course American bond, suggesting that this part of the house probably dates from the early 19th century. *Visible from the road; privately owned. (Map C)*

Holly Springs (78)

Greenfield (Smith) (79) Built in either the late 18th or early 19th century by Samuel Smith, the son-in-law of James Webb of Harewood (76), Greenfield has essentially retained its original size and features. It is a 1¹/₂ story, three-bay center-hall plan frame house set on a low basement laid in English bond. The chimneys on either side of the house are laid in five-course American bond, suggesting that perhaps the present house was built on the foundations of a much earlier one. The home features a clipped, or hip-on-gambrel roof, the only one to be found among early houses in the county. *Not visible from the road; privately owned. (Map B and Map C)*

Greenfield (Smith) (79)

Travelers Rest (80) Also known as Cauthorn's Place, this mid-19th century house is one of several Cauthorn properties in this area of the county. The original portion is a two-story, three-bay dwelling that sits on a high English basement. Being one room deep, with two rooms on each floor flanking narrow center hallways, the

Travelers Rest (80)

oldest part of this home is a good representative of the so-called I-plan. A two-story wing off the rear of the house was added in the 1930s, transforming the house into a T-plan dwelling. *Not visible from the road; privately owned. (Map C)*

Rose Hill (Hundley) (81) It is now believed that a house already stood here when Robert Hundley—thought to be the earliest Essex County ancestor of this old Essex County family—purchased this property in 1759. That dwelling was a 1¹/₂ story hall and parlor structure, with a bedroom above, set atop an English basement, and it may have been preceded by an even earlier house on this site.

Hundley's grandson, Capt. Larkin Hundley, inherited the property in 1856 and hired a German-born architect, Louis Kuindz, to design the present frame house for one of his sons, a five-bay full two-story structure built partly with materials from the upper story of the original house. Now a center-hall plan home, the original parlor and new dining room feature marble mantels and decorative plaster designs surrounding the chandelier mountings. The kitchen was moved in 1905 from the basement to a new addition on the rear of the house. Rose Hill has remained in the Hundley family for some 250 years. *Not visible from the road; privately owned. (Map C)*

Rose Hill (Hundley) (81)

Montague (82) Capt. Larkin Hundley had this house built for one of his sons in 1855, several years after he had Colnbrooke (83) remodeled for another son, and one year before he had Rose Hill (81) enlarged for yet another son. Unlike the other two houses, Montague was not an enlargement of an earlier house. Designed by the German-born architect Louis Kuindz as a five-bay Federal style frame center-hall two-over-two home, Montague has a hip roof with end chimneys, together with a two-story extension with its own chimney off the rear of the dwelling. Marble mantels identical to those at Rose Hill frame the fireplaces in the parlor and dining room. *Visible from the road; privately owned. (Map C)*

Montague (82)

Colnbrooke (83) The first of three homes built by Capt. Larkin Hundley for his three sons, (see (81) and (82)) Colnbrooke was constructed in 1847 by adding the main part of the new house onto the front of an earlier house dating from

Colnbrooke (83)

the late 18th century. The two-story, five-bay brick house with a hip roof and interior chimneys is more than 50 feet wide, and was constructed with bricks made on the property. The front door has unusual colored sidelights, and the wide center hall is flanked by two spacious parlors. The older, rear wing contains the dining room and the stairway leading to the second floor. *Visible from the road; privately owned. (Map C)*

Tappahannock

(All sites are visible from the street unless otherwise indicated.)

Topahanock Indian site (84) The Rappahannock Indians, members of what the early British visitors termed the Powhatan Confederacy, lived in this region, in numerous villages on both sides of the river. The Indian homes were typically large huts made of saplings interwoven with grass and rush, with a hole in the center of the top serving as a chimney. One of these villages, which was located nearby, the English called Topahanock. The Rappahannock Indians, then the dominant group on the river, clashed with John Smith and his exploratory party in August 1608. *Historical Marker N-25. Exact whereabouts of the village site is unknown. (Map D)*

Beale Memorial Baptist Church (85) The front portion, built in 1728, was originally the Essex County courthouse. Partially destroyed by the British in 1814, the courthouse was soon restored and continued in use until 1848, when it was replaced by the present Courthouse (89). The building was purchased from the county in 1875 and initially served as Centennial Baptist Church. It was later re-designated Beale Memorial Baptist

Essex County, Map D
Town of Tappahannock

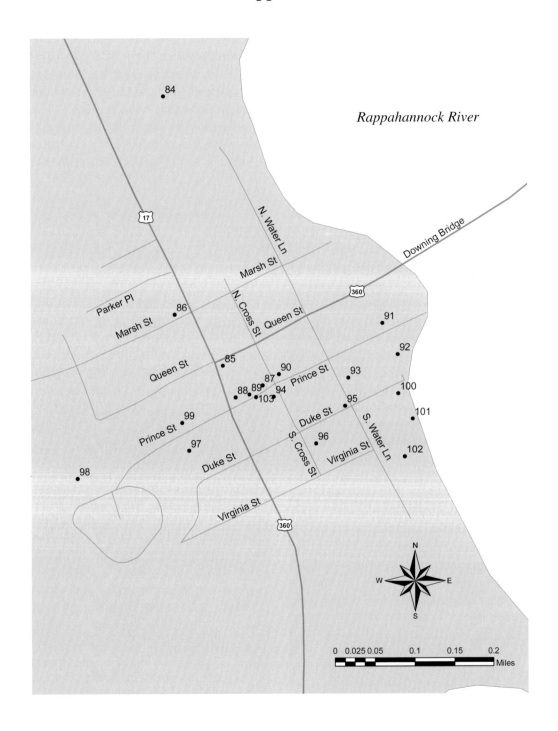

Rappahannock River

Church in honor of its first pastor. In 2007, a new Beale Memorial church was erected north of town, and this old building again became county property. *(Map D)*

Beale Memorial Baptist Church (85)

First Baptist Church (86) This centrally located church in Tappahannock was organized in 1867 by freed blacks who had left white churches in the area. They initially met at the inter-denominational Town Chapel on West Duke Street. In 1874, the congregation moved to a modest newly built frame structure on Virginia Street, and in 1893 it built the present Greek Revival church located on the corner of Marsh Street and Route 17. This church was constructed on land acquired from the son of William Breedlove Jr., a respected blacksmith who had been freed before the Civil War, and who during Reconstruction had served as an Essex delegate to the 1867-68 Virginia Constitutional Convention, and later, was a member of the Tappahannock Town Council. *(Map D)*

First Baptist Church (86)

County Clerk's Office (87) In 1808, the Essex County Court ordered the building of a Clerk's office to be located on the southeast corner of the Public Square. Completed and in use by February, 1810, this building later saw service as an ordinary (tavern) and a shop. At one point, the county issued a prohibition against the structure being used for the storage of grain, as a restaurant, or as a place for the storage or consumption of liquor.

After the Civil War, the county jail was destroyed by fire, and the old clerk's office was converted for use as a jail, with grids of heavy strap iron installed to secure those rooms used for confinement. Later, the county jail was moved, and in 1923 this building was renovated again, this time through the generosity of Mr. and Mrs. Alfred I. duPont. It became the home of the Essex County Woman's Club, shared until 1978 with the County Library, which the Club had actually established. *(Map D)*

County Clerk's Office (87)

Debtor's Prison (88) In 1769, the Essex County court designated a part of Tappahannock as "prison bounds," an area within which imprisoned debtors were allowed to frequent after putting up bond. This building is believed to date from that time. Its inmates were removed in 1809, however, and the structure was given over to other purposes. Following its use as a law office, it became the County Treasurer's Office. *(Map D)*

Debtor's Prison (88)

Essex County Courthouse (89)
Built in 1848, this courthouse is said to be the successor to at least four earlier courthouses dating respectively from: (1) 1656, near Sabine Hall (41) in today's Richmond County, the two counties then being parts of one called Rappahannock County; (2) 1685, on lot 16 in Tappahannock (then usually called Hobb's Hole); (3) 1694, near Caret, in upper Essex County; and (4) 1728, the building that became Centennial and then later Beale Memorial Church (85) in the last quarter of the 19th century.

Renovations to the present courthouse, mainly sponsored by Alfred I. duPont in 1926, included the addition of a bell and clock tower. A fire in 1965 damaged not only the structure, but also much of the large portrait collection housed here, although there still remains an impressive array of Essex County leaders' images on the walls of the courthouse. *(Map D)*

Essex County Courthouse (89)

Ritchie House (90) What is today known as the Ritchie House began as a smaller house erected by Thomas Meriwether before 1708. The property was purchased by Thomas Heard, a London merchant, in 1742, who in short time added a storehouse and another building that would later house a tavern. He also had installed ceiling-high paneling that ended up being sold to the Winterthur Museum in Delaware in 1929. After Heard's brief ownership of the house, it passed through several hands until purchased by the Scottish merchant Archibald Ritchie in 1768.

Ritchie added the five dormer windows on the Prince Street side of the building, and had a brick wall (no longer standing) erected around the entire block on which the house stood. Although a leader in Essex County throughout his active live, Ritchie ran afoul of local patriots who protested passage by the British Parliament of the Stamp Act in 1765. After announcing that he would conform to the Act, on February 27, 1766 Ritchie faced the wrath of 400 local Sons of Liberty—partly inspired by Richard Henry Lee of Westmoreland County, who earlier had drafted the Leedstown Resolves (see Leedstown (13) in Westmoreland County)—who proceeded to confront the merchant. Ritchie ended up signing an apology and promised not to use the stamps, which were effectively a tax on the colonists.

Ritchie's sons were prominent in Virginia affairs. Two of them fought against the British in the War of 1812, and another, Thomas Ritchie (1778-1854), founded one of the South's leading newspapers, *The Richmond Enquirer*, and was a co-founder of the Bank of Virginia. The Ritchie House passed through a number of hands in the 19th and 20th centuries until local attorney Alexander Dillard oversaw a thorough restoration of the house in the early 1990s, most of the work being undertaken by local craftsmen.

Today the Ritchie House, at the corner of Prince and Cross streets, is a 1½ story house with a clipped gable roof, set atop a rough basement. Its siding is Flemish bond with a belt course at the bottom and a brick splash-guard, and the elaborate chimneys at either end of the building are laid in Flemish bond and capped. The Prince Street entrance has a low, pyramid style porch and double doors. A little door at the southwest corner opens into the basement. A crowned brick wall helps to block off the lawn in the back of the house. Much of the interior hardware is original. *Historical Marker N-22; privately owned. (Map D)*

Ritchie House (90)

Customs House (91) Believed to have been bought by the merchant Archibald Ritchie in 1756 (see Ritchie House (90)), this two-story brick structure sits on a hill immediately overlooking the Rappahannock River. An ordinary (tavern) with a rather notorious reputation was established here by one John Whitlock in 1766.

Customs House (91)

In 1800 the house was purchased by Lawrence Muse for the purpose of conducting his duties as Collector of Customs for the Port of Tappahannock, a designation the town had received in 1786 during the first years of the new republic. Since then the building has been known as the Customs House. *Privately owned. (Map D)*

Dobyns House/Riverside Hotel site (92) The Dobyns House, standing right on the Rappahannock riverbank, was built by George and Judith Hoskins Dobyns in 1836 on the site of several earlier houses, taverns and storehouses. It was a three-story brick structure with a two-story riverside porch. Each floor had a central hall flanked on each side by two rooms, each with a fireplace. This building, also popularly known as the Riverside Hotel, which occupied the site from 1899 to 1967, was torn down in 1972 and is now the site of a large condominium building. *Privately owned. (Map D)*

Dobyns House/Riverside Hotel site (92)

Henley House (93) Also known as Emerson's Ordinary, the original section of this house, a 1½ story structure with dormers, is clearly quite old, and may date from the 1720s. The addition in the rear of the house was added in the 19th century. Although records show that James Emerson ran an ordinary (tavern) on or near this site in the mid-18th century, it is unclear whether he operated his business out of this house, or one close by. The

Henley House (93)

house is now undergoing an extensive restoration. *Privately owned. (Map D)*

Lucy Gray's School site (94) The original part of this house was a 1¹/₂ story brick structure probably dating from the mid-18th century. After her husband's death, Lucy Yates (Wellford) Gray opened the Tappahannock Female Seminary on this site in 1818. At some point she added a two-story frame wing for boarding students, and the original part of the structure was later raised to two full stories. Over 700 young women were educated here before Mrs. Gray's death in 1860. Later the building became the Virginia Hotel, and still later reverted to a private home and was called Monument Place, as it faced the Confederate Monument (103) in the middle of Prince Street. Monument Place was torn down in 1965. *(Map D)*

Moore Wright House (95) Located on the northwest corner of Duke Street and Water Lane, this house was built by Dr. Lawrence Roane in 1851. One of the largest houses in Tappahannock, the two-story five-bay Greek Revival structure has a hip roof and sits on an English basement. Its brick walls are covered with white stucco. Both the front and back porches are original and have fluted columns. Fireplaces in each of the house's twelve rooms are served by four chimneys. Servants' quarters, an old laundry and a kitchen stand at the rear of the house and may date from the 1840s.

During the Civil War, the structure was still known as Roane's House, and as its size and location presented a good target, it was pillaged by Union soldiers. The son, Capt. Roane, sold the house to Judge Croxton in 1875, Croxton later serving two terms in the U. S. Congress. Late in the 19th century the house passed to Moore Wright, a prosperous local merchant. At the turn of the 21st century the house was significantly renovated, and it opened as the Essex Inn. *(Map D)*

Moore Wright House (95)

St. John's Episcopal Church (96) This church, dating from 1850, is a lineal descendant of two late 17th-century churches of South Farnham Parish (1665 and 1683) that were lost to post-Revolution disestablishment of the Church of England followed by neglect and vandalism. A side door once led to stairs to the balcony where black members worshipped. During the Civil War, the steeple bell was removed and donated

St. John's Episcopal Church (96)

to the Tredegar Iron Works in Richmond as scrap for the Confederate war effort. St. John's is a frame structure of the Carpenter Gothic genre, most unusual in this area. *(Map D)*

The Sycamores (97) The original part of this house dates from 1750-65. It now is a very large two-story frame home with fifteen rooms, five chimneys, a basement and a number of porches and balconies. The entry hall has a very old staircase, and the downstairs rooms have particularly high ceilings. The exact plan of the original, and presumably much smaller, structure is as yet unknown. *Privately owned. (Map D)*

The Sycamores (97)

Little Egypt (98) It was the rich soil of the farm property on which this 1½ story Dutch colonial house originally stood that accounts for its name. The house is believed to date from before the Revolutionary War, although its original owner is unknown. Post and beam construction and hand

Little Egypt (98)

wrought nails are found throughout the house. Four fireplaces with original mantels are served by two original chimneys. Extensive restoration and preservation work began in the 1980s and continues to this day. *Privately owned. (Map D)*

Hilton House (99) James Griffing is considered to have built this two-story three-bay frame home on Prince Street in 1729. Although it may well have begun as a smaller and simpler house, little evidence has been found that it has changed much in the meantime. The house is built over a rough basement, and one of the two gable-end chimneys appears to be an original. The floors are irregular heart of pine and also appear to be original, and the eight-inch beams in the basement are hand hewn. The front foyer connects into a dining room and a living room, and the lathed plaster interior walls in most rooms have a waist-high railing. *Privately owned. (Map D)*

Hilton House (99)

Anderton House (100) This frame house may have been built by Robert Coleman in the first quarter of the 18th century. Dr. John Brockenbrough, a surgeon in the U.S. Navy during the Revolution, bought the house in 1803. His son John, Jr. became president of the Bank of Virginia, and built the home in the city of Richmond that became known as the White House of the Confederacy. Another of his sons, William, represented

Essex County in the Virginia House of Delegates, and was appointed Judge of the Supreme Court of Appeals in 1834. By 1812, the house had been sold out of the Brockenbrough family, and after passing through many hands, was purchased in 1947 by the Episcopal Church Schools of the Diocese of Virginia and is now a dormitory of St. Margaret's School.

The original house likely had two stories and a center-hall plan. By 1801, the house was 48 feet long and 20 feet deep, standing on a foundation rising three feet above ground. The four fireplaces were served by two exterior end chimneys. Various additions were made in the 19th and 20th centuries. *One of several buildings of a private school. (Map D)*

Anderton House (100)

McCall-Brockenbrough House (101)
A home stood on this river front site as early as 1706. After passing through several hands, the lot on which it stood was sold by Robert Beverley (see Blandfield (20)) to wealthy Essex County merchant Archibald McCall in 1763. McCall either built the present house or added to an existing one.

Like his Scottish compatriot, Archibald Ritchie (see the Ritchie House (90)), McCall—who was also at that time King's Attorney for Essex County—initially said he would abide by and indeed, given his own position, enforce the unpopular Stamp Act passed by the British parliament in 1765. Unlike Ritchie, however, he refused to give in to the patriot rioters, and he moved to Glasgow, not to return until 1786.

Neighboring Thomas Brockenbrough, one of the five sons of Dr. John Brockenbrough of Anderton House (100), bought the McCall house at auction in 1811 and two years later sold it to his brother Austin, a physician and later a member of the House of Delegates. The house remained in the extended Brockenbrough family until 1927, when it was purchased by the Episcopal Diocese of Virginia as the second building for St. Margaret's School.

The house inhabited by Archibald McCall and later the Brockenbroughs has experienced a number of additions and renovations over the past 200 years. The original house likely was a relatively simple center-hall structure. Although some of the original paneling is intact, most of it is now in the Tappahannock room of the Winterthur Museum in Delaware. *One of several buildings of a private school. (Map D)*

McCall-Brockenbrough House (101)

Gordon-Wright House (102) Now known as St. Margaret's Hall, it is the heart of the girls' school of that name on the banks of the Rappahannock River. The white frame house that formed the basis for the Hall was erected by Dr. Thomas C. Gordon in the 1840s. It was built in the Greek Revival style, with a high one-story porch with fluted columns, over a high English basement. The house's twelve fireplaces are served by four exterior chimneys, and the hip roof has a balustraded deck. The staircase in the wide center hall faces the riverside, and the landing has a Palladian window.

The Episcopal Diocese of Virginia purchased the Gordon-Wright House and its property when it was deciding to establish St. Margaret's School, which opened in 1921, in Tappahannock. *One of several buildings of a private school. (Map D)*

Gordon-Wright House (102)

Confederate Monument (103) The monument was erected in 1909 by the Women's Monument Association of Essex County. It is 27 feet high, and crowned by the statue of a Confederate soldier facing north. All the names of Essex Civil War veterans appear on the monument, which contains an inscription in their honor. *(Map D)*

Confederate Monument (103)

Selected Bibliography

Arnold, Scott David. *A Guidebook to Virginia's Historical Markers*. Charlottesville: University of Virginia Press, 2007.

Harrower, Gordon. "Civil War and Reconstruction in Essex County," *Essex County Museum and Historical Society Bulletin* 54 (September 2010): 1-5.

La Follette, Robert, Anita Harrower and Gordon Harrower. *Essex County Virginia: Historic Homes*. Lancaster, Va.: Anchor Communications for the Essex County Museum, 2002.

Lee, Edmund Jennings. *Lee of Virginia*. Baltimore: Genealogical Publishing Co., 1974; orig. published in 1895.

Loth, Calder. *The Virginia Landmarks Register*. Charlottesville: University Press of Virginia, Fourth Edition, 1999.

Lounsbury, Carl R. *An Illustrated Glossary of Early Southern Architecture and Landscape*. Charlottesville; University Press of Virginia, 1994.

McGuire, Lillian H. *Uprooted and Transplanted: From Africa to America*. New York: Vantage Press, 1999.

O'Dell, Jeffrey M. *Essex County Historic Site Survey*. Richmond: Virginia Historic Landmarks Commission, early 1970s.

Rountree, Helen C., Wayne E. Clark and Kent Mountford. *John Smith's Chesapeake Voyages, 1607-1609*. Charlottesville: University of Virginia Press, 2007.

Scarborough, William Kauffman. *Masters of the Big House: Elite Slaveholders of the Mid-Nineteenth Century South*. Baton Rouge: Louisiana State University Press, 2003.

Slaughter, James B. *Settlers, Southerners, Americans: The History of Essex County, Virginia 1608-1984*. Salem, West Va.: Walsworth Press, Inc., 1985.

Webb, Willard J. and Anne C. Webb. *The Glebe Houses of Colonial Virginia*. Westminster, Md.: Heritage Books, Inc., 2003.

Woman's Club of Essex County. *Old Homes of Essex County*. Richmond: Williams Printing Co., Revised Edition, 1957.

Chapter 9

Some Conclusions and Lessons for Historic Preservation in the Northern Neck Region

Although European settlement in the Northern Neck and in Essex County dates from the 1640s and 1650s, the rather complete inventory of historic structures in this *Guide* for the period prior to the Civil War has shown that only about 130 sites in the six counties studied have identifiable portions (other than possible foundations of earlier structures) that date from before 1800, and only about 55 of those look more or less the way they did in that period. Given an estimate of some 3,000-odd dwellings occupied by the free population of this region in 1790, this suggests that perhaps only about four to five percent of these dwellings still exist in some above-ground form, and that possibly less than two percent would be recognizable today to their late 18th-century inhabitants.

Going back earlier in time, it would seem that the number of 17th-century structures still standing in this region, in some form or another, could be counted on the fingers of two hands. This is less surprising, though, since most structures built before 1700 in this area were of earthfast construction (i. e., lacked brick or stone foundations), and did not survive long in the region's humid climate.

The vast majority of these surviving early buildings (mostly houses, but also some brick churches and public buildings) are well-maintained and cared for, but a number of structures from this early period have disappeared just in the last decade or two, whether due to general neglect and then abandonment, accidental fires, or "controlled burns." The devotion of individual preservationists aside, the fact that only some four to five percent of structures remain from the 17th and 18th centuries (whether more-or-less standing alone as they were originally, or as part of larger encompassing structures) is highly regrettable and very worrisome to those interested in preservation and our historical heritage more generally. A number of the more obviously endangered sites in this *Guide* have, as noted, been identified as such in the individual site descriptions.

One way to help preserve an old structure or complex is to work with the Virginia Department of Historic Resources (DHR) to place an eligible site on the Virginia Landmarks Register (VLR). This, in turn, normally leads to the site's inclusion on the National Register of Historic Places (NRHP), maintained by the U.S. Department of the Interior. Inclusion of a site on these registers should help in its preservation by bringing attention to its age and significance.

Of the 460 stand-alone sites listed in the *Guide*, only 92, or one-fifth, had been placed on the VLR as of January 2010. Many others have been preliminarily judged by the DHR to be eligible for possible inclusion on the VLR. It is hoped that the owners or stewards of those sites, as well as of many of the other sites described in this *Guide*, will also decide to apply for register status. But without also placing a site under an historic easement—which thus far has been done for only about 15 of those places on the

VLR for this region—simply being listed on this register is unlikely to ensure its preservation in perpetuity.

It should be pointed out, however, that probably not all properties listed in this *Guide* are eligible for listing on the VLR and NRHP. To be eligible, a resource must inter alia be a tangible property, be at least 50 years old, have reasonably good architectural or archaeological integrity, and be considered to be of some historical importance. It has to meet at least one of the several National Register criteria. The criteria are even more stringent for religious properties, a relocated building, a birthplace or grave, a cemetery, a reconstructed building, a commemorative property, or those that are less than 50 years old.

At the same time, it is important to keep in mind that there exist other options for helping to ensure the preservation of properties deemed historic. These include historic zoning overlays; the promotion of tax credits for renovations and restorations that adhere to the Standards for Rehabilitation established by the U.S. Secretary of the Interior; partial real estate tax abatement at the local level, which may not be tied to the historic status of a property; and of course public education more generally about the importance of historic preservation.

The archives of the DHR in Richmond were an incomparable source of information for the preparation of this *Guide*. These files have been compiled mainly on the basis of surveys by architectural historians over the past fifty years. Nevertheless, those volunteers directly involved in this project at the county level were pleased to be able to add information and usually photographs for 69 additional sites to those archives. Most of these additional sites have not been subject to examination by professional architectural historians or archaeologists, however, so much remains to be done in terms of investigating and describing them beyond what is reflected in this *Guide*.

At the same time, the project volunteers found it to be quite sobering, and indeed saddening, that a large number of sites identified in the DHR archives on the basis of professional surveys carried out two to five decades ago have in the meantime disappeared and are thus lost forever. This possibility of future destruction was often clearly anticipated by the architectural historian in times past, who might have noted, for example, that "unless measures are taken to stop the present deterioration, this structure is likely to collapse within a few years."

The authors of this *Guide* would recommend that professional countywide archaeological surveys be carried out in each of the six counties covered by the *Guide*. Furthermore, it would be very useful for thorough architectural surveys to be conducted for all resources 50 years or older, for each of these counties for which such studies have not already been made.

Finally, and as noted in Chapter 1, in an essentially rural setting such as the Northern Neck region, the threat of loss of open land, whether to housing or commercial development or to shoreline erosion or other factors, cannot really be separated from the interest in preserving historic structures. These homes, churches, schools, old commercial buildings and various public structures were all built in specific natural environments, whether rural or riparian, or in the context of an 18th or 19th century village setting. It is hoped that future historic preservation and land conservation efforts in the Northern Neck region will be carried out with full recognition of the complementary nature of these activities. The original historic and cultural "landscape" in which these structures existed had both indoor and outdoor aspects, and both need to be preserved for future generations.

Glossary of
Architectural Terms

American Bond A modified English bond brick pattern in which each row (or course) of headers is separated by several courses of stretchers or, as in most contemporary buildings, there are no headers

American Four- Square An early 20th-century hip roof house plan, two piles deep and square

Architrave The bottom part of an entablature (see below), which is usually a lintel or beam resting on the capitals of columns

Asymmetrical plan Uneven placement of windows or doors

Bay Any window- or door-opening in a structure. For example, a building with two windows and a door in the middle is a three-bay structure

Balloon construction Wall studs run continuously from the sill plate to attic joists

Bead A small, convex rounded molding, often found on the bottom edge of early clapboards or weatherboards

Board-and-batten Wooden door, shutter or partition where a vertical set of parallel boards is secured by a plank or other wooden strips nailed more or less horizontally across them (or vice-versa)

Braced-frame construction Each post and beam is mortised and tenoned, and diagonal corner braces are used to provide lateral stability to the wooden framework

Ceiling medallion Ornamental object, usually of plaster composition, placed in the center of the ceiling of a fine home

Center-hall plan A house with a central hall flanked by one or more rooms on either side

Clapboard An exterior covering consisting of horizontally placed, overlapping boards

Corbelled cornice The projection of masonry courses, usually in a stepped series at the top of a brick chimney or brick or plastered wall, usually used to support weight or for decorative purposes.

Cornice The top part of an entablature (see below), but also simply a horizontal molded projection crowning the wall or chimney of a building

Course A row of bricks in a wall or chimney

Cruciform plan Structure, usually a church, built in the form of a cross

Decorative snow birds Devices set in roofs to retard the sliding off of snow

Dentils An ornamental pattern made of small rectangular blocks, usually in rows, lining a mantelpiece or the cornice of an interior or exterior wall of a building

Diapering A pattern formed by small, repeated geometrical motifs set adjacent to one another, used to decorate masonry surfaces

Eave That part of a roof which extends beyond the exterior wall

English basement   A basement rising substantially above ground, usually with windows

English bond   A brick pattern of repeated single rows (or courses) of stretchers between single rows of headers

Entablature   The horizontal part of a classic order above columns, usually consisting of three parts, an architrave at the bottom, a frieze in the middle, and a cornice at the top.

Façade   Exterior face of a building

Fascia board   The trim board below an eave

Flemish bond   A brick pattern in which each row (or course) has alternating headers and stretchers such that a header in one row always appears directly above (below) a stretcher in the row beneath (above).

Flue stack   The passage within a chimney that vents the smoke and heat from the fireplace to the air above

Frieze   The middle section of a classical entablature (see above), between the architrave below and cornice above

Gable roof   A roof in the shape of an inverted V, composed of rafters with a single slope, where the gables are the triangular sections of the exterior walls at each end of the roof

Gambrel roof   A roof with two pitches, the lower one being steeper than the other

Glazed header   A brick fired on the end to give a dark glaze

Half Story   The top story of a building in which the ceiling follows the pitch of the roof and the square footage and ceiling height is less than that of the stories below, but is not usually intended for use simply as a storage attic

Hall and Parlor plan   A more public room in front, with a smaller, more private room to the rear, usually with a loft above

Header   In masonry bonding, a brick or rectangular stone laid so that only its short end appears on the surface of a foundation, wall, or chimney

Hip roof   A roof that has sloping rafters rising from all sides

I-plan   A structure one or two bays deep and all in one plane, with no front or rear extensions

Jack arch   A flat (or straight) arch over a door or window, as opposed to a point-arch

Joist   Horizontal framing timber that supports the floor

Kneewall   A bracing wall, most commonly found along the inside of a half story, helping to support the roof rafters

Loft   An upper story or attic

Mortice and tenon construction   A means of fastening wood, in which the tenon, or the stub at the end of one board or rafter, is inserted into a slot, or mortise, in a second board or rafter

Newel   A post that supports the framing, handrails, and stringboards of a staircase at its beginning, turning points and end

Overlights   Glass above doors or windows

Pediment   A low, triangular gable with a horizontal cornice and two inclined cornices atop a portico, colonnade or wall

Piano Nobile   The principal floor of a large house

Pilaster   A slightly-projecting column built into or applied to the face of a wall

Pile   The depth of a structure measured in rooms; a house one room deep is a single pile house

Plinth   The flat square-shaped piece under the base moldings of a column, pilaster or pedestal

Rafter Framing timber that supports the covering of the roof

Saltbox (or catslide) roof A gable roof that slopes down at the rear of the house, virtually to the ground

Shouldered brick chimney A chimney with sides that narrow with height, with inclined sides connecting the lower wider sections with the narrower sections above

Side-hall plan A house for which the entrance door is set near one end of the house rather than in the center of the façade

Sill A square, thick horizontal timber that supports the vertical members—posts and studs—of a building

Sidelight Window(s) at the side of a doorway

Splayed eave A roof eave that is curved upwards

Standing seam roof A tin roof that has vertical ridges covering the joints

Stretcher In masonry bonding, a brick or rectangular stone laid so that its long side runs horizontally along the surface of a foundation, wall or chimney

Stud One of a series of slender vertical timbers, interspersed between larger structural posts, used in framing walls and partitions

T-plan A structure with a rear or sometimes a front extension

Vernacular house A house designed and constructed largely on the basis of locally-produced designs and traditions

Water table The sloping top of a brick foundation, protruding from the wall above, designed to deflect rainwater away from the foundation

Weatherboard Horizontal overlapping siding boards, similar to clapboards, but thicker

Wicket door A small door within a larger door

Window lights The separate compartments of a window, usually panes of glass

Appendix

Historical Societies, Preservation Groups, and History Libraries and Museums in the Northern Neck Region

Essex County

The Essex County Museum and Historical Society, 218 Water Lane, P. O. Box 404, Tappahannock, VA 22560. (804) 443-4690.

King George County

King George County Historical Society, 9483 Kings Highway, P. O. Box 424, King George, VA 22485. (540) 775-9477.

King George County Museum and Research Center, 9483 Kings Highway, P. O. Box 424, King George, VA 22485. (540) 775-9477.

Lancaster County

Foundation for Historic Christ Church Museum, P. O. Box 24, Irvington, VA 22480. (804) 438-6855.

Genealogical Society of the Northern Neck of Virginia, 50 Fox Tail South, Irvington, VA, 22480.

Kilmarnock Museum, 76 North Main Street, Kilmarnock, VA 22482. (804) 436-9100.

Mary Ball Washington Library and Museum, 8346 Mary Ball Road, Lancaster, VA 22503. (804) 462-7280.

Morattico Waterfront Museum, P. O. Box 80, Morattico, VA 22523.

Steamboat Era Museum, 156 King Carter Drive, Irvington, VA 22480. (804) 438-6888.

Northumberland County

Northern Neck Farm Museum, 12705 Northumberland Highway, Heathsville, VA 22473. (804) 443-1118.

Northumberland County Historical Society, 86 Back Street, P. O. Box 221, Heathsville, VA 22473. (804) 580-8581.

Northumberland Preservation, Inc., P. O. Box 65, Wicomico Church, VA 22579.

Reedville Fishermen's Museum, 504 Main Street, Reedville, VA 22539. (804) 453-6529.

Rice's Hotel/Hughlett's Tavern Foundation, 73 Monument Place, P. O. Box 579, Heathsville, VA. (804) 580-3377.

Richmond County

Menokin Foundation, 4037 Menokin Road, Warsaw, VA 22572. (804) 333-1776.

Preservation Northern Neck and Middle Peninsula, Inc., P. O. Box 691, Warsaw, VA, 22572.

Richmond County Museum, 5874 West Richmond Road, Warsaw, VA 22572. (804) 333-3607.

Richmond County Public Library, Library Center, Rappahannock Community College, 52 Campus Drive, Warsaw, VA 22572. (804) 333-6710.

Westmoreland County

Armstead Tasker Johnson High School Museum, 18849 Kings Highway, Montross, VA. (804) 493-7070.

Colonial Beach Historical Society and Museum, 128 Hawthorne Street, Colonial Beach, VA 22443. (804) 224-3379.

George Washington Birthplace National Monument, 1732 Pope's Creek Road, Washington's Birthplace, VA 22443. (804) 224-1732.

Jesse Ball duPont Memorial Library, Stratford Hall Plantation, 483 Great House Road, Stratford, VA 22558. (804) 493-8038.

Kinsale Museum, 449 Kinsale Road, P. O. Box 307, Kinsale, VA 22488. (804) 472-3001.

Northern Neck of Virginia Historical Society, 15482 Kings Highway, P. O. Box 716, Montross, VA 22520. (804) 493-1862.

Westmoreland County Museum, P. O. Box 247, Montross, VA (804) 493-8440.

Note: Most of these historical societies, museums and other organizations also have websites that provide additional information, including operating hours.

Photography Credits

Chapter 2: Historical Overview
Gillions and Coates Cannery: Frank Delano for *The Northumberland Echo* in 1969, and included in John C. Wilson, *Virginia's Northern Neck: A Pictorial History*, first published by The Donning Company/Publishers in 1984.

Edward J. White: All 2010 photos

Chapter 3: King George
Elizabeth Lee: Sites 1-3, 5-6, 10, 18, 20, 30, 33-36, 39, 43-44, 48, 50-52, 55, 58, 65

Edward J. White: Sites 11, 21, 53, 59

Jean Hudson: Site 4

Ruth Taliaferro: Sites 7, 47

Jean Graham: Sites 14, 42

Gloria Sharp: Sites 49, 56

DHR archives: Sites 8-9, 12, 15-17, 22-26, 28-29, 32, 37-38, 40-41, 45-46, 53-54 , 57, 60-62, 64, 67

King George Museum: Sites 13, 68

Library of Congress: Site 63

Internet photos: Sites 19, 27

Chapter 4: Westmoreland
Edward J. White: Sites 1-4, 8-11, 14, 21-22, 24, 26, 28-41, 44-53, 55-59, 61, 63-65, 68-69, 73-83, 85-91, 93

DHR archives: Sites 6, 12, 15-19, 23, 42-43

Paul Ventura: Site 70

Bryan Fairfax: Site 72

Chapter 5: Northumberland
Edward J. White: Sites 4-5, 17-20, 24-26, 28-29, 31-32, 34, 36-38, 41-42, 44-45, 48-50, 53-68, 70-73, 75-78, 80, 84

DHR archives: Sites 1-3, 7-13, 15-16, 22- 23, 27, 30, 33, 35, 40, 46, 51-52, 69, 74, 79, 81-83, 85

Internet: Site 43

Chapter 6: Lancaster
Edward J. White: Sites 1-2, 4, 9, 13, 16, 21-25, 28-29, 38-39, 40, 43-44, 46, 48, 50-53

Lancaster County Historic Resource Commission: Sites 3, 5-8, 11-12, 14-15, 17-19, 26-27, 30-37, 40, 42, 45, 47, 49, 54, 56-58, 61-62

Chapter 7: Richmond
Edward J. White: Sites 1, 10-11, 13, 15-16, 18-21, 23, 26-30, 32-40, 43,

DHR archives: Sites 2, 5, 7, 9, 17, 24, 42, 45-46

Kathryn Murray: Sites 41, 47-48

Rebecca Marks: Sites 6, 14

Francene Barber: Site 12

Chapter 8: Essex
Edward J. White: Sites 4b, 12-13, 15, 21-22, 26, 38-39, 44, 58, 61-62, 70, 86-88, 91, 93, 96, 98-102

Kathryn Murray: 47

Essex County Museum and Historical Society: Sites 29, 43

DHR archives: Sites 1-4a, 5-11, 14, 16-20, 23-25, 27-28, 30-37, 40-42, 45-46, 48-57, 59-60, 63-69, 71-77, 79-83, 85, 89-90, 95, 97, 103

Index of
Historic Sites

General Index

Cabell, Mary Walker Carter, 156
Caledon Natural Area, 56
Callao, 29
Calvary Baptist Church, 130
Camden (Caroline Co.), 11
Camp of Confederate Veterans (KG), 56
Campbell, Rev. Archibald, 71
Campbell Memorial Presbyterian Church, 156
canneries, 26-27, 34, 108, 230
Canning (early KG county seat), 56, 61
Capitol (Virginia State), 79
Caponka (cargo ship), 202
Caret (hamlet), 240
Carey, William, 102
Carey's Corner, 102
Carmichael, Daniel, 75
Caroline County, 11, 20, 33, 66, 208
Carter family, 18, 63, 153
Carter, Addison L., 173
Carter, Charles, 13, 63, 153
Carter, Charles, Jr., 67
Carter, I., 165
Carter, Job, 169
Carter, John, 8, 156
Carter, Landon (1710-1778), 13, 195, 198, 214
Carter, Landon, Jr., 148
Carter, Priscilla, 201
Carter, Robert "King" (ca. 1663-1732), 13, 63, 67, 97, 155-56, 165, 198
Carter, Robert, II, 13, 97
Carter, Robert, III ("Councillor"), 16, 97, 192, 201
  emancipation of slaves, 16, 97
Carter, Robert W., 146
Carter, Robert Wormeley (son of Landon), 148
Carter, Robert Wormeley, II, 198
Carter's Creek, 28, 158
Carter's "Great Mill", 165
Cat Point Creek, 193
Cauthorn family, 220, 222
Cauthorn's Place, 236
Cauthorn, James, 233
Cedar Grove (KG), 46, 57
Cedar Grove (R), 188
Centennial Baptist Church, 237
Central High School (N), 135
Century Farm, 48, 155
Champlain, 20
Champlain (hamlet), 215

Champlain Colored School, 215
Chantilly, 14, 84, 86, 102
Chantilly Acres, 85
Charles I, King, 73
Charles II, King, 9, 12-13
Charles Co., Md., 33, 73
Chase family, 163
Chase, Lawson, 165
Chatterton Landing, 51
Cherry Point (KG), 62
Cherry Point (N), 12, 17, 21-22, 99, 117, 120, 125, 173, 178
Cherry Walk, 222
Chesapeake Bay, 5, 7-8, 22, 26, 28, 34, 115, 120, 136, 145-47, 153, 202
Chesapeake Beach, 32
Chicacoan Oak, 128
Chickakoan (Chicawane) District, 8-9, 115
Chilton family, 85
Chilton, Robert H., 155
Chiltons (hamlet), 86
Chinn family, 183
Chinn, John, 183
Chinn, Joseph, 177
Chinn, Joseph W., 184
Chinn, Justice Joseph William, 198
Chotank, 48
Chowning, Robert H., 103
Chowning, Capt. William, 176
Chowning ferry, 11
Christ Church, Historic, 15, 143, 163, 165, 188, 198
  Episcopal Vestry of, 156
  Foundation for, 156
  Glebe, 157
  Parish, 173
Christmas Cove, 144
Church of England (Anglican), 10, 12, 15
  disestablishment of, 15, 55, 57, 110, 143, 156, 188, 207, 210, 223, 242
"Circus House", 224
Citizens Bank of Callao, 28, 117
Civil War, 1-3, 5-6, 18-23, 28, 41-42, 49, 52, 53, 55-58, 60, 62, 65-66, 77, 84-85, 98, 102, 108, 111, 134, 141, 145, 149, 158, 163, 171-73, 187-88, 197, 207-08, 214, 242, 247
Civilian Conservation Corps (CCC), 83
Claiborne, Col. William, 8
Claraville (hamlet), 135
Clarksville Baptist Church, 193
Claughton, William, 118

McCall-Brockenbrough House, 227
McCarty, Billington, Jr., 184
McCarty, William Jr., 186
McClellan, Gen. George B. (USA), 20, 48, 219
Meade, Bishop William, 15, 80
Meadow, The, 20, 48
menhaden fishing and processing, 28, 135-36, 138-39, 141, 162
Menokin, 84, 97, 193, 201
  Foundation, 194
  Martin Kirwan King Conservation and Visitors Center, 194
Menokin Baptist Church, 199
Meriwether, Thomas, 240
Merrimac (ship), 117
Merriweather, Francis, 228
Merry Point Ferry, 168
Methodist church, 16, 22, 110, 166
Methodist Episcopal church, 127
Methodist Protestant church, 127
Metropolitan Museum of Art (N.Y.), 51
Micou, James Roy, 225
Micou, Mary, 205
Micou, Paul, 205
Middle Peninsula, 5, 8, 34
Middlesex County, 9, 11, 176
Middleton, Dr. Benjamin Smith, 189
Midway (E), 223
Midway (L), 173
Midway Female Academy, 220
migration (outward), 16
Milden (village), 186
Milden Hall, 186
Milden Lodge, 186
Milden Presbyterian Church, 186
militia (county), 12
Mill Creek, 145
Mill Stream, 228
Miller, Mr., 223
Millers Tavern, 14, 19
  Resolutions, 19, 223
"Millionaires Row" (Reedville), 28, 135
mills (grist), 80, 84-85, 122, 165, 192, 194, 212, 228
Minor, Dr. Jefferson, 220, 223
Minor, Dr. John Thomas, 53
"Miss Addie's School," 187
Mitchell, Carter, 201
Mitchell, Daniel P., Jr., 169
Mitchell, Robert, IV, 201
Monaskan, 173
Monitor (ship), 117

Monroe, James (1758-1831), 1, 14, 60, 74, 77
Mont Calm, 89
Montague family, 225
Montague, Abram, 218
"Monte Carlo", 73
Montross, 71, 86, 89, 112
Monument Place, 242
Moore, Rt. Rev. Richard Channing, 194
Morattico, 178, 183
Morattico Baptist Church, congregation, 15-16, 93
Morattico Creek, 183
Morattico Hall, 153
Morattico Waterfront Museum, 177
Morgantown, Md., 33
Morris, Albert, 28, 135, 139
  widow of, 135
Morris-Fisher menhaden complex, 28, 135, 138-39, 141
  smokestack, 135
Mosby's Rangers (CSA), 102
Mosquito Creek, 161
Mosquito Point, 161
Moss Neck Manor (Caroline Co.), 60
Mothershead House, 125
Motley, Claude Douglas, 197
Mottrom, Col. John, 8, 122
Mount Airy, 13, 16, 62, 68, 183, 188, 193
Mt. Airey Stock Company, 84
Mt. Olive Baptist Church, 130
Mount Pleasant (KG), 61
Mount Pleasant (Lees, (W)), 98
Mount Rose Cannery and Pickle Factory, 26
Mount Vernon, 44, 95
Mount Vernon Ladies Association, 44
Mt. Zion Baptist Church (E), 219, 225
Mount Zion Baptist Church (R), 22, 181
Mumford, L. E. Bank building, 186
Munday House, 215
Mundy Point, 17, 115
Murdock, Jeremiah, 110
Murphy family, 107
Murphy, Helen & Tayloe (Conference Center), 83
Murphy, Robert, 95
Murphy, W. Tayloe, 190
Muse, Lawrence, 241

Nalley's Landing, Md., 50
Nanzatico Bay, 67
Nanzatico Indian Archaeological site, 67
National Historic Landmarks, 83, 110, 156,

194, 198-99
National Monuments, 80-81
National Park Service, 4
National Register of Historic Places (NRHP), 4, 71, 115, 153, 205, 247-48
Native Americans (Indians), 5-8
  Algonquian dialect, 7
  Chicacoans (Sekakawons), 7, 122
  Corrotomans (Cuttatawomens), 7, 161
  Massawomecks, 7
  Moratticos (Moraughtacunds), 7, 177, 183
  Nanzaticos (Nandtaughtacunds), 8, 67
  Pissasecks, 8, 67
    Pissasec village, 76
  Potomacs (Patawomecks), 52-53
  Powhatans, 7
    Alliance (confederacy), 7-8, 237
  Rappahannocks, 9, 237
  Topahanocks, 8, 237
  early settlement patterns of, 6-8
  fortifications, 7, 102
navies (Revolutionary War)
  Continental, 15
  Virginia, 15
Naylor's Beach, 201
Nelson, Rev. George Washington, 194
Newton, Willoughby, Sr., 99
Newton, Willoughby, Jr., 17, 99
Nice (Harry W.) Bridge, 3, 33
Ninde, 43
Nomini Baptist Church, 16
Nomini Church (Episcopal), 17
Nomini (Nominy) Creek, 11, 94-95, 97
Nomini Hall, 13, 16, 18, 94, 96, 99, 192, 201
Nomony Meeting House, 193
Norfolk, 68
Norris (Robert O.) Bridge, 3, 33
North Farnham Parish, 12, 188, 194-95
North Texas (tract), 118
Northern Neck Baptist Association, 31, 184
Northern Neck Industrial Academy, 31, 90
Northern Neck Planning District Commission, 117
Northern Neck Proprietary, 13, 51, 155
Northumberland Academy, 18
Northumberland County Courts Building, 127
Northumberland County Historical Society, 128, 141
Northumberland County Public School Board, 130
Northumberland County Training School, 31, 135

Northumberland Court House (now Heathsville), 29
Northumberland Home Guard, 134
Northumberland House, 122
Northumberland Preservation, Inc., 147

Oak Grove, 74
Oakley (L), 184
Occupacia, 215
Office Hall, 43
"Old Church Store", 213
Old Monrovia Baptist Church, 112
Oldhams, 112
Oldhams, Thomas, 187
Omohundro, T. E., 194
Opie family, 117
Opie, Thomas, Jr., 118
Orange County, 65
ordinaries (see taverns)
Owens (hamlet), 43

Panorama site, 58
Parks' Cannery, 27
Payne, Addie Veazy, 187
Payne, Robert, Jr., 217
Peachey, Samuel, 186
Peachey, William, 186
Peckatown's Field, 103
People's Bank of Reedville, 28
Petersburg, 26
Phi Beta Kappa, 123
Pickett, Gen. George (CSA), 212
Piedmont, 14, 65
Pierce, F. A., 174
Pierce, Capt. Joseph, 93
Pierce, William, 168
Pinckard, Thomas H., 168
Piscataway Baptist Church, 219
Piscataway Creek, 228
Piscataway Post Office, 219
Plainview, 107
Plainview Cottage, 107
Pocohantas, 53
Polk, Robert, 84
Pop Castle, 17, 20
Pope, Col. Nathaniel, 80, 83
Pope, Nathaniel, 80
Pope's Creek, 81
population
  of counties in region, 6, 39, 71, 115, 153, 181, 205
  of Northern Neck region, 5-6, 17, 247

St. John's Church (Wash., D.C.), 188
St. John's Rectory (KG), 61
St. Margaret's School, 244-45
St. Mary's White Chapel Church, 15
St. Paul's Episcopal Church, 15
St. Stephen's Baptist Church, 43
Sale family, 207
Sale's Church, 12, 213
Salem Baptist Church (KG), 43
Salem Baptist Church (W), 112
Sanders, James, 161
Sandy, Capt. P. A., 224
Sanford, William H., 85
Saunders family, 209
Saunders, John, 208
Saunders' Wharf, 23
Scorpion (gunboat), 85
Segar, Randall, 232
Selden, Richard, II, 172
Senate, U.S., 214
Senate (Virginia), 172, 186
Settle family, 194
settlement,
   European, 5, 8-10
   Native American, 6-8
Shalango, 141
Sharp, Dewitt Clinton, 186
Sharps wharf 23, 186
Shears, Abraham, 145
Shenandoah Valley, 51
Shiloh, 41
Shiloh Baptist Church (KG), 39
Shiloh Baptist Church (N), 130, 135
Shiloh Baptist Church (W), 112
Shiloh School (KG), 31
Shiloh School (N), 22
Shuck, Henrietta Hull, 165
Sigourney, James Butler, 109
Siloam Baptist Church, 112
Sittingbourne Parish, 12
Skinker, Samuel, 63
slavery, 6,10
   abolition of, 21
   falling profitability of, 16
   legislation relating to, 10, 16-17
slaves, 6, 10, 232
   emancipation of, 16, 97, 220
   escapes, 21
Smith, Capt. John 1, 7-8, 53, 67, 76, 122, 161,
   183, 237
Smith, Columbia (Turner), 63
Smith, Gov. George W., 228-29

Smith, James, 122
Smith, James M., 18, 122
Smith, Meriwether, 16
Smith, Samuel, 236
Smith, Gov. William ("Extra Billy"), 41, 43
Smith, William F., 234
Smith, William Taylor, 63
Smith's Wharf, 52
Smoot, Ann Hopewell, 50
   Caledon Natural Area, 56
Smoot, Lewis Egerton, 50
   Library, 56
Society Hill, 45
Somervill, Margaret (Bellows) house, 162
Sons of Liberty, 14, 240
South Farnham Parish, 12, 223, 242
South Texas (tract), 117
Southern Maryland shore, 33, 50, 108-09
Southside Rappahannock Baptist
   Association, 31
Speake's Mill, 85
Spence, Thomas, 87
Spence, Dr. William A., 87, 89
Spindle family, 212
Spindle, John, 210
Spindle's Mill, 212
Spriggs family, 159
Spring Grove, 99
Spring Hill, 60
Springfield farm (E), 215
Springfield (N), 18, 123, 125, 132, 147
Spy Hill, 43, 46
Stafford County, 12, 48-49, 63, 153
Stamp Act protests, 14, 76, 217, 240, 244
Standards for Rehabilitation (U.S. Secretary
   of the Interior), 248
Station Number 1 (Civil War), 108
Statute for Religious Freedom (Virginia), 15
Steamboat Era, 26, 108
steamboats, 6, 22-26, 50, 73, 209
   steamboat wharves, 24-26, 157, 186-87,
      209, 232-33
Stebbins, Laura W., 130
Stebbins School, 22
Stern, Richard and Yelverton (architects), 65,
   67
Sthreshley, Thomas, 217-18
"Store Home", 61
Stratford Hall, 4, 13-14, 73, 76, 79-80, 83-84,
   86, 96-97, 99, 101, 193
Stratford-Langthorne (England), 83
Stretchley, John, 173

Wilder, Michael, 157
Williamsburg, 10, 63
Williamson's School, 187
Willow Hill, 31
Wilson, John E., 81
Wilton, 103
Windmill Point, 161, 163
Windsor, 45, 51
Winterthur Musueum (Delaware), 176, 181, 240, 244
Wirt, Dabney Carr, 77
Wirt, William (U. S. Attorney General), 77
Wirt, William Jr., 77
Wirtland, 18, 77
Wishart, Rev. James, 53
Woman's Missionary Society, Methodist Episcopal South Church, 127
Women's Monument Association of Essex County, 245
Wood family, 221-22, 224
Wood, Waddy Butler (architect), 96
Woodbury, 87
Woodlawn (KG), 11, 66
Woodlawn site (KG), 56, 61
Woodlawn-Trible (E), 224
Woodstock, 20
Woodville, 221-22, 224
World War I, 26, 46, 128
World War II, 28, 33, 46, 128
Works Progress Administration (WPA), 171 architectural historians, photographers, 46, 52, 176
Wright, Albert Terry, 31, 158
Wright, Edward, 218
Wright, Moore, 242

Yeocomico Church, 15
Yeocomico River, 108-09
York County, 8-9, 153, 181, 205
York River, 8
Youell, Thomas, 94
Young family, 221
Young, Ambrose, 221
Young, Capt. Henry, 232

Zion Baptist Church, 22, 130